Imperialism and Terrorism: Dissertation

Imperialism and Terrorism: Dissertation

...

Hani Montan

Panania, NSW, Australia
Title: *Imperialism and Terrorism: Dissertation*, by Hani Montan

Edited and printed by CreateSpace
7290 B. Investment Drive
Charleston, SC 29418
United States of America

ISBN-13: 9781977647511 (paperback)
ISBN-10: 1977647510

Includes notes, bibliographical references, and index

Subjects:
1. Nationalism
2. Ideological
3. Global conflict
4. Tribalism
5. Far right movements

Library of Congress Control Number: 2017915185
CreateSpace Independent Publishing Platform
North Charleston, South Carolina

National Library of Australia ID: 60839855
Canberra ACT 2600

A catalogue record for this
book is available from the
National Library of Australia

BISAC (category): POL047000—Political science / imperialism
POL011000—Political science / international relations / general

Contents

Preface

...

AFTER WRITING SEVERAL BOOKS (OFTEN on the subject of political science) that cover the themes of psychology, philosophy, socioeconomics, international relations, human relationships, and general politics and political systems, I felt it was time to write a dissertation as a summary of my previously expressed thoughts but supported with further research. Those who are familiar with my earlier works will be aware of my advocacy for moderation in human and international relations—an advocacy that is based on the "give and take" and "live and let live" principles rather than the prevailing "winner takes all" approach. Throughout my advocacy, I have often felt I was shouting into a void, my voice drowned by the loud voices of extremists and vested interests. These voices shout a powerful message that embodies the emotive slogan of the "clash of civilizations" that is currently sweeping the less informed sections of society. The message proposes a "them and us" idea that places Muslims (on the "them" side) against Christians and Jews (on the "us" side). The less informed people blindly follow often sinister leaders, while the moderate (but silent) majority sits on the sidelines, not realizing that the clash of civilizations can lead to catastrophic consequences for the following generations—consequences that necessitate our participation in the debate and our action to counter the mounting threat.

For this reason, I have come to the conclusion that writing a dissertation and receiving recognition could make my voice heard; my voice might then be added to the voices of reason that is calling for tolerance, for diversity, and for creating a more peaceful and harmonious world than the current fragmented one in which we currently live. We cannot achieve these goals without the middle class, the intellectuals, and the silent majority becoming alert to the brewing danger so that they might shake their complacency and start to fight for the security and the future of the following generations. That security and future, after all, are threatened from the current conflicted world, especially from the threat of various far-right movements and religious fanatics. I feel the world is now driven by protectionism, nationalism, xenophobia, excessive greed, and ideological extremism, all of which need to be confronted before it is too late.

In writing the dissertation, I was guided by conventional wisdom and by quotes from both famous and not-so-famous people. In discussing the subjects of imperialism and terrorism, I have adopted several arguments based on the following quotations.

- Newton's third law of physics: "For every action, there is an equal and opposite reaction."
- Lord Acton: "All power tends to corrupt, and absolute power corrupts absolutely."

- Martin Luther King Jr.: "No justice, no peace." This message has a similar meaning to an earlier quote by Pope Paul VI: "If you want peace, work for justice."
- Joseph S. Nye: "US security hinges as much on winning hearts and minds as it does on winning wars."
- Niccolò Machiavelli: "Wars begin when you will, but they do not end when you please."
- Noam Chomsky: "You can't bomb your way to peace."
- Simone Weil: "Modern life is given over to immoderation. Immoderation invades everything: actions and thought, public and private...There is no more balance anywhere."
- President Franklin D. Roosevelt: "Let me assert my firm belief that the only thing we have to fear is fear itself."
- President Dwight D. Eisenhower: "A people that values its privileges above principles soon loses both."

The dissertation is not about the battle between good and evil, but it *is* about the battle against the two evils of imperialism and terrorism, which ignite each other and feed on each other, thus creating a dangerous snowball effect.

Some of the following bits of paraphrased conventional wisdom—not necessarily in order—have guided me throughout my earlier works and in writing this work.

- In politics, there are no principles, only interests; the self-interest of individual politicians to preserve their power is the greatest of these.
- Propaganda is when rhetoric trumps reality.

- The concentration of media power in the hands of super-rich and far-right proprietors, who use that power for political ends, is the biggest threat to Western democracy.
- Partial truths or half-truths are often more insidious than total falsehoods.
- Diplomacy is a reflection of the balance of power, not the balance of rhetoric.
- In diplomacy, it is not a matter of who is calling for the talks but who is calling the shots, both on the ground and in the negotiations.
- US foreign policy is centered mostly on military power.
- Imperialist countries will always promote values when their national interest is served; in international relations, politics will always trump values.
- Western values can also be measured by the killing and displacing of millions of civilians throughout the Middle East while hiding the West's real motives.
- The current conflict in the world has resulted from a mixture of Jewish, Islamic, and Christian fascism.
- Wisdom can be directed toward creating a peaceful and harmonious world instead of a world at war.
- If you love something, set it free. If it comes back, it's yours; if it doesn't, it never was.
- Terrorism is the outcome of ignorance and the capacity of leaders to brainwash their followers.
- Terrorism stems from ignorance, extremism, and radicalization.

- Religious schools are often the incubators of radicalization.
- Terrorism is also the outcome of misguided Western foreign policy.
- Terrorism uses shock and random violence to create psychological fear that exceeds the actual threat posed by the capability of the perpetrators.
- Imperialism is the outcome of extreme capitalism and excessive greed.
- America and its allies should refrain from provoking religious wars that will have no winners but will result only in mutually assured destruction.
- Economic sanctions target the people, not the rulers.
- The poorest of the people fight other people's wars.
- The line between insurgent and freedom fighter has always been blurry.
- The success or failure of an empire depends on the number of enemies it creates.
- Politics and elections in the Western world are no longer run on traditional issues such as the economy or equality; instead, they are run on the national mood, which is manipulated by politicians.
- Moral authority is never retained by any attempt to hold on to it; it comes without seeking and is retained without effort.
- Hatred and antipathy do not grow in a bubble. They fester and grow over years, fed by rhetoric that is, at its core, dehumanizing of the targeted group.

- Before you look down on people, you should first think about your own history.
- United we stand; divided we fall.
- The greatest ingredient in any democracy is trust between people and their government.
- Fear doesn't make us safer; it makes us weaker. No one in the world deserves to be afraid.
- Violence breeds violence.
- Prevention is better than the cure.
- The political apathy of one generation can destroy the hopes of the next.
- People who live in the shadows must be given a chance.
- Military power can bring fear and destroy people, but fear can drive people by triggering their survival instinct to fight.
- Power can be both addictive and corrosive.
- The most successful results are obtained when talks are conducted with goodwill.
- Individuals in history do matter.

Some of the above snippets will appear directly or in spirit throughout the text.

Throughout the dissertation, I have relied on the earlier work of many distinguished writers and academics who have inspired me to make my humble contribution to political science.

Among the many writers who have promoted the wisdom of moderation in human and international relations, and whom I have especially relied on throughout my work, the following stand out: Noam Chomsky, Jeffrey Sachs, Jacqueline Rose, Samuel Huntington, Norman Finkelstein, John Mearsheimer, Steven Walt, Daniel Goleman, Howard Gardner, James Petras, Niall Ferguson, Ilan Pappe, Richard Immerman, Paul Findley, William Blum, Michael Scheuer, and many more. They have all made it their mission in life to serve humanity.

Hani Montan
Panania, New South Wales, Australia
February 2018

Introduction

...

THIS WORK'S GOAL IS TO analyze the main causes of the conflicts that are destabilizing the world today. These causes include the imperialistic ambition for domination through aggression, on the one hand, and the terrorism that reacts to it on the other. This dissertation is about scrutinizing political and international relations from a perspective different from the mainstream view—which often subjectively categorizes countries and sects as either good or evil. Such a view chooses who deserves to be rewarded and who is to be punished, and which ideology deserves to survive and which one deserves to be destroyed. In this way, the powerful and the influential leaders ignore, or at least gloss over, the facts that "violence breeds violence," "no justice, no peace," and "for every action, there is an equal and opposite reaction." Above all, these leaders gloss over the fact that in many instances, state terrorism fuels other forms of terrorism. (See chapters 1 and 2 for details.)

The analyses in this book will also show that, throughout history, religion, nationalism, and economic expansion have been behind genocides, destruction, the rise and fall of empires, and the clash of civilizations. I've discussed these subjects in my earlier books, including *Thorny Opinion* (2008), *Israel vs. America vs. the World* (2011), *Voice of Reason: In 7 Essays* (2015), and *Axis of Evil: Imperialism – Religion – Nationalism* (2016).

This work sets out to prove that imperialism, in all its forms—and the reaction to it—is an extension of the historic tribal conflicts that occur when a powerful and aggressive tribe (or its aggressive tribal leader) finds a pretext to attack other tribes, whether for an economic, religious, or nationalistic purpose or some other purpose. This attack results in an opposite reaction, with an opposite pretext, or simply in order to fight for survival. In an uncivilized world, the conquest and subjugation of weaker tribes meant the superior tribe was destined to rule all others. Unfortunately, it was then—and still is—part of human desire to want more and more; the conqueror endlessly seeks to obtain wealth, power, and prestige. And, on the opposite side, it's human nature to try to prevent oneself from being conquered or being destroyed by others.

But in the long run, and as history shows, the end result was the opposite of the aggressor's intended goals, which we can see in the history of the rise and fall of aggressive imperialistic powers. This was mainly because overambitious imperialistic power extends beyond its capacity to control bigger targets; it creates many enemies through the process of abuse, exploitation, and impoverishing other nations by stealing their wealth. In the end, the imperialistic process creates enemies; the more enemies it creates, the sooner it collapses. [1]

The process of destroying a nation to steal its wealth is clearly illustrated in the invasion of Iraq to control its oil reserves, which became the root cause of the current terrorism. (The invasion of Iraq is discussed in chapter 2.)

Other parts of the dissertation discuss the rise of various far-right movements, especially in the United States, Europe, and Israel. The increased popularity of these movements is entrenching the religious-nationalistic conflicts in the world, which in turn is leading to a catastrophic clash of civilizations. This clash is taking the world into dangerous territory that demands the awakening of the silent majority to take action before it is too late. Using racism, populism, and bigotry, far-right movements are capable of dividing the citizens of not only their own countries but also the whole world. Their behavior can be construed as flipping around the conventional wisdom of "united we stand, and divided we fall" into the catastrophe of "divided we stand, and united we fall." These groups promote fear to achieve popularity, when people can in fact feel safer by getting rid of fear. In the United States, for example, the adoption of a politics of fear contradicts President Franklin Roosevelt's bold declaration about the United States: "This great nation will endure as it has endured, will revive and prosper...The only thing we have to fear is fear itself." [2]

Far-right leaders achieve their objectives by creating slogans that twist words to exercise power and control over people's minds. For example, with far-right leaders' patriotic slogan of "protecting the West from Islamic terrorism"—which Western countries, especially the United States and

Great Britain, helped create in the first place—such leaders plunge their countries and the rest of the world into a major conflict that will have no winner. This is when a simple question must be asked: how can leaders claim to be patriotic by destroying the social fabric of their own countries by division, as well as by fragmenting the world? Unfortunately, in the process, the United States is producing bigoted leaders like Donald Trump with the help of the religious-right Tea Party and the white supremacists who make up Trump's power base. During the 2016 presidential election, these groups were able to highjack the Republican Party using populist slogans. The United States, being a country of immigrants, cannot afford to have racist leaders or to adopt an evangelical religious nationalism that can lead to deep social divisions and ultimately upheaval in the country.

I believe this work can add to the moderate voice of reason that is currently being drowned out by the louder voices of fanatics, the religious right, and the ultranationalists with their powerful propaganda machine that includes many influential members of the right-wing media and press. The current debate about terrorism is subjectively focused on its evil and its effect while ignoring or glossing over its main causes, which are imperialism, nationalism, and religion.

I hope the readers of this dissertation will make an allowance for my occasional drifting from an academic mode into a counterpropaganda mode; I feel this is necessary to do because propaganda is always aimed at diverting people's attention from reality. My approach is intentional. My hope is that this work will also become useful to the many readers who are systematically fed purposefully misleading information that is designed for manipulation and mind control. I also take this approach because, without devaluing knowledge, sometimes opinions can be as important as facts. In some cases and in certain situations, opinions have been more important than facts, especially when things that people believe are true turn out to be wrong. For example, people believed the sun revolved around the earth, which was a "fact" until Copernicus proved the opposite. People also believed the earth was flat until Ferdinand Magellan, Vasco da Gama, and Christopher Columbus proved otherwise.

In this work, my purpose is to use my intellectual freedom to challenge the effect of the prevailing propaganda. It is my belief that understanding the subjects under discussion can help many people shed their apathy and start to care about the future and the safety of the generations who follow. The work is for not only the benefit of students of political and social sciences but also people who are interested in learning and understanding the world as it is in reality, rather than in the way the vested interests present it.

Readers will notice I try to avoid interrupting them with critical citation-related notes that are traditionally placed at the end of a book. In this book, important notes and definitions are provided immediately after the paragraph in which they appear, to give readers immediate descriptions, meanings, and clarifications with minimum disruption to the smooth flow of thoughts, while other notes and the original sources can still be found at the end of the book.

CHAPTER 1

Imperialism and Conflicts

•••

VARIOUS DICTIONARIES AND OTHER RESOURCES define "imperialism" as an action of extending a country's power and influence on other countries through colonization, the use of military force, or other means. The aggressor in this case could be a powerful country or group of countries that dictate political change or influence the way people live in other countries; the aim is domination and economic benefits.

To distinguish between imperialism and empire, historian Richard Immerman wrote in his book *Empire for Liberty* (2010) that "in contrast to empire, imperialism refers to a process by which one state employs instruments of power to acquire control over peripheral peoples and territory. This process may result in the extension of liberty for some (for example, the liberty to attain more wealth and power), but the loss of others' liberty is unavoidable. As such, from the beginning *imperialism* was a much more value-laden term than *empire*, freighted with negative weight." [1]

In political scientist James Petras's July 2014 article titled "Foundation of the US Empire: Axes of Evil," in the *information clearing house*, the author wrote:

Imperial difficulties are multiplied when an empire is in economic decline (loss of market shares with growing debt), facing domestic unrest as the economic costs to the taxpayers exceed the returns by a substantial margin, and when the political elite is internally divided between the militarists and the free market advocates.

The US Empire today is in the midst of a long-term decline, during which it has suffered a series of costly defeats. In addition, Washington has assumed long-term burdensome commitments to allies who have imposed their own ambitions of seeking mini empires (Israel, Turkey, and Saudi Arabia).

The US White House has increasingly adopted a military definition of the imperial leadership at the expense of reconfiguring imperial relations to accommodate potential new political and economic partners.

As the empire slides, the political elite, operating with a highly militarized mind set, has expanded its intrusive global intelligence networks to spy on allies, adversaries and its own citizens. Washington has risked deepening hostilities among key allies (Germany and Brazil), and exacerbating conflicts with conciliatory competitors (Russia), by refusing to curtail its massive espionage. Spying is a clear hostile act and part of the policy of military-driven empire building. [2]

In the same article, Petras wrote that "Today, the US empire builders are making their transition back to the 19th century colonial model. The Pentagon has been moving from reliance on US ground troops to recruiting colonial troops under US military command.

To that end, Washington's empire has turned toward creating alliances with regional powers to sustain imperial pre-eminence. These alliances are in place in Africa, Latin America, Asia, and, in particular, in the Middle East." [3]

Imperialism occurs when a country—such as Germany and Britain in the past, and the United States in the present—begins to convert its growing economic resources into military power and political influence. It occurs when the country's economic development is accelerated at a high speed that may necessitate market expansion, which in turn may necessitate the acceleration of military and political influence. Imperialism is achieved by direct territorial acquisitions or by gaining indirect control over the political or economic lives of other countries through surrogate governments. Historically, countries achieved imperialism by installing an imperial government and imposing the imperial system in other countries. In the modern era, we have witnessed the creation of vast empires, primarily colonial ones. Between the fifteenth century and the middle of the eighteenth century, England, France, the Netherlands, Portugal, and Spain built empires in the Americas, Africa, India, Australia, and the East Indies. The decades between the middle of the nineteenth century and World War I were characterized by intense imperialistic policies and conflicts. Russia, Italy, Germany, the United States, and Japan were added as newcomers among the imperialistic states, especially during what is sometimes called the second British Empire (1783–1860), when indirect economic control became a preferred form of imperialism. [4]

This situation may be contrasted with the earlier British philosophy in place during the first British Empire, when the British acted as agents to encourage free markets, the rule of law, investor protection, civil society, and culture, and, importantly, they installed relatively noncorrupt governments in most of their colonies. The British also did quite a bit during the earlier period of their empire to encourage similar attitudes and approaches among the leaders of other countries, especially those that were outside Britain's formal imperial domain but under its economic influence through the imperialism of free trade. It is worth noting that the first British Empire was the creation of explorers and traders and was based on an economic relationship between colonies and the mother country—a relationship that produced the United States, as one example. The first British Empire was built in competition with Spain, Portugal, Holland, and France to exploit the world outside Europe, while the second British Empire was built by enlightened government power and was created by bureaucrats and generals. This second empire was based on the political relationship known as imperialism that produced Canada, Australia, and New Zealand. [5]

The focus in this chapter is on the role of imperialism as a form of state terrorism that contributes to the current spread of other forms of terrorism—especially to Islamic terrorism (discussed in chapter 2). Vested interests (the beneficiaries of imperialism) often gloss over the role of state terrorism in provoking a counteraction. Such interests often use their power of propaganda to articulate to less informed people a one-sided message that distorts reality and diverts their anger away from the aggressive imperialistic actions. Though the vested-interest groups are the main beneficiaries of acts of imperialism, such as the invasion of Iraq, thus far they have been able to convince the unwary that the other side is ultimately responsible for terrorism because the other side hates the Western way of life. These vested interests also pretend they want to rid the world of unwanted dictators while failing to admit terrorism could be a reaction to an aggressive act of domination, or a fight for survival, or a fight of ideologies.

I wrote the following in my book *Thorny Opinion* (2008):

> Often political and religious leaders justify their fight against Islamic extremism on the basis of their hatred for the Western way of life, but they forget to mention that this intolerance works both ways. The Western way of life has been built on the exploitation and wealth grabbing of weaker countries, some of which happened to be Islamic countries. Unfortunately, Western media and press tend to [overlook or gloss over] basic facts and blame one extremist group, instead of implicating both. [6]

Propaganda is when rhetoric trumps reality, which plays a major role in forming public opinion and in diverting the anger of the masses to a direction that suits the beneficiaries. Forming public opinion is always critical for the desired outcome, which can be illustrated by the following comparison: resisting Nazi imperialism during World War II was considered heroism then, but resisting American imperialism or Israel's illegal occupation of Palestine are considered terrorism today.

How can anybody forget America's act of "shock and awe" that resulted in killing half a million Iraqis—with many more killed and displaced in the civil war that followed—under the pretense of getting rid of a dictator and imposing on the country a manufactured democracy through the barrel of a gun? And all this happened without America considering the unintended consequences of unleashing a wave of Islamic terrorism. Can any politically aware person now distinguish state terrorism from religious or other forms of terrorism? What has been proved to date, however, is that propaganda can manipulate people into believing in anything that suits them.

It should be mentioned that the propaganda employed before, during, and after the destruction of Iraq has proved to be the opposite of what the United States had portrayed to the world before invading Iraq. Iraq didn't have weapons of mass destruction and had no connection with al-Qaeda; rather, the invasion was a matter of oil and the protection of Israel. The liberation of Iraq was a smoke screen advanced by Paul Wolfowitz and other neoconservatives and far-right Zionists in the George W. Bush administration. (For more on neoconservatives and far-right Zionists, see chapter 2.)

It should also be mentioned that throughout the book, where Zionists or Zionism are in focus—for clarity—Zionism is not the same as Judaism. Zionism is a narrow ethnic and nationalistic movement, whereas Judaism is a pluralistic religious movement that advocates tolerance, coexistence, and peace. In contrast, Zionism is about ethnic cleansing, racism, and vengefulness.

The outcome was catastrophic not only because of the civil war that devastated Iraq but also because it devastated America's reputation as a champion of liberty and human rights; the global war on terror exposed America's torture of prisoners and the rendition of prisoners to other countries for torture. Needless to say, the US Army's behavior in Abu Ghraib prison, where the Iraqi prisoners were in jail and defenseless when subjected to sadistic criminal abuses, amounted to tyranny. How can anybody forget the images of the Americans seemingly taking great delight in denying dignity to their prisoners in tyrannical and barbaric ways? Images were taken of American soldiers smiling, cigarettes dangling from their mouths, while pointing to one another with hoods over the prisoners' heads. [7, 8]

In his 2006 book *A Question of Torture: CIA Interrogation, from the Cold War to the War on Terror*, history professor Alfred McCoy points out that the CIA funded research in experimental psychology for the investigation of human ecology for the purposes of mind control. The aim of the research was to identify key behavioral components in the CIA's emerging psychological torture technique, especially the devastating impact of sensory deprivation. According to

McCoy, victims worldwide have also endured the CIA's tortures, as highlighted by its methods in Abu Ghraib prison following the invasion of Iraq. [9]

The CIA's main objective in torturing prisoners following the September 11 attacks was to find any links between Saddam Hussein and al-Qaeda to justify America's planned invasion of Iraq. In his May 2009 article "The Torture Memos," historian, linguist, and philosopher Noam Chomsky details the testimony in the Senate Armed Services Committee report on Vice President Dick Cheney's and Defense Secretary Donald Rumsfeld's desperation to find these links, which were irrelevant "facts" that were later concocted as justification for the invasion. In his testimony, former major army psychiatrist Charles Burney stated that a large part of the time, Cheney and Rumsfeld were focused on trying to establish a link between al-Qaeda and Iraq. The more frustrating it became to try to establish such a link, the more pressure was applied, using measures that might produce more immediate results—that is, torture. [10]

This is what happens when a country that has led the world to believe it is a symbol of liberty and human rights does not act in the way it presents itself. This is also what makes it difficult for America to reconcile its claim to be a champion of freedom and democracy while much of the world sees it as a hypocritical country driven by self-interest and the monopolistic desire to control the world. This is not a reflection of the American people, however, because Americans themselves are victims of the misinformation and propaganda perpetrated by vested interests and manipulative political leaders. (For more on the invasion of Iraq, see chapter 2.)

On the topic of trusted and mistrusted American leaders, it is worth mentioning a satirical remark that American syndicated columnist Mark Shields made on the TV program *PBS NewsHour* in May 2017 about Donald Trump's administration: "I cannot overstate how unbelievable…this administration has become…It was said that George Washington was the president who could never tell a lie, and Richard Nixon was the president who could never tell the truth. Donald Trump is truly the president who can't tell the difference." [11] Shields should have had added that George W. Bush was the president who declared "Mission accomplished" when it had just started and had no end in sight.

For some awareness about the negative aspects of imperialism as a form of terrorism, people should again ask themselves these questions: What is the difference between state terrorism and sectarian or tribal terrorism? Does violence breed violence? Does injustice bring peace? Is there a reaction to an action? The discussion continues.

American Imperialism (Neocolonialism)

The modern form of imperialism as practiced by the United States is generally termed "neocolonialism." Under neocolonialism, economic, political, cultural, or other means (such as temporary military interventions) are used to control or influence other countries, especially by installing puppet governments. Under American imperialism, civil wars, corrupt governments, and lawlessness—as we can see in the Middle East, North Africa, and parts of Asia—have condemned many countries to decades of conflict, displaced citizens, and poverty. This situation contradicts what America preaches about free trade and helping poor countries stand on their feet. Instead, these countries now produce people who lack hope and become lawless and a threat to Western civilization. The US imperialism generally relates to the policy of a strong country targeting a weaker country for political and economic hegemony or for extending the country's sphere of influence; it involves the use of the weaker country's resources to strengthen and enrich the stronger country and is an imperialistic geopolitical practice of capitalism and business globalization. [12] Modern imperialism, as practiced by the United States, causes turmoil in the world, especially in the oil-rich Middle East, which is described below.

As Immerman states in *Empire for Liberty* (2010), in 1783, the year the United States formally gained independence from Great Britain, George Washington described the newborn republic as a "rising empire." [13] The concept of an American empire was first popularized during the presidency of James K. Polk, who led the United States into the Mexican-American War of 1846 and the eventual annexation of California and other western territories via the Treaty of Guadalupe Hidalgo and the Gadsden Purchase. [14]

In his annual message to Congress in 1904, President Theodore Roosevelt proclaimed that the United States, because it was a civilized nation, had the right to stop "chronic wrongdoing" throughout the Western Hemisphere. "Any country whose people conduct themselves well can count upon our hearty friendship," he said. "Chronic wrongdoing, however, may force the United States to exercise an international police power." [15] Unfortunately, following World War II, when the United States became a major superpower, it often behaved as judge, jury, and executioner. America often acted above the law in a unilateral way or with its allies by using military power, as the world saw during the wars in Vietnam, Cambodia, Afghanistan, Pakistan, Iraq, Libya, Nicaragua, and elsewhere.

Following the demise of the British and French empires as a result of World War II, the United States emerged as a superpower rivaled only by the Soviet Union. The race between the two superpowers to expand their respective spheres of influence was a race between the two economic/political systems of capitalism and socialism, which eventually ended in capitalism prevailing over socialism. To date, the United States has no rival, especially since the collapse of the Soviet Union in 1991.

America's lending of money to a Europe that was devastated after World War II and its establishment of a foothold in the Middle East to control its energy resources were the foundation stones of modern American imperialism. This new power came at the expense of the French and British, who had become heavily indebted and their power drastically diminished. The country's financial and military power benefited from the "brain drain" following World War II—especially of highly educated and motivated European immigrants—as well as America's own embrace of technical education. These two factors placed the United States on a growth path that drove it to evolve into an expansionist imperialistic power. The rapid growth and industrialization required new markets and the control of energy sources, especially when the country started to live beyond its means. This is similar to what had happened before the decline of the British and French empires.

The problem for America was the ease with which it had gained its new power and its sphere of influence (especially following the demise of other empires), which gave it the overconfidence that soon led it to ignore the responsibilities that came with its new power. The world is still waiting for America to realize that influence, and not power, is ultimately the most valuable strategy. Influence comes through generosity of the spirit, which reaps greater gains than mere power. The use of power and constant military interventions, on the other hand, results in resentment and counteraction, which ultimately weaken and destroy the aggressor. America should be able to learn from the lesson of history of the rise and fall of empires for its far-reaching ambition of world domination. America instead is following a similar path of earlier empires, which is leading the world into plunder, wars, corruption, famines, exploitation, impoverishment, massacres, and genocides. If only America understood imperialism in the context of industry and trade, without repeating the old cycle of hegemony and without employing the element of forceful market expansion, then the world, including America, would be better off.

American imperialism evolved to become mainly characterized by economic and military influence on other countries. Such influence often goes hand in hand with expansion into foreign territories. To control the world and its resources, America needed to do the following:

1. Create suitable financial institutions and a global financial system with minimum regulation, as well as allow the commercial banks to become investment banks, which enabled them to deal with derivatives and to trade outside the banking regulations by moving the bulk of their dealing outside their balance sheets and transferring the risk to the unregulated insurance sector. Subsequently, these banks grew too big and too rich and became a dominating force on the international financial market.

2. Help the expansion of its rich multinational corporations grow bigger and more powerful, which then entrenched America's extreme capitalism. This happened by the process of allowing large companies to take over smaller companies, which reduces competition and increases the profit of the larger companies.

3. Expand the militarization of the country, as well as enhance its national security agencies, which are designed for controlling the world and protecting the nation's puppet regimes.

4. Expand its sphere of influence. To do so, it needed to enter into alliances, especially with the North Atlantic Treaty Organization (NATO) countries and Israel, the latter of which is spearheading US expansion in the Middle East.

In targeting countries such as Iraq for expansion, America considers three main points before acting, which Noam Chomsky addresses in his 2004 book *Hegemony or Survival: America's Quest for Global Dominance*: "The target of preventive war must have several characteristics."

1. The targeted country must be virtually defenseless.
2. It must be important enough to be worth the trouble.
3. There must be a way to portray it as the ultimate evil and an imminent threat to our survival. [16]

The main problems with America are discussed below.

What Is the Problem with America?

Following the collapse of the Soviet Union and the end of the Cold War, upon becoming an undisputed single superpower, America chose to adopt an aggressive approach to international relations in its quest to dominate the world. Behind its aggression is the alliance between the religious-right groups and the neoconservative hawks, who are a combination of certain far-right Zionists and other far-right Christian groups, such as the Evangelicals. (For more on the neoconservatives, the Evangelicals, and the Tea Party, see chapter 2.) These groups constitute the essential part of the Republican Party structure, not only for its conservative attitude and its total commitment to Israel but also for its commitment to an extreme-capitalist platform and the use of military power to achieve America's control of the world. These groups believe in "American exceptionalism," that America is an indispensable empire, and that its national interest has no limit.

The feeling of America being an indispensable empire contradicts what history has shown—namely, that America is unable to reach the status of empire because it has evolved to become an imperialistic country. In his *Empire for Liberty* (2010), Richard Immerman describes how prominent British historian and Harvard Business School professor Niall Ferguson wishes the United States wore the mantle of empire proudly instead of creating a national delusion. As Ferguson wrote (quoted in Immerman [2010]), "The great thing about the American Empire is that so many Americans disbelieve in its existence. They think they're so different that when they have military bases in foreign territories, it's not an empire. When they invade sovereign territories, it's not an empire." [17]

In my 2016 book *Axis of Evil*, I wrote about American imperialism/neocolonialism:

It was necessary for imperialistic America to build an elaborate military machine and naval power that included the establishment of military bases all over the world, estimated to be over 730 bases spread… over 130 countries. Most of these bases are designed for attacking other countries, expansion, and protecting America's strategic interests, rather than what its propaganda claims—that they are for America's defense—when everyone knows that no country [in] the world is capable of attacking America in a convention-al way with conventional weapons. [18]

To draw an analogy with the Russia-US conflict following the Russian Revolution of 1917, the invasion of Russia was justified because of the fear of the threat to the survival of the capitalist system and that this Russian development might infect Western and other countries. In *Hegemony or Survival* (2004), Chomsky says the following:

> Attack is therefore defense, another "logical illogical-ity" that becomes coherent once the doctrinal appara-tus is properly understood. On the same grounds, we can understand the persistence of basic policies of the US and other leading Western powers before, during, and after the Cold War, always in self-defense. Note that the defensive invasion of Russia in 1918 is another precursor for the doctrine of preventive war declared in September 2002 by radical nationalists pursuing their imperial vision. [19]

By embarking on simultaneous unnecessary wars—earlier in South America and later in Afghanistan and Iraq, as well as during covert wars in Pakistan, Yemen, and Syria—America is often stamped as an aggressive and imperialistic power that is currently provoking Islamic insurgency, all of which is placing the country on a path of steep decline. For its lack of diplomatic skills and inability to conquer people's hearts, its life as an empire is destined to be short. America, before considering its weakness, is challenging the world and creating a huge backlash and many enemies, all of which is proving to be beyond its ability to control, no matter how many rockets it is able to fire. In its endeavor to control the world, America is provoking major resentment and resistance, which is contributing to its decline—a much worse decline than it suffered following its defeat in Vietnam, because the current war has a religious overtone and is aimed against the world's 1.7 billion Muslims.

In their book *Unintended Consequences: The United States at War* (2007), professors Kenneth J. Hagan and Ian J. Bickerton demonstrate that America often embarks on unnecessary wars without proper analysis and often under total ignorance of local conditions. The authors detail America's wars from the War of Independence to the war in Iraq and reach the conclusion that every war America has engaged in has led to unforeseen and unintended consequences. The authors make their position clear when they quote Machiavelli: "Wars begin when you will, but they do not end when you please." [20]

The wars in Afghanistan and Iraq are the ones that will produce probably the highest level of unintended consequences. The war in Afghanistan will eventually engulf the Asian region in a nuclear war, especially between India and Pakistan, or at least will lead to the collapse of Pakistan and the triumph of Muslim fundamentalists in both Afghanistan and Pakistan. The war in Afghanistan is proof that America plans for a war first with engagement of the CIA and then with the military, complete with the "mother of all bombs," as it is known, but without an exit strategy and without a nation-building plan for the country's destroyed infrastructure and government institutions. America and its allies are still fighting the Taliban insurgency after spending more than $1 trillion over the past seventeen years (from the date of publication of this book). There's no end in sight, especially with a new American military surge announced in 2017.

As for the engagement of the CIA, in Steve Coll's book *Ghost Wars: The Secret History of the CIA, Afghanistan, and Bin Laden, from the Soviet Invasion to September 10* (2004), the journalist and president of the New America Foundation—a nonpartisan think tank in the United States—provides comprehensive details of the CIA's involvement in the rise and evolution of the mujahedeen and al-Qaeda in the years before the September 11 attacks. Coll shows how the CIA miscalculated its engagement with Afghanistan and the emerging power of the Taliban after the end of the Soviet war. He also demonstrates how Afghanistan became a deadly playing field for international politics where Soviets, Pakistani, and American agents armed and trained a succession of warring factions. [21]

Unfortunately, the training and arming of warring factions as its foot soldiers—as has also happened in Iraq, Yemen, Libya, and Syria—is one of America's misguided methods of aiming for a positive outcome; in the absence of appropriate resources, however, the situation often gets out of control, and the opposite happens. Covert CIA activities often involve the mobilization of local military personnel and right-wing groups financed and trained to overthrow their governments so that America can have a new mob of foot soldiers who are totally dependent on it, loyal to it, and happy to serve its national interests. To achieve its objectives, the CIA employs every trick possible, including extortion, blackmail, kidnapping, torture, intimidation, conducting fraudulent elections, and, if necessary, the assassination of opposition leaders.

The war in Iraq, on the other hand, had different unintended consequences, especially in America's support of Saudi Arabia and Turkey. This support has caused ongoing ethnic and sectarian conflict between Sunnis and Shiites, at the same time strengthening Iran's influence in the region, thus causing a major threat to the Sunni Arab regimes in the Middle East. This situation will likely turn into a major threat to oil supplies when a major war breaks out between the two camps. This is in addition to exposing millions of Christian citizens in Islamic countries to genocide as a consequence of the religious/nationalistic clash between the Jewish and the Christian Zionists, on the one hand, and the Arabs and the Islamic world on the other. (For more on Christian Zionists, see chapter 2.) America's and Israel's aggression in the Middle East is making Christians an easy target for Islamic insurgency and revenge. The killing of Christians and the attacks on their churches have already started, and nothing will stop them. Over the past fifteen years—between the removal of Saddam Hussein and the publishing of this book—Iraqi Christians have been the target of violence many times, including murder and abductions. Hundreds of Christians in other Middle Eastern and African countries have been killed, and several churches have been attacked since the US-led invasion of Iraq in 2003. These killings and attacks on churches are now spreading widely, especially against Egyptian

Christians, who have become the softest targets for Islamic insurgency.

Hagan and Bickerton have correctly predicted that, as a result of a catastrophic foreign policy, the unintended consequences of America's wars would be far worse than their originally desired benefits. The miscalculation of consequences is reflected in the continuation of America's involvement in the defeated countries' chaotic messes for many years after wars, with negative impacts on the US economy, national security, and the security of the world. [22] Furthermore, America's foreign policy is causing its decline, partly because allowing Israel to spearhead American aggression in the Middle East is causing the rise of Islamic terrorism, which in turn is endangering America's security, as well as the security of its Western allies. Its foreign policy is influenced by far-right Zionist groups, to the benefit of Israel but with little regard for America's national interests. The far-right Zionists' influence is also negatively reflected in America's domestic and economic policies, because of the Israeli lobbying groups' control of Congress. (For more on Israel's role in the Middle East conflict, see chapter 2.)

America's wars and its foreign policy are mainly driven by its need for market expansion and the acquisition of cheap resources, as dictated by the country's expansionist capitalist system, which has been the cause of vast numbers of crises and conflicts around the world. An extreme-capitalist system leads to an expansionist foreign policy that causes the creation of many enemies because the imperial power impoverishes people in the targeted countries and installs corrupt puppet governments. In the process of controlling the world, such a power also attempts to weaken competing countries, especially the rising and ambitious emerging superpowers China and Russia, which provokes a nationalistic backlash. (America's extreme capitalism and its foreign policy are discussed below.)

What is frightening is that the conflicts and the enemies America creates can endanger the world's security by the potential for terrorists to acquire biological and nuclear materials, which will sooner or later become a reality. It is worth highlighting the problem associated with the security of Pakistan's nuclear arsenal, which will be extremely difficult to manage and could lead to an unpredictable and catastrophic outcome if some of the material gets into the hands of terrorist groups. Worse yet, the most frightening scenario is if and when North Korea or any other rogue state—as an act of economic desperation, survival, or revenge—decides to sell nuclear materials to anybody who is willing to pay, including to terrorist organizations. Beyond the possibility of theft and the use of nuclear material, other looming future terrorist threats are extremely difficult to predict or control, such as the use of biological weapons or drones in attacking a number of easy targets.

In February 2017, in a speech at the Munich Security Conference, Microsoft cofounder Bill Gates warned of the possibility of tens of millions of deaths by bioterrorism:

Whether it occurs by a quirk of nature or at the hand of a terrorist, epidemiologists say a fast-moving airborne pathogen could kill more than 30 million people in less than a year. And they say there is a reasonable probability the world will experience such an outbreak in the next 10 to 15 years...It's hard to get your mind around a catastrophe of that scale, but it happened not that long ago. In 1918, a particularly virulent and deadly strain of flu killed between 50 million and 100 million people...Getting ready for a global pandemic is every bit as important as nuclear deterrence and avoiding a climate catastrophe. Innovation, cooperation and careful planning can dramatically mitigate the risks presented by each of these threats. [23]

As for the use of drones to attack targets, I wrote the following in *Axis of Evil*:

The war on Islam resulted in the expansion and the creation of more extremist organizations that are morphing into even more extremist ones than Al-Qaeda, such as the Islamic State, al-Nusra Front, Jund al-Aqsa, and others. These extreme Muslim fanatics have the capacity to destabilize not only the Middle East but the rest of the world by adopting terrorist activities on soft targets that are difficult to control, such as car and truck bombings, lone-wolf attacks, suicide bombings, and future local chemical attacks and bombing with drones. The unmerciful drone attacks will become a common feature in the next phase of terrorism's evolution. Drones are based on American technology, especially when they were deployed in Afghanistan, which resulted in civilian casualties [that] are now contributing to creating more enemies for America…

In the midst of the fast advancement of technology and lagging international legislation, other countries and terrorist organizations will be competing in spreading the use of drones everywhere in a devastating way so that no country in the world will be safe. If drones currently can be used for mail and parcel delivery with the help of GPS technology, what will stop the parcel being a bomb or a dirty bomb? Is America playing with fire? Worse yet, what will stop downing passenger planes with drones? [24]

The difficulty of dealing with drone threats is illustrated in an article published on BBC's website in March 2017 by technology reporter Chris Baraniuk: "A patriot missile—usually priced at about $3m—was used to shoot down a quadcopter drone that cost 200 bucks purchased from Amazon.com. Patriots are radar-targeted weapons more commonly used to shoot down enemy aircraft and ballistic missiles while the improvised weapons consist of a plastic tube attached to a consumer camera drone to carry explosives." Similar weapons were used by Islamic State terrorists (IS) in Mosul from early March 2017 in their fight against the Iraqi army. [25] (For more on the Islamic State [IS], see the "Islamic Terrorism" subsection in chapter 2.)

Beyond all the above threats, another major problem is the controlling of emerging technologies such as 3-D printing when no government structure is in place to control this technology. Such a fast-growing technology that allows for making one's own products or weapons—where the sky is the limit—falling into the hands of terrorists should be of great concern to all countries of the world. (For a description of 3-D printing, see note 26.) UN Secretary General Ban Ki-Moon gave a speech in August 2016 to the UN Security Council in which he voiced his concern that humans were not properly dealing with the potential dangers of producing weapons using 3-D printing. In addition to paying heed to the standard trio of chemical, nuclear, and biological threats, Secretary General Ban also advised that the world should pay more attention to the destruction made possible through advanced emerging technologies. The contribution that 3-D printing makes to this morass of fearful possibilities is the opportunity the technology provides for terrorist groups to simply make the things they are unable to procure by other means. [27]

The Problem with America's Partisanship and Racism

Generally, politicians' partisanship is a reflection of the people's partisanship, which often revolves around various social and economic issues. The economic issues relate to the extreme-capitalist system that is practiced in America today—where the rich get richer and the poor get poorer—which we will discuss in the following subsection.

The social issues that are causing internal conflicts and are contributing to America's national decline mainly relate to discrimination, racism, and generally unfair treatment. In a social setting, discrimination is the manifestation of insecurity and fears, especially when a threat of competition from individuals or groups is perceived and exacerbated by the natural laws of the "survival instinct" and "survival of the fittest." The perception and the effect of these natural laws could become a cause for discrimination. Overcoming the negative social effects of these natural laws in a civilized society is usually done through (1) the provision of proper education; (2) social conditioning to develop self-awareness (emotional intelligence, or EI) and the awareness of others (social intelligence, or SI); and (3) enacting laws that promote equality, tolerance, and social harmony. These steps can be helped and reinforced by the fact that human beings are a social species; we are naturally equipped with the instinct to exchange empathy.

On the other hand, far-right politicians' and commentators' division of communities often leads to minorities being marginalized and despised, which leads to oppression, which in turn breeds resistance and violence. Looking down at others to achieve a feeling of superiority from the perspective of bigotry, humiliation, injustice, and discrimination will always result in resentment and counteraction, which then creates conflict and acts against the interests of a nation. Often the ground for discrimination and bigotry may be found in gender, sexual orientation, physical disability, skin color, and ignorance and lack of compassion because of religious beliefs.

As often happens, because of religious beliefs, because of racial heritage, because of physical disability, because of gender, and because of sexual orientation, people are denied their civil rights, their dignity, and the chance to reach their full potential. It should be stressed that the poorest, the most often unemployed, and the most jailed people in America are black.

Racism, which is the fear of difference, is the ugliest form of discrimination. It occurs when members of a community assume they are superior to others because of the group's ancestry, the color of their skin, or other features that make them feel entitled to more social and political privileges. Race and inequality have always been the causes of social conflict, as they have real impact on the lives of many people—an impact that cannot be ignored, especially when the loud voices of the extremist fringe are calling for dividing people and driving them into conflict. Because of racism, inequality is not imagined; it is real and often leads society to self-destruction because of the resentment and revolt it engenders. Racism is a pervasive and very harmful problem in any country of the world. It can increase the risk of mental illness, limit educational and employment opportunities, destroy social cohesion, increase crimes, and incite violence. Building a strong sense of cultural identity and perceived cultural respect buffers minorities from the negative effects of racism, especially the harsh impact of disempowerment. To prevent society from self-destruction, minorities must be treated with respect and equity. Dividing the community with bigotry and hatred weakens the country's stability and its productive capacity; it makes people lose their creativity and innovation to build a better future for the following generations. For any country's survival, perpetrators of unpatriotic social division should be treated with contempt. For any nation, it is important to work together for the betterment of society rather than focus on the differences that lead people into discrimination and bigotry. A united country that has a good and free secular education system based on equality and belief in equality as a constitutional human right helps give equal opportunity to all people to reach their potential. Out of this system, a better society and better politicians can emerge. [28]

Historically, humanity has always progressed by overcoming ignorance through the acquisition of wisdom within education. Teaching tolerance from childhood can be an important way to minimize human fear and insecurity. This can be achieved by objective social psychologists producing a carefully structured and secular school curriculum that will be beneficial to parents and children to ensure that future generations are developed in a psychologically stable manner and are able to live in harmony. Eventually, a country that uses this new concept of education could produce higher-quality politicians with less prejudice and bigotry than those who—for their own political survival—often play the race and religious cards or other forms of populism to appease specific groups of society through psychological manipulation.

In addition to having a good education system that embodies fairness and equality, a country must first acknowledge the existence of discrimination and institutionalized racism in order to eliminate their threat to society. Second, a country must develop a program to fight these evils at all levels of society, from home to schools to government. Although governments in many countries have enacted laws against racism, these laws will not stop people from displaying their nasty side. But the existence of laws can make bigoted and prejudiced people pause for thought before they cause harm. It is understandable that criminal laws can be a powerful tool to rein in bigots, but the law is also blind to many injurious behaviors. The enactment of laws and the provision of proper, free education for all can help society reach the level of psychological awareness of equality that can lead to social harmony—such that living by the motto of "United we stand and divided we fall" will be considered the better option.

We should remember that racism and discrimination originate from the more powerful groups in society and countries and toward countries and groups that have less power. Power is not necessarily bad in itself; it is the way it is used that is the problem. The exploitation of that privileged position is what causes so many harmful and detrimental acts against the underprivileged. We should also remember that some of the worst forms of institutionalized racism have been those that have been well documented: those of Nazi Germany and the apartheid regime of South Africa. Similarities today may be found in Americans' treatment of blacks and Latinos and in Israelis' treatment of Palestinians in building an apartheid separation wall, as well as ethnic cleansing, institutionalized discrimination against Palestinians, and the collective punishment of the Arab population. [29] (For more on Israel's role in the Middle East conflict, see chapter 2.)

Racism is often promoted by politicians' racist rhetoric and by political and media commentators, many of whom directly or indirectly advocate white supremacy or an attack on certain minorities or members of different religions they consider to be inferior. Although using racism has historically proved to be dangerous, far-right and populist politicians often use it for political gain. These far-right politicians and commentators are somehow ignoring the fact that racism is even more dangerous for America. This is simply because in America, there are over three hundred million weapons in the hands of its citizens and where a huge number of underclass and discriminated-against citizens have nothing left to lose, so they may as well revolt.

Racially and religiously motivated politicians and populist commentators stoke fear to gain advantages, and they don't care about society's future. They are more concerned with satisfying their large egos and toxic **narcissism*** rather than worrying about the damaging consequences. They have no concern that, to prevent society from self-destruction, minorities must be treated with respect and equity. [30]

* **Narcissism** goes beyond the natural, healthy form of a normal ego that provides one with a sense of self-esteem and becomes an unhealthy, antisocial personality disorder that often leads to violating the rights of others. "Unhealthy narcissism" refers to a person who has a profound inability to empathize with others; such people are obsessed with self-love, which means that they become preoccupied with self and their needs and how they are perceived by others. Unhealthy narcissism is a mental state in which people

engage in self-worship and take excessive interest in their own perfection. People with unhealthy narcissistic personalities often blame anything that goes wrong on others, display volatility and mood swings, and tend to be self-important and to need constant attention and admiration, which essentially means that such people are totally absorbed in the self and obsessed with self-image. The disorder's ultimate stage is megalomania, which refers to having delusions of grandeur and is a form of paranoid schizophrenia. The condition often affects people in power, especially obsessive politicians, crusading religious leaders, army generals, extreme capitalists, and any other people who show signs of aggression and ruthlessness toward others. (For more on other aspects of narcissism, see chapter 5 of my book *Psyche and Personality* [2013], as well as Daniel Goleman's books *Emotional Intelligence* [2006] and *Social Intelligence* [2007]. And, on the subject of intelligence, Howard Gardner's book *Multiple Intelligences: New Horizons* [2006] is highly recommended.)

Sinister political leaders and far-right commentators, who are blinded by bigotry and prejudice, might appeal to the less informed section of the community, but these leaders lose their creativity and become divisive. In the best interests of the country, their advocacy should be rejected. People should ask a simple question about them: how can people claim to serve their own country by dividing its people? This is when the unity of any nation and collective patriotism are paramount to the country's survival and prosperity. This is when wisdom—in the context of human relationships, and of being the human virtue of intellect—embodies the interdependence of knowledge, reasoning, and experience. This interdependence has always been the ultimate guide to human progress and survival. Wisdom guides people to the commonsense principle of "flexible moderation," which allows for diversity in social environments and in each individual's intellectual creativity. Applying flexible moderation means taking into consideration the emphasis and interpretation of meanings assigned to values in many cultures and civilizations; this could be the best path toward harmonious human relations.

Furthermore, wisdom, as an essential part of culture, can be defined as an evolutionary social process that coincides with the sophistication of people relative to their scientific, social, and economic progress. Wisdom encompasses all aspects of life, especially customs, traditions, religion, arts, language, common sense, and scientific and technological achievements. Common sense and scientific and technological achievements are the mental components of culture, while customs, traditions, arts, and religion are the spiritual components. Wisdom, generally, is the catalyst of all components. Variations and the degree of emphasis on any particular component within various groups and nations are the determining factors behind the world's multicultural structure. The Western world—especially America, as a multicultural nation—is mature enough to develop a secular school curriculum for teaching logic, rational thinking, common sense, and associated subjects to develop a new generation of nation builders equipped with wisdom and objectivity. Through secular education and experience, people can develop intuition, perception, spontaneity, free expression, creativity, and a free spirit, so that they are devoid of prejudice, bigotry, irrationality, subjective religion, and negative politics. I hope that America, as a civilized country, can become a clarion call for the world in setting up a process that can produce better politicians who are committed to uniting people instead of dividing them; doing so will ultimately stop the fragmentation of society and the world. Good citizenship occurs when people accept one another and reject racism and discrimination. A good politician is one who constantly promotes equality, individuality, diversity, and "fair play" principles. [31]

Unfortunately, white Americans have always displayed racial discrimination against African Americans, Native Americans, Latino Americans, Muslim Americans, and illegal immigrants. (Illegal migrants are generally allowed in America during times of high labor demand but are hounded out and demonized during slow times.) Furthermore, racial discrimination is not being eliminated, because Americans are electing politicians who play the race and religion cards, lead their country through populism, and promote the clash of civilizations. (For more on the clash of civilizations, see chapter 2.) The country's attitude must be changed. America needs a genuine, wise, committed, psychologically powerful, and trusted leader to emerge with a revolutionary agenda to save the nation, and the other nations of the world, from its current awful fragmentation. But American leaders are in no hurry to overcome the problem of racism in the country, as illustrated in the following example. As reported in the press in May 2017, following LeBron James's ordeal of suffering racism after the "N word" was spray painted on his Los

Angeles home, James said, "No matter how much money you have, no matter how famous you are…being black in America is tough…We've got a long way to go for us as a society and us as African-Americans until we feel equal in America." It should be noted that at the time of the incident, James was the Cleveland Cavaliers' team superstar; he became the all-time leading scorer in the NBA playoffs, surpassing Chicago Bulls legend Michael Jordan's record.

From the above description, one could observe that in America, discrimination and racism are alive and well. In *Israel vs. America vs. the World* (2011), I address the subject of racism in America:

Historically, the country has been dominated by white people and the rest were treated as second-class citizens. Prejudice and racism [are] often directed toward Native Americans, African Americans, Muslim Americans, Asian Americans, Mexican Americans, Hispanic Americans, illegal immigrants, and other minority groups.

It is estimated that there are 11 million badly exploited illegal immigrants in America who have no legal or social protection. During economic growth, illegal immigrants, especially Mexicans, are allowed in the country to work for low wages, but they are hounded or deported during economic slow-downs. Illegal immigrants, whose cheap labour has for many decades helped build American economic growth, are now being demonized.

Racial discrimination has occurred in employment, housing, education, and by government. American legislators had earlier recognized that people come to America for either money or freedom. Accordingly, they decided to end the formal racial discrimination, which was officially banned in the mid-twentieth century. Since then, racial discrimination has become socially unacceptable, except in racial politics, where it remains a major problem, especially in racist attitudes and prejudice against African Americans, illegal immigrants, Hispanics, and Muslims. [32, 33]

Discrimination and racism expose America's split personality in its constitutional and cultural aspects, which means that equality has lost its meaning in the US Constitution. This blatant discrimination comes in addition to the discrimination that is practiced against all economically disadvantaged groups who are left behind by America's extreme capitalism and globalization. The eventual revolt and uprising of these groups will add to the causes that are driving America's decline.

From the above social polarization stems political polarization, especially when the Democrats and Republicans are now driven by toeing their respective parties' lines on a party-loyalty basis; they have abandoned the earlier conscience-voting approach in Congress. Congress's previous capacity to hear the voices of minorities is now lost. The move to party authoritarianism usually results in placing power in the hands of a few influential members of the party, which makes a mockery of any democracy.

Partisan politics places the interest of one political party and its ideology above the interest of the country, especially when one party is determined to defeat the other party at any cost. The polarization between the Republicans and the Democrats and the use of the filibuster rule in the Senate to obstruct legislation, even when such legislation is in America's national interest, impede America's progress. The constitutional rules of the filibuster were originally designed for the purpose of debating in order to reach a better outcome for the country; it is now having the opposite effect. Unfortunately, the ideology-driven interest of one party is becoming more important than the needs of the country. The political polarization is happening at a time when maximum national unity is needed to restore America's strength to face the threats of terrorism and nuclear proliferation and, importantly, to arrest its economic decline, which is being accelerated by the country's huge national debt while the United States militarizes and wages unwinnable wars around the world.

Ironically, partisan politics do occasionally become bipartisan, such as when Congress, by overwhelming majority, decided to impose economic sanctions against Russia in a July 2017 bill that deliberately included measures to ensure that President Trump would not be able to lift them. The bill, at the time, was based on unproven speculations that Russia had interfered in the 2016 American election. These sanctions are generally not anticipated to contribute to improving international relations or to improving trade and the world economy.

Political polarization in the United States has been further aggravated by the Supreme Court's ruling on political campaign finances that it handed down in January 2010. In a March 2010 article on the website of the law firm Curtis, Curtis & Brelinski, PC, Brad Brelinski analyzed the implication of the ruling. The ruling struck down a longstanding prohibition by businesses and unions against campaign financing and advocacy. The ruling allows corporations to act as "individuals," which allows them to donate anonymously to parties or candidates. The ruling has the potential to encourage huge corporations to sponsor legislation directly or indirectly. It is a decision based on freedom of speech and the First Amendment, but in this case it has entrenched the influence of money on election results. It is the single biggest political decision by the Supreme Court and will have massive implications on all future elections' outcomes. The ruling has the potential to further poison the political atmosphere by entrenching the role of money in elections that are driven by propaganda, the distortion of facts, and the art of deception. Corporations are now able to bankroll candidates, especially by paying for the advertising of candidates who are willing to sponsor legislation that is to their advantage. Because payments for costly advertising are not considered donations under the law, they are not subject to disclosure. [34]

Another decision based on the freedom of speech and the First Amendment that has resulted in the degradation of American democracy was President Donald Trump's executive order of May 4, 2017, which gives members of the clergy the freedom to endorse candidates without the fear of losing their tax-exempt status. The president signed an executive order that did away with an IRS rule that stated that religious organizations and other nonprofits that endorse political candidates risk losing their tax-exempt status. The IRS rule that was repealed by Trump's order is known as the Johnson Amendment and was sponsored by then senator Lyndon Johnson. The regulation went into effect in 1954 and became a provision in the US tax code that barred any nonprofit organization from endorsing or opposing a political candidate. [35]

The new order allows churches and other religious organizations to flaunt the electioneering restrictions and grants preferential treatment to religious organizations, while secular groups must still abide by the law. Completely tax-exempt religious organizations can raise huge amounts of money and donate that tax-deductible money to their preferred political party or candidate, which is only adding to the corruption of American partisan democracy. The move is a backward step that puts America on equal footing with several Islamic countries in which religion and politics are inseparable.

I should add that the separation of religion from politics and often-violent clashes in the civilized world has never been fully accomplished. They are embedded in the history of all religions. [36]

The Problem with America's Extreme Capitalism
Since the years of benign moderate capitalism under President Franklin Roosevelt, when the fair distribution of wealth and a safety net for the disadvantaged applied, America has moved into an extreme economic system that is anchored mainly by exploitation—the rich get richer and the poor get poorer. It is a system that is unrestrained by a moral code; it is just about money and extreme greed, which are addictive and destructive. The extreme-capitalism model that has been adopted is characterized by income inequality and the concentration of wealth in the hands of ultrarich capitalists, the banks, and Wall Street. Generally, this has resulted in polarization within American society and with other nations because of extreme capitalism's exploitative and expansionist nature. It is the ultimate stage of capitalism that fundamentally results in economic power combined with political power that is directed to exploit the masses within a country and other nations for economic expansion; this expansion is the driving force behind American imperialism (neocolonialism). It is the stage where capitalists become obsessed in their quest to make a profit, without taking into consideration the unintended consequences of their actions. Under extreme capitalism, the emphasis on self-interest and the overlooking of accountability have resulted in ignoring the cultural advantage of having a compassionate and moderate capitalist system that operates with a fair distribution of wealth and a reasonable safety net for the disadvantaged and for those who are left behind by advanced technologies and globalization. In adopting such an economic model, America has

introduced corruption, dishonesty, and the element of extreme exploitation, where "dog eats dog" becomes socially normal. Capitalists in such a system develop a culture where people succeed for the capitalists rather than for themselves. They become obsessed with profit, they push the law as far as possible to obtain advantage, and they corrupt democracy with their wealth. They build their wealth by ripping others off and by avoiding taxes, legally and illegally, which results in the government spending more on militarization and less on social security, health, and education, all of which are disadvantageous to the majority.

Under extreme capitalism, having a safety net for the disadvantaged is not a priority. People who are left behind by globalization and by an unfair economic system are left to fend for themselves. It is also when the economic system and the social environment aren't taken into consideration when people are left behind because of lack of proper education, training, or retraining and the entrenched discrimination and racism in the country. The same system doesn't consider that creating social injustice and an economic underclass will eventually lead to the breakdown of social order and will result in violence. This is when the same system that entails the exploitation of other nations creates more and more enemies to fight against the empire; the larger the number of enemies, the sooner the end will come. This is the history of the rise and fall of empires.

Wall Street—the symbol of extreme capitalism—controls the international financial system, which has no foolproof international coordination. This gives Wall Street the capacity to manipulate other countries' financial and monetary systems to achieve its objectives of enriching the selected few among the megarich financial engineers. In today's global economy, the big banks, hedge funds, private-equity funds, and other traders have the capacity to attack any market and target any country's currency, which makes the financial and monetary management of other countries much harder for these countries' own governments. This group of financial engineers and institutions use computer technologies that surpass other countries' capacities, which gives them a huge advantage in manipulating and stealing the wealth of other nations.

The nature of extreme capitalism—which is driven by extreme greed and operates under the principle that the winner takes all—is that the strong will gobble up the weak.

In a March 2017 *Wall Street Journal* article, investing columnist Jason Zweig stated that "modern capitalism is built on the idea that as companies get big, they become fat and happy, opening themselves up to lean and hungry competitors who can under-price and overtake them. That cycle of creative destruction may be changing in ways that help explain the seemingly unstoppable rise of the stock market."

New research by economists Gustavo Grullon of Rice University, Yelena Larkin of York University, and Roni Michaely of Cornell University further argues that US companies are moving toward a winner-takes-all system in which giants get stronger, not weaker, as they grow. Why might it be easier now for winners to take all? Professor Michaely suggests two theories. One is that the declining enforcement of antitrust rules has led to bigger mergers, less competition, and higher profits. The other is technology. "If you want to compete with Google or Amazon, you'll have to invest not just billions, but tens of billions of dollars." [37]

Unfortunately, on a longer-term basis, such a system has no chance of survival, as it has built-in self-destruct mechanisms called extreme greed, excess credit, and lack of social justice. Extreme capitalism has the capacity to destroy the social fabric of the United States, and it will eventually lead to the nation's own economic system destruction. The excess-credit aspect associated with such a system is far from being similar to the moderate credit associated with moderate capitalism, where businesses and individuals borrow and spend within their capacity. Instead, under extreme capitalism, borrowing and spending often get out of control. Big spending, which is often fueled by financial engineering, is done for the benefit of a few to become richer at the expense of others. Above all, extreme capitalism has destroyed the real American dream of a secure job and a home, a better life for the family, upward social mobility, and a dignified retirement, most of which are now out of reach for many people, including the middle class, while the rich get richer and the poor get poorer.

I wrote the following in *Axis of Evil*:

In its quest for profit without taking into account moral and human values, extreme capitalism creates many losers and resentful underclass social groups, which results in social instability and eventually revolt, whether large or small scale. But social stability can be achieved; one way is by the fair distribution of wealth, which begins with providing equal opportunity to all children to reach their full potential through free and quality education, which is the key element of upward social mobility.

One of the most damaging aspects of extreme capitalism is that the owners of capital and the vested interests control the political system to the extent that politicians cannot innovate and reform without their approval. Additionally, extreme capitalism has turned the financial markets into a gravy train for executives and their boards of directors while investors and workers are relegated to the bottom of the food chain. [38]

This is why many Americans feel angry and betrayed by their politicians for their poor decisions, especially those that involve the waging of unnecessary and expensive wars, the global financial crisis, the protection of vested interests, the tax avoidance by the rich, and the various emerging technologies that are making jobs disappear. [39]

The impact of extreme capitalism may be found in the system's capacity to create the opposite extreme: the revolt of the exploited against the exploiters, who are blinded by their short-term self-interest rather than worrying about the eventual consequences of their actions, which will have the potential to destroy not only the social fabric of their country but also their own wealth. This destruction will be the consequence of believing in the fiction that, under capitalism, the market regulates itself and that if they inflate asset prices, those prices will eventually go back to fair value.

America is in desperate need of a new economic model and policies that focus on revitalizing the middle class and raising the minimum wage to recover the nation's spending power. But due to partisan politics and ideological polarization, the Republican Party has made itself a stumbling block by preventing any reform that doesn't make the rich richer and the poor poorer. For example, the Republicans often advance the argument, especially when America enters a recession, that raising the minimum wage causes businesses to cut jobs because they can no longer afford to pay all their workers. The Republicans' argument doesn't take into consideration that when the economy is in recession, it has to be stimulated by additional spending. Stimulating spending depends largely on improving people's spending power to increase demand, while the opposite happens when the working and middle classes are getting poorer and their wages are depressed. Furthermore, spending cannot be stimulated when America has the greatest concentration of wealth in the top 2 percent of its population. This situation is when the unfair distribution of wealth makes America a country where upward social mobility is no longer in sight and where investment in the future is drastically diminished. Extreme capitalism leaves many people behind, with no hope and with nothing left to do but beg, turn to crime, or, ultimately, revolt. The history of revolutions suggests that, in the absence of social justice, what has happened in other countries will happen in America, no matter how farfetched this might sound today. History also shows that when a major social vacuum is created and an underclass that has nothing left to lose is established, an upheaval will follow. (The laws of physics, too, say that a vacuum will be filled.) The entrenchment of poverty is the first ingredient of social disintegration and the seed of eventual upheaval and revolt. [40]

The social and political vacuum is further amplified by degrading and sidelining the middle class economically and in political representation. This decline is caused by the American polarized two-party system of the Republicans versus the Democrats. (For a description of the middle class, see note 41.) The two-party system in America and in a few other Western countries leaves their democracies at a huge disadvantage because of polarization. Major decisions about a country's national interests are forsaken for vested interests from the leftists and the rightists, with no moderating force in between, which is the moderate majority who have no direct representation in Congress. The absence of a middle-class party has resulted from three main reasons. First, the middle class sits in an economic comfort zone relative to the working class and the capitalists. Second, as a consequence of its economic comfort, the middle class has developed political apathy because it belongs outside the traditional "class warfare" between the other two polarized economic groups. Third, the middle class, historically and to a certain extent today, remains loyal to a top-down system of power. Besides the middle class being in an economic comfort zone, this class's political apathy is entrenched because the group's moderate voice is drowned out by the loud voices of the far right and religious-right groups, which are enhanced by the power of the generally dominant right-wing media and press.

As it stands, certain sections of the middle class, such as a few politicians and political administrators, are employed by the two polarized groups in serving their interests rather than worrying about forming a middle-class political structure. During elections, being part of the swinging voter group, the middle class's vote is appealed to by both leftists and rightists with false promises that cause the middle class to become undistinguishable from the working class. I should mention that under extreme capitalism, one reason that the rich get richer and the poor get poorer is by depressed wages and salaries, which in turn results in the country ending up with an unfair distribution of wealth. Couple this situation with the wealthy paying fewer taxes (through both legal and illegal methods) while the working and middle classes pay more. Depressing middle-class income will sooner or later lead to the middle class's political awareness and engagement in class warfare, especially because of the class's transition from an economic comfort zone to economic disadvantage. The middle-class awakening will be further stimulated by its predicament, caused by extreme capitalism; its survival in the commercial world will largely depend on political activism. The awakening of the middle class and the forming of its own independent party will be vital for restoring American democracy, which is currently controlled by the elites and by the power of money. Democracy can be restored by creating a moderate, middle-class party that in turn can restore young people's engagement in politics and democracy, as well as making democracy a tool in the hands of the majority, who are currently discouraged from having a stable ideology. The governing elites are never serious about the nation's political awareness or the people's engagement with politics and democracy. If they were, they would have insisted on introducing an objective **political science**** subject as part of a secular high school curriculum—in an introductory format—that would be free from subjectivity and manipulation.

**** Political science**: The general and traditional definition of political science, as provided by various authorities, is a science that examines the political system; the state; and the state's organs and institutions, political activities, and political behavior. The field borrows heavily from social science, which focuses primarily on ethical, empirical observations and system of governance. [42]

In this dissertation, however, for the purpose of a possible future design of a basic introductory-format high school curriculum for grades eleven and twelve, the components of political science should include the following:

- the political systems and institutions of key countries
- socioeconomics
- human relationships
- international relations
- psychology
- philosophy

I should add that basic financial management and the role of money in everyday life should be taught earlier, wherever possible. These subjects are essential for stimulating the youth's engagement in politics through an understanding of the democratic process and through helping students become aware of themselves and the world around them, especially while they are approaching voting age. If the West is serious about arresting the decline of Western civilization, then it should start by arresting the decline of its democracy, which has been hijacked by vested interests and the power of money, which is now in the hands of the ultrarich 2 percent of the population and the loud voices of Christian and Jewish lobby groups.

To revive Western civilization and to become a beacon for the world, America and its Western allies should set the example and then encourage the others to follow the path of adopting a free and secular education system that can bring the world together instead of suffering from the prevailing fragmentation, especially in countries where religious education is dominant. Through secular education, students—Muslim, Christian, and Jewish—can avoid the subjectivity and sectarianism that embolden bigotry and prejudice. In turn, secular education can produce secular politicians who promote equality, individuality, diversity, and fair-play principles. America is well equipped to lead the world in an education revolution by its own reformation, or at least by going back to its roots instead of becoming preoccupied with dominating the world by force. [43]

Because of America's drastic imbalance in the distribution of wealth—for either evolutionary or revolutionary reasons—the country could become the first extreme-capitalist country with no other option but to adopt a third-party concept. The "evolutionary" aspect refers to how social inequality progresses at a certain pace until it becomes intolerable, through a constant exploitation of the working and middle classes that brings them to poverty or below the poverty line, especially when the economy is burdened with a massive national debt. The "revolutionary" aspect refers to the exploitation and the absence of a safety net and reasonable health and welfare systems; when these failures reach the boiling point, they turn into major dissent and upheaval. This can happen when people lose hope, as has happened in other countries, such as in Russia in the early twentieth century. This caused the emergence of socialism there in order to achieve political and economic rights for workers, which eventually led to the socialist revolution.

As a general rule, society is divided into social classes. In a traditional Western democracy, a social class is represented by a political class. The two-party system was mostly copied from the old British Empire's structure, which still exists in Britain today and in some of its old colonies; it is called the Westminster system of government. Over the years, the Labour Party in Britain represented the working class, while the conservative Liberal Party represented the capitalists and middle classes. The equivalents in America are the Democratic Party and the Republican Party, respectively. Conversely, the American Democratic Party is generally known as the liberal party, and the Republican Party is known as the conservative party. [44]

The two parties have always complicated and manipulated the voting system and put legislative hurdles in place to ensure that no third party can emerge to challenge their dominance, especially when the middle class wasn't large enough and while it was accommodated mostly within the conservative political wing. The intensive industrialization of the West after World War II, however, has coincided with better education and the development of various high-tech and service industries, which in turn has resulted in the continuous growth of the middle class and the intelligentsia. This combined class is now becoming as large as the working class—and even larger in some Western countries. The economic mobility between social classes usually causes ideological distortion and conflicts of interest within a party if adjustments are not made for this mobility, since the status quo will become unsustainable.

The turmoil, polarization, instability, and partisanship in American politics provide a good example of the ideological distortion that occurs under a two-party system when a moderate middle-class party doesn't yet exist. Under the two-party system, the demagogues on both sides often play the class-warfare card in their ideological confrontations, which often leads to social discord.

The contradiction in American politics is that both parties are ignoring the class struggle that is simmering in the country, yet what they have in common is maintaining the American Empire and its leadership of the world—and at a time when America doesn't have the capacity to play a leading role because it is creating many enemies, and even its friends are losing faith in the nation. This has occurred because the country is afflicted by the conflicted Democratic and Republican Parties and because no intelligent or moderate party exists to show them the way. Above all, both parties are subservient to the extreme capitalists and the religious lobby groups. And to date, no president has been capable of taking these powers on. Furthermore, both parties have continued to cause America's decline because of their commitment to military interventions around the world, especially in Afghanistan, Iraq, Libya, Yemen, and Syria (indirectly and directly), and earlier in Korea, Vietnam, Cambodia, Somalia, Granada, Serbia, Panama, and so on. The delusion of building an empire through interventions is leading America into the opposite direction—the direction of gradual decline and eventual demise. All this is occurring simply because both parties are overlooking the fact that spending trillions of dollars on avoidable wars is depriving the economy of the money necessary for the country to be productive. Worse yet, both parties have sought to deregulate the financial sector, which has wreaked havoc not only on the American economy but also with the economies of the world. This deregulation caused the great financial crisis, and economic observers predict many more future crises. Especially if a new moderate leader doesn't emerge to stop the rot, then America's future doesn't look bright. [45]

According to a *Huffington Post* census published in September 2014, America's extreme capitalism has already left over forty-five million people, or over 14.5 percent of the American population, living below the poverty line, and still more are becoming trapped in entrenched poverty. Worse yet, many Americans who work full time are living below the poverty line because of depressed wages. When wages are continuously depressed so that the rich can get richer, the incentive to improve productivity on the management side proportionally diminishes. At times like this, the drive to meet the demands of international competition dictates that management must adopt innovations, invest in new technologies, improve systems, and generally cut costs. Depressing wages results in removing the incentive for manufacturers and other business leaders to aim for restructuring as a method of boosting efficiency and productivity. Destroying the morale and the upward mobility of the workforce by cutting wages is counterproductive.

Despite the setbacks and the lessons it should have learned from history, America still persists with its economic model, which is leading it into the kind of economic expansionism that entails control of other countries' markets and resources. This in turn has led the United States to wage wars on countries that are rich in resources and on other countries that resist American domination. Waging wars entails borrowing money to fight those wars, which has led to an unsustainable public debt. [46]

Worse yet, while the nation directs its funding to wars, other essential growth factors become ignored, such as education, science, health, infrastructure, and protection of the **environment**.*** These are the essential elements of progress and prosperity. This environmental destruction may be demonstrated by the attitude of the far-right politicians who advocated pulling out of the Paris Accord for political reasons, without considering the negative impact of fossil fuels on the planet or the positive economic benefits from embracing and developing lower-carbon-emission technologies that will make coal and other fossil fuels more expensive.

*** The **environment**: As reported by various sources, in June 2017, President Donald Trump followed through on his promise to pull out of the Paris Accord with this declaration: "We're getting out. And we will start to renegotiate and we'll see if there's a better deal. If we can, great. If we can't, that's fine." The decision represents a great win for the minority of the vocal, conservative climate deniers and a betrayal to the future of the planet. This minority told the world that climate change is not a problem, when the scientific investigations say otherwise. The decision met with swift worldwide condemnation and undermined America's credibility and its claim of world leadership. Luckily, in the face of the decision, China, India, and Europe then pledged to unite to save the planet and to save the Paris Accord, despite losing the world's second-largest carbon polluter from the climate-change pact. (The United States contributes about 15 percent of global carbon emissions, which will make it difficult to keep global temperature increases well below 2°C above preindustrial levels, a goal that was part of the Paris agreement.) China, India, and Europe, along with the United States, make up the four biggest emitters of carbon dioxide into the atmosphere from industry, transportation, agriculture, and other areas. The Paris Accord was reached in 2015 between 195 countries and was meant to limit the global rise in temperatures attributed to emissions. By America's divorce from reality and morality, according to global leaders and the scientific community, the nation lost its moral leadership of the world.

America has spent over \$6 trillion so far on various wars in the Middle East and Afghanistan. Donald Trump stated this fact in many of his speeches, both before and after his election in 2016. Can anybody imagine what would happen if \$6 trillion were to be spent on America's **soft power instead of hard power**,**** the former of which includes its foreign-aid budget, and the latter of which includes its excessive military budget?

**** **Soft and hard power**: America's continued dominance is based on its ability to project both hard and soft power. It has formidable military power and spends around 40 percent of the total amount that other countries spend on defense globally, which is six times the amount spent by second-place China. Many Western and other allies rely on American technologies in their defense systems, which is why America insists that its allies allocate 2 percent of their gross domestic product (GDP) on defense to recover some of the costs. The nation's soft power, in contrast, includes the quality of American universities, innovation, and its leadership in high technology and research and development, with an expenditure of 2.5 percent of GDP, which is four times greater than that of China. [47]

In his book *Soft Power: The Means to Success in World Politics* (2004), Joseph S. Nye Jr. states that with the help of US companies, foundations, universities, churches, and other institutions of civil society, American culture, ideals, and values have been crucial in helping Washington attract partners and supporters. Nye acknowledges the limits of soft power, stating that it tends to have diffuse effects on the outside world and is not easily wielded to achieve specific outcomes. Indeed, societies often embrace American values and culture but resist US foreign policies. Overall, Nye's message is that US security hinges as much on winning hearts and minds as it does on winning wars. Nye chided the George W. Bush administration (in power at the time) for wantonly or foolishly destroying the country's image abroad. The brutal use of hard power may yield results, but it won't yield dividends. The "shock and awe" campaign may have cowed Iraq's resistance, but it also spawned resistance to American leadership worldwide. In the end, power is exercised through either force or legitimacy. A regime that has lost its legitimacy can survive through terror for a while, but in the end it will be toppled, as other nations will view it has having "lost the mandate of heaven," to borrow a term from Chinese history. A defining feature of soft power is that it is noncoercive; the currency of soft power is culture, political values, and foreign policies. [48]

In the same book, Nye wrote the following:

It is not smart to discount soft power as just [a] question of image, public relations, and ephemeral popularity. As we argued earlier, it is a form of power—a means of obtaining desired outcomes. When we discount the importance of our attractiveness to other countries, we pay a price. Most important, if the United States is so unpopular in a country that being pro-American is a kiss of death in that country's domestic politics, political leaders are unlikely to make concessions to help us. Turkey, Mexico, and Chile were prime examples of the run-up to [the] Iraq War in March 2003. When American policies lose their legitimacy and credibility in the eyes of others, attitude[s] of distrust tend to fester and further reduce our leverage. [49]

Throughout his books, Nye always recommends that America become a nation that other nations will look up to and want to follow, thus setting an example for other countries to achieve global harmony and respect for international law.

THE PROBLEM WITH AMERICA'S FINANCIAL SYSTEM AND INSTITUTIONS

The 2008 failure of the American international financial institution Lehman Brothers rocked the global economy and was one of the signals that heralded the global financial crisis (henceforth "GFC").

Wall Street insiders Lawrence G. McDonald and Patrick Robinson, in their book *A Colossal Failure of Common Sense: The Inside Story of the Collapse of Lehman Brothers* (2009), answer a few of the questions of why Lehman Brothers was allowed to fail. McDonald and Robinson reveal the culture of arrogance, ambition, greed, and brilliance typical of Wall Street—a culture that ignites prosperity and the occasional destruction of wealth. It was the addiction to growth and greed that resulted in the destruction of America's oldest investment bank. Its destruction was a pivotal event that led to the GFC and served a major blow to America's extreme capitalism, which manifests itself in lies and deception, high leverage, and extreme greed. [50]

The GFC exposed the weakness in American-style capitalism and its link to the economies of other countries, which forced many governments to adopt a semisocialist system to bail out the banks and large companies that are essential to their economies. This has resulted in a massive demand for state-owned investment funds (sovereign funds,) which will take years before a return to normalcy and before public capital is replaced by private capital. This situation has become one of the causes of America's decline and the slow growth of other economies.

America's decline is directly linked to its growing and unsustainable national debt, incurred largely because of financing the bailouts and the nation's unnecessary wars. Its debt reduction is hindered by the nation's partisan political structure, which could cause sociopolitical upheaval, especially if the United States speedily attempts to extricate itself from its central bank's earlier assets purchases with money it has created electronically through its quantitative easing program and to shrink its massive balance sheet. (The US national debt stood at over $20.6 trillion as of January 3, 2018.) Based on current trends, the nation's debt could reach 300 percent of GDP by 2050, up from 10 percent of GDP in 2010. This and other detailed analyses may be found in *The Ascent of Money: The Financial History of the World* (2009), by the aforementioned Niall Ferguson:

> The fall of empires in history occurs for many reasons but there is one thread through most falls, which

is overextending the empire's commitment past its ability to resource. Most empires fell because the desired-expected-anticipated return on the investment of expansion failed to materialize. Rome fell because it failed to bring all its conquered territories into its hegemony; the territories always retained their sense of tribal/racial identity and regarded the Romans as overlords. The British Empire decayed (rather than fell) because it lacked the will and resources to continue after the Second World War but its core remained untouched. The US will probably go the same way unless its creditors determine that destruction of the economy is a more commercially beneficial outcome than allowing it to decay. [51]

Under America's current extreme-capitalist system, the country's next financial crisis will be caused by some greedy capitalists who don't know the difference between the right ways to make money and the wrong ways. This can be seen before the GFC in the way Goldman Sachs executives traded messages saying they would make "some serious money" betting against the housing markets. Another message released by the US Senate Permanent Subcommittee on Investigations stated that "we lost money initially; but we later recovered by making negative bets." (Negative bets, known as short positions, are designed to profit as housing prices plummet; a short position refers to the sale of borrowed securities, commodities, or currencies, with the expectation that the asset will fall in value.) Another message reads, "Of course we didn't dodge the mortgage mess; we lost money, but then made more than we lost because of shorts."

The US Senate Permanent Subcommittee on Investigations, in its July 2011 report entitled "Wall Street and the Financial Crisis: Anatomy of a Financial Collapse," estimated that Goldman Sachs made almost $4 billion by betting against mortgage-related securities as the housing market collapsed. Other messages revealed at the hearing clearly indicate the bank's awareness of what was happening. One of the messages reads, "But a free market was never meant to be a free license to take whatever you can get, however you can get it." And another, "Some on Wall Street forgot that behind every dollar traded or leveraged, there is [a] family looking to buy a house, pay for an education, open a business, or save for retirement. What happens here has real consequences across our country." [52]

It is worth noting that Gary Cohn, a shining star of extreme capitalism and (at the time) president of Goldman Sachs, was earlier the head of Goldman's fixed income, currency, and commodities division and the cohead of global securities businesses. He was accused of playing a major role in the Greek government's attempts at concealing and deferring debt in order to meet various criteria for inclusion in the eurozone by obscuring billions in debt from the European Commission's budget supervisors. [53] It is also worth noting that Cohn was the president and chief operating officer of Goldman Sachs from 2006 until he took office as director of the National Economic Council (NEC) in President Trump's administration in January 2017.

Goldman Sachs, which many financial commentators consider to be among the smartest, greediest, and most dangerous investment banks (together with a few other major American financial institutions), is at the head of the cartel that is causing a calamity not only for America but also for the rest of the world. This is because large American financial institutions operate internationally, and without foolproof international coordination, they have the capacity to corrupt the international financial system to achieve their objectives. [54]

The US Securities and Exchange Commission (SEC) fined Goldman Sachs for defrauding investors and for misleading them into buying toxic mortgage-related securities just before the US housing-market collapse. This occurred in addition to creating and selling collateralized debt obligations linked to subprime mortgages in 2007, when the bank was fully aware that the US housing market was faltering yet failed to disclose this information to the market. Worse still, according to John C. Coffee of Columbia Law School, was that before the onset of the financial crisis, Goldman Sachs offloaded numerous toxic products on its clients and generally made profits from trading against the bank's customers.

Goldman Sachs and other top American financial institutions have converted the financial markets into a gambling casino and created several associated toxic assets through the corrupt financial practices of derivatives trading, such as credit-default swaps, which brought America and the rest of the world to the brink of economic depression. These institutions created a financial crisis that has driven many countries to cut spending and increase taxes to pay debts, to balance budgets, to avoid banking crises, and to avoid loan defaults. Subsequently, the purchasing power of many nations has become drastically reduced, which in turn has limited their growth and productivity, as is reflected in world growth and trade since that time.

Despite all the troubles that Goldman Sachs went through following the GFC, the bank, together with its executives, became richer. Many commentators and lawmakers describe this in the following terms: the bank today has been accused of numerous charges, including playing a key role in the subprime loan fiasco, pushing several of its competitors into bankruptcy, helping nations such as Greece hide their deficits and then speculating on their downfall, causing the euro to fall, and influencing the consumer-price index. Still, the bank has emerged from the latest crisis more powerful and more wealthy than ever before. Although Goldman Sachs was not solely responsible for the 2008 GFC and the ensuing worldwide recession, it had plenty to blame for.

In an interview with *Al Jazeera* in June 2014, Robert Weissman, president of Public Citizen, a nonprofit consumer rights advocacy group and think tank, stated the following points:

[On market complexity] Goldman has been a key innovator and exploiter of the most complicated and complex financial products—the kinds of financial products about which boosters often claim miraculous returns or social benefits, but which typically are revealed over time to be dangerous for both investors and the stability of the financial system…

[On too-big-to-fail subsidies] Like other giant banks, Goldman benefits from the implicit guarantee of a bailout in the event its viability is threatened. The Dodd-Frank Act included many important reforms, but Goldman remains too big to fail. In the wake of the financial crisis, Goldman was aided by a $10bn infusion from the US government, along with access to super-cheap loans from the Federal Reserve's discount window. Gaining coverage under the government's protective umbrella required Goldman to convert itself, in legal terms, from an independent investment bank into a bank holding company, a manoeuvre remarkably performed in just a matter of days…

[On criminal immunity] For all of its shenanigans, no criminal charges have been brought against Goldman or its executives. Nor have any criminal charges been brought against any other leading Wall Street bank or executives for illegalities in the run up to the financial crash. Perhaps this is because no crimes were committed. But perhaps it's because prosecutors have been frightened about bringing criminal charges against firms they have deemed "too big to jail"…

Over the last few decades Goldman has become emblematic of the problem. Wall Street firms have grown too big, and Wall Street has taken over too much of our economy and gained too much influence in and over our government. The financial services sector is supposed to serve the rest of the economy, not the other way around. And the government must control Big Finance, not the other way around…

What should be clear is that we cannot "put the matter behind us." Banks wrecked the economy once—forcing millions out of their homes, throwing tens of millions out of their jobs, throwing entire nations into crisis—and they will do it again, unless we take steps to prevent it. [55]

What happened in America was the result of turning a blind eye to the financial institutions' speculative investment, lack of risk assessment, rampant credit growth, and inflated asset prices. The crisis resulted in a few becoming extraordinarily rich while others became very poor. This is an economic system that allows financial institutions, together with other major enterprises, to become engaged in schemes to minimize and avoid taxes by using loopholes and offshore tax havens. [56]

THE PROBLEM WITH AMERICA'S CORPORATIONS
In *The Price of Civilization: Reawakening American Virtue and Prosperity* (2012), Jeffrey D. Sachs, an economist from Columbia University, says that "the US economy is caught in a feedback loop. Corporate wealth translates into political power through campaign financing, corporate lobbying, and the revolving door of jobs between government and industry; and political power translates into further wealth through tax

cuts, deregulation, and sweetheart contracts between government and industry. Wealth begets power, and power begets wealth." He adds, "Four key sectors of US business exemplify this feedback loop and the takeover of political power in the United States by the corporatocracy." [57] (A "corporatocracy" is a political system in which powerful corporate interest groups dominate the policy agenda.)

Sachs identifies the four key sectors as follows:

1. First is the military-industrial complex, which President Eisenhower famously warned about in his farewell address in January 1961. The linkage of the military and private industry created a political power so pervasive that the United States has been condemned to militarization, useless wars, and fiscal waste on a scale of many tens of trillions of dollars since that time.

2. Second is the Wall Street–Washington complex, which has steered the financial system toward control by a few politically powerful Wall Street firms, notably Goldman Sachs, JPMorgan Chase, Citigroup, Morgan Stanley, and a handful of others. These days, almost all treasury secretaries—from the Republican Party or the Democratic Party—come from Wall Street and go back there when their terms end. According to Sachs, the close ties between Wall Street and Washington "paved the way for the 2008 financial crisis and the megabailouts that followed, through reckless deregulation followed by an almost complete lack of oversight by government."

3. Third is the "Big Oil"–transport–military complex that has put the United States on the trajectory of heavy oil-import dependence and a deepening military trap in the Middle East. Since the days of John D. Rockefeller and the Standard Oil Trust a century ago, "Big Oil" has loomed large in US politics and foreign policy. "Big Oil" teamed up with the automobile industry to steer the United States away from mass transit and toward the gas-guzzling vehicles driven on a nationally financed highway system. "Big Oil" has consistently and successfully fought the intrusion of competition from other energy sources, including nuclear, wind, and solar power. The industry has been at the side of the Pentagon in making sure that the United States defends the sea-lanes to the Persian Gulf, in effect ensuring a more than $100 billion annual subsidy for a fuel that is otherwise dangerous to national security. Sachs adds, "And 'Big Oil' has played a notorious role in the fight to keep climate change off the US agenda. Exxon-Mobil, Koch Industries, and others in the sector have underwritten a generation of antiscientific propaganda to confuse the American people."

4. Fourth is the health care industry, the United States' largest industry, which is currently absorbing no less than 17 percent of US gross domestic product. Sachs says, "The key to understanding this sector is to note that the government partners with industry to

reimburse costs with little systematic oversight and control." Pharmaceutical firms set sky-high prices protected by patent rights—Medicare for the aged and Medicaid for the poor—and private insurers reimburse doctors and hospitals on a cost-plus basis. The American Medical Association (AMA) also restricts the supply of new doctors through the control of placements at medical schools. [58]

The results of this pseudo-market system are sky-high costs, large profits for the private health care sector, and no political will to reform. Sachs says that the main thing to remember about the corporatocracy is that it looks after its own. Absolutely no economic crisis is happening in the corporate United States. Consider the pulse of the corporate sector as opposed to the pulse of the employees working in it. Corporate profits in 2010 were at an all-time high, and CEOs' salaries in 2010 rebounded strongly from the financial crisis. Wall Street compensation in 2010 was also at an all-time high, and although several Wall Street firms paid civil penalties for financial abuses, no senior banker faced any criminal charges, and no adverse regulatory measures were put in place that would lead to a loss of profits in finance, health care, military supplies, and energy. The thirty-year achievement of the corporatocracy has been the creation of the United States' rich and superrich classes. [59]

The starting point for a resolution to stop America's decline is for its politicians to deal with the social inequalities in which over forty-five million of its citizens live below the poverty line, most of whom are black or Latino. Through proper analysis of its extreme capitalism, which is based on the winner-takes-all principle, America should learn to adopt a more equitable capitalist system with a fair distribution of wealth based on "give and take" and "win-win" principles for its own security and prosperity; the country should then apply genuine principles in its dealings with the rest of the world. [60]

THE PROBLEM WITH AMERICA'S FOREIGN POLICY AND ALLIANCES
Modern international relations are embedded in the history of the twentieth century, which was driven by industrial and technological revolutions that resulted in wars between nations for market expansion, control of resources, and the desire to dominate the world. Several key events shaped and continue to shape the modern world, especially the major conflict of World War II, which involved the vast majority of the world's nations, including the great powers of the United States, the Soviet Union, the United Kingdom, France, Germany, Japan, and Italy.

The participants in the war threw their entire economic, industrial, and scientific capabilities behind the war effort, thereby erasing the distinction between civilian and military resources. The war was marked by the mass civilian deaths caused by the strategic bombing of industrial and population centers, and it culminated in the use of American nuclear weapons against Japan's civilian populations. Other than the deaths of some six million European Jews by Nazi Germany during the Holocaust, World War II is estimated to have caused the deaths of between fifty million and eighty-five million people. It is, so far, the deadliest war in human history. With the proliferation and the sophistication of modern nuclear weapons, the next war will wipe out most of the world population and send the world into another Stone Age.

Following World War II, the political and military landscape of Europe changed with the formation of new alliances. The collapse of the British and French empires brought Europe under the influence of the new superpowers of the United States and the Soviet Union. To cement their newly found spheres of influence, the two nations formed two new major alliances: the Western bloc, which included the United States and its NATO allies, and the Eastern bloc, which included the Soviet Union and its allies in the Warsaw Pact. The two new superpowers had completely different economic and political systems: the Soviet Union had a single-party Marxist-Leninist socialist dictatorship, while the United States had a capitalist democratic system. The two superpowers evolved to become mainly characterized by economic, political, and military influence on other countries through policies of expansion of their respective spheres of influence.

Following the development of their nuclear-deterrence strategies, they were prevented from engaging in direct military confrontation because of the threat of mutually assured destruction (MAD). But this threat did not prevent the two nations from engaging in regional confrontations as part of their attempts to widen their spheres of influence and to weaken each other. Such regional wars may be seen in the Americans' Korean and Vietnam wars and the Soviets' Afghanistan war.

Rather than using their nuclear arsenals, the two superpowers developed and deployed conventional military forces to support proxy wars around the globe as part of their struggle for dominance. They also engaged in psychological warfare, propaganda, espionage, and technological competitions, such as the space race. After the end of World War II, the Soviet Union adopted a policy of consolidation of control over the Eastern bloc, while the United States adopted a strategy of global containment as a challenge to the Soviets by providing military and financial aid to Western Europe, as well as by supporting all anticommunist movements around the world.

Until the collapse of the Soviet Union in 1991, the world was polarized between the two camps and in a state of an arms race and Cold War. The two camps were divided by economic, political, cultural, nationalistic, and occasionally religious or antireligious causes. [61]

For self-preservation, weaker countries often had to align with stronger countries; in other instances, stronger countries aligned to create formidable powers, as was the case with Germany and the Ottoman Empire in World War I and with Germany and Japan in World War II. For cultural and religious reasons, and due to their general feeling of insecurity, the Anglo-Saxon countries have always acted in unison and as a military bloc in alliance with the United States, which then encouraged America's adoption of an aggressive foreign policy. I should note that a few countries' passive leaders, such as many of those in Europe, have not always acted in accord with their citizens' feelings for their countries' sovereignty, which leaders often ignore because of a lack of dynamic political participation and opposition.

In Europe's case, citizens of the NATO countries need to shed their apathy and understand that their leaders are letting them down by their blind support of the Americans' imperialistic ambitions in the hope that the United States will throw a few crumbs their way, or in their wish that America will protect them. This situation is despite the fact that the threat for which NATO was established—the threat of communism from the Soviet Union—no longer exists. Despite the fact that Russia is not an innocent bystander, the current Cold War mind-set of the NATO countries' animosity against Russia over Ukraine is a conflict the Americans have designed to destabilize and weaken Russia, with the aim of a regime change as part of the expansion of the American Empire's sphere of influence. Economically, Europe may be better off if it treats Russia as a natural ally instead of an enemy. America, in creating the Ukraine conflict, intentionally or unintentionally, is causing the economic decline of Europe. Furthermore, the mood among some in America is that the US commitment to NATO should be scaled back, which the main Republican candidate, Donald Trump, suggested during the 2016 presidential election campaign and should be taken into consideration. It could be that he was reflecting the mood of the American political class, especially in the Republican Party.

To avoid the influx of refugees to Europe, as well as to shift the focus of jihadi terrorists away from that continent, the nations of Europe would be better off if they didn't participate in America's and Israel's adventures in the Middle East and North Africa.

On the subject of refugees, who are causing major problems for many European countries, I wrote the following in *Axis of Evil*:

The refugee problem, which is a consequence of America's military interventions and Israel's atrocities in the Middle East, is causing the division in Europe. Accordingly, European leaders should be in a position to refrain from participating in America's and Israel's dangerous game. Alternatively, they should stand up to America and Israel, just like friends who would stand up against a friend when the friend is wrong. As a good friend, you make a stand, or the least you can do is to give sensible advice instead of cheering on or being part of their atrocities. The shortsighted European leaders have overlooked the fact that the refugee problem will affect Europe much more than America. This is because of the following:

First, the geographical location of America relative to the Middle East and North Africa makes Europe an easier target for terrorists.

Second, the Islamic jihadists have negligible ties with American Muslims, which makes it much harder for the jihadists to establish an elaborate terror network compared to Europe, which is a much softer target for terrorism.

Third, America has [a] much higher level of sophistication in border security and in its integrated surveillance system than does Europe. [62]

I should mention that America's national security agencies were dramatically boosted following the September 11 attacks. According to a July 2010 *Washington Post* report on the CIA by Dana Priest and William Arkin, the organization had become so large and secretive by that time that no one knew how many people it employed, how many programs it ran, and how many other agencies were doing the same work. The report stated that more than twelve hundred organizations and more than nineteen hundred private companies worked on counterterrorism, homeland security, and intelligence in ten thousand locations across the United States. The report estimated that the CIA and its affiliates employed 854,000 agents, including 265,000 contractors. [63]

It is clear that America has a powerful antiterrorism structure that is not possible for Europe to match, despite being much more vulnerable than America is to terrorism. This advantage has encouraged America to be more aggressive toward Muslim countries, which doesn't give the United States the incentive to worry much about its European allies' vulnerability and their budget restraints. At the same time,

European people remain poorly informed by their leaders about the leaders' unconditional support of America's foreign policy. The leaders fear a backlash against their inability to stand up to America's adventurism, which is having a negative impact on their lives.

American aggression is one of the key causes of fragmentation and the ongoing conflicts in the world. As I've stated in the introduction to *Axis of Evil*, "America is following a similar path of earlier empires that is leading the world into plunder, wars, corruption, famine, exploitation, impoverishment, massacres, and genocides. If only America understood imperialism in the context of industry and trade without the element of forceful market expansion, the world would be a better place." Benjamin Franklin himself fervently believed that both Britain and America would grow stronger through harmony than through conflict. [64]

America versus the World

Toward the end of the twentieth century, the American development and use of sophisticated modern technologies—satellites, telecommunications interception, and the Internet—have encouraged it to sink deeper into the desire to dominate the world. This situation comes in addition to the nation's use of military-warfare technologies such as drones, laser-guided missiles, and so on, all of which are designed to destroy infrastructures and kill people remotely.

Unfortunately, the aggressive approach to international relations has caused poverty, refugee crises, and resentment around the world. The more killing and destruction of other countries occurs, the harder it becomes for Americans to have a physical presence in many places around the world, because they become the target of revenge, either as groups or as individuals. This situation also makes it impossible for America to control the world, since no empire in history has been able dominate other countries by remote control or from the air without a presence on the ground.

In the June 1999 issue of *Z Magazine*, historian William Blum listed a brief history of US interventions around the world. Blum showed that American foreign policy was fueled not by devotion to any kind of morality but rather by the necessity to serve other imperatives, which can be summarized as follows:

- making the world safe for American corporations
- enhancing the financial statements of defense contractors at home who have contributed generously to members of Congress
- preventing the rise of any society that might serve as a successful example of an alternative to the capitalist model
- extending political and economic hegemony over as wide an area as possible, as befits a great power

Blum wrote on interventions in the Middle East during the period from 1956 to 1958:

America's doctrine is preparedness to use armed forces to assist any Middle East country requesting assistance against armed aggression from any country controlled by international communism. This meant that no power would be allowed to dominate, or have excessive influence over the Middle East and its oil fields except the United States, and that anyone who tried would be deemed "communist." In keeping with this policy, the United States twice attempted to overthrow the Syrian government and staged several shows of force in the Mediterranean to intimidate movements opposed to the US. It supported governments in Jordan and Lebanon, landed 14,000 troops in Lebanon, and conspired to overthrow or assassinate Qasim of Iraq and Nasser of Egypt for their troublesome Arabic nationalism and their dealings with the Soviet Union. [65]

America's overambition in extending its control of the world has included in its foreign policy the **encircling of Russia and the containment of China******* (thus making them active enemies), which is far beyond its present capacity to handle. Such a policy will sooner or later bring these two nuclear powers into a formidable alliance that will spell the end of America's ambitions and the eventual demise of its empire. America, after winning the Cold War, instead of creating economic and political stability in the world, has adopted an old course of the cycle of hegemony.

***** **Encircling of Russia and the containment of China**: Since the collapse of the Soviet Union in 1991, the United States, through its NATO allies, has relentlessly pursued a strategy of encircling Russia in bringing its military forces directly to Russia's borders. It was part of American neoconservatives' advocacy to resurrect the "permanent dominance" doctrine as spelled out in the Defense Planning Guidance (DPG). It also was part of the neocons' advocacy for the policy of conflict over diplomacy in establishing America's dominance. The policy included the global militarization against potential challengers and America's main rivals, especially Russia and China, by encircling them with military bases and strategic weapons. Part of Russia's encirclement was the inclusion of ten Warsaw Pact countries to NATO, with the prospective of new candidates such as Georgia and Ukraine. The containment of China, on the other hand, was simply because it has the greatest potential—militarily and economically—to offset traditional US advantages. To prevent China's expansion in Asia, the United States has been establishing military, economic, and diplomatic ties with countries adjacent to China's borders, frustrating it from attempting alliance-building and economic partnership.

America's current agenda is to control other countries, their people, and their resources not through diplomacy but by force, intimidation, threat of using force, and bullying. The United States often backs up its foreign policies by military solutions and constant interventions, or often by imposing economic sanctions that target the people, not the governments, with the intent that people will demand regime changes to serve America's strategic interests. These policies bring America into conflict with nations that resist economic exploitation and military interventions, especially when they are amplified by the nationalism of a targeted country or the presence of ideological and cultural clashes. What worries people of other nations is living in a world dominated by an aggressive America.

In *Hegemony or Survival* (2004), Chomsky wrote the following:

> After 9/11, at a time of enormous global sympathy and solidarity with the United States, George Bush asked, "Why do they hate us?" The question was wrongly put, and the right question was scarcely addressed. But within a year, the administration succeeded in providing an answer: "Because of you and your associates, Mr. Bush, and what you have done. And if you continue, the fear and hatred you have inspired may extend to the country you have shamed as well." On that, the evidence is hard to ignore. For Osama bin [Laden] it is a victory probably beyond his wildest dream. [66]

America's aggressive approach to international relations was especially amplified immediately after winning the Cold War when it embarked on the establishment of a new world order to suit its unlimited strategic interests. Under George H. W. Bush and following the demise of the Soviet

Empire, America decided to take direct control over the Middle East's oil supply and its vast oil reserves by manipulating regional geopolitics to create suitable ground for the first Gulf War and Operation Desert Storm in 1991, when over one hundred thousand Iraqis were killed. At the end of that war, America decided to establish a military base in Saudi Arabia, which the Saudi Wahhabis saw as an assault on the Islamic holy land of Mecca by the infidel Americans. This became the catalyst for the birth of al-Qaeda.

The American quest to control the oil reserves in Iraq was aggravated further under George W. Bush following his post-9/11 declaration of the clash of civilizations, which was aimed at all Muslim extremists. (For more on the neoconservatives, Israel's role in the Middle East conflict, the invasion of Iraq, and the clash of civilizations, see chapter 2.)

America's aggressive approach is embedded in the historical fact that its foreign policy has been centered mostly on its military power, which has often caused it to forget the corrosiveness of power and to overlook the difference between influence and the use of power. The use of power results in resentment and reaction, which ultimately weakens and destroys the aggressor. To have influence is first to understand the social and political culture of the nation you want to win over and how to approach grievances and, if legitimate, how to address them instead of bombarding the country, which only multiplies the number of your enemies. Having influence is also to understand that the most successful results will come when talks are conducted with goodwill. (For more on the rise and fall of empires, see chapter 1 of my 2011 book *Israel vs. America vs. the World* [67].)

In *Hegemony or Survival* (2004), Chomsky also indicts the prevailing American foreign policy. He observes that the policy had led to disaster not only for America but also for the rest of the world. He provides a commonsense analysis with undeniable evidence of the dangerous course of American military interventions around the world, especially since the beginning of the first Bush administration and after September 11. These interventions were characterized by America's quest for global domination, which convinced the world that America's leadership was not trustworthy. Chomsky argues that America's policy in response to September 11, and the invasion of Afghanistan and Iraq, were consistent with the country's attempt to maintain its hegemony through the threat or use of military force as an "imperial grand strategy" that had been going on for over sixty years in Cuba, Central America, Vietnam, and the Middle East. He criticizes America's use of the term "terrorism" to describe others when the term is an exact description of America's unlawful use of force and its contempt for international law. [68, 69]

Based on his work in *Culture of Terrorism* (1988) and *Necessary Illusions* (1989), Chomsky wrote the following:

Contempt for international law and institutions was particularly flagrant in the Reagan-Bush years—the first reign in Washington's current incumbents—and their successors continued to make it clear that the

US reserved the right to act "unilaterally when necessary," including the "unilateral use of military power" to defend such vital interests as "ensuring uninhibited access to key markets, energy supplies, and strategic resources." But the posture was not exactly new. [70]

Instead of centering its foreign policy on aggression, threats, and bullying for its excessive power (i.e., hard power), America can dominate the world peacefully through its tremendous technological capacity and highly educated human resources (i.e., soft power). Unfortunately, however, America has relied on the precivilization instinct of aggression, of which Stephen Hawking once had this to say: "I fear evolution has inbuilt greed and aggression to the human genome. There is no sign of conflict lessening, and the development of militarized technology and weapons of mass destruction could make that disastrous. The best hope for the survival of the human race might be independent colonies in space."

In a civilized world, through genuine globalization and free trade, America has the capacity to engineer mutual and sustainable global economic growth by producing more consumers by lifting these consumers' purchasing power, rather than producing poverty and more enemies to fight the empire. It can do this by refocusing and expanding its economy away from the manufacture and sale of weapons and military technologies and toward other peaceful technologies, which have already benefited and will benefit huge numbers of consumers around the world. The use of weapons will always lead to mass destruction and poverty, which will retard world growth and will benefit no one. Instead of frightening the weaker countries of the world into submission, America could revert to its history of great contributions to world progress in many aspects of life.

Before its recent adoption of far-right policies, America was a positive symbol for the world to look up to for its soft power—its ability to export great culture and technology to the world, especially in cinema, music, TV, computers, mobile phones, literature, the arts, and sports. Furthermore, nobody can deny America's role in helping Europe triumph over the nightmare of Nazi Germany. (From a historical perspective, however, the main cause of Adolf Hitler's defeat could be said to have been the German invasion of Russia during the summer of 1941, in which he failed to take into account the fact that the campaign might spill over into the harsh Russian winter, which ended up crippling his troops across the entire Eastern front.)

The world will unfortunately have no respite as long as America's attitude is corrupted by its excessive power and its desire to expand without taking into consideration its limited capacity. With any luck, however, the nation's decline will reach a stage that may result in a new breed of leaders emerging to rescue America and to spare humanity a major catastrophe. The first and foremost goal for such leaders will be to once again earn for America the world's trust. This trust has declined because of the nation's hypocrisy and because it has placed its undefined national interests ahead of any other principle. Its hypocrisy may be found in its overthrowing of democratic governments, its support of dictators, and its deposing of many others when it suits American national interests—but not those of the world.

THE MILITARY OPTION VERSUS TRADE AND DIPLOMACY

Once the United States won the Cold War, following the formal dissolution of the Soviet Union in December 1991, America became the only superpower in the world. Since that time, it has decided to follow a similar path to earlier imperialistic powers in its attempt to dominate the world. This means that America has often employed its excessive military power with military interventions or by bullying and intimidating other countries. Instead of adopting a humanistic approach, which would eventually lead to a stable and mutually beneficial world, it embraced the neoconservatives' advocated theory of "unilateral and assertive wars as an essential strategy in achieving world hegemony and in shaping the international environment to the advantage of the United States." (For more on this theory and on the neoconservatives, see chapter 2.)

Unfortunately, because of the urgency the United States has placed on implementing this theory, the nation has lost the ability to distinguish between strategy and tactics in order to achieve a suitable outcome. America's dual track of maintaining both military and diplomatic approaches has often driven it toward using projected power over diplomacy. And, as stated earlier, its projection of power is aggravated by its current foreign policy, which includes the encirclement of Russia and the containment of China, thereby making them active enemies. This is especially problematic at a time when both Russia and China are too big to alienate and too power-ful to antagonize.

What emboldened America's projection of power over diplomacy is its alliance with the NATO countries, especially with Britain, for British military power and for being an Anglo-Saxon country with a natural history of cultural, political, and military connections. As noted earlier in this chapter, the Anglo-Saxon countries generally have always acted in unison and as a military bloc. Other reasons for encouraging America to project power over diplomacy include its development and use of sophisticated modern technologies and military-warfare technologies, including drones, laser-guided missiles, the Terminal High Altitude Area Defense (THAAD) system, and so on. These new trillion-dollar technologies reflect the realities of modern warfare, where battles are fought remotely through air surveillance and strikes; this is gradually making ground combat redundant. For this reason, it will not be easy for America to control the world from the air without military and civilian personnel on the ground. Because of the widespread destruction, the civilian casualties, and the large number of enemies the United States has created, American personnel on the ground have become easy targets for revenge. [71]

American defense companies, including their subsidiaries, such as General Dynamics, Northrop Grumman, Boeing, Lockheed Martin, and so on, account for more than

60 percent of arms sales in the world and represent a huge source of revenue from the arms trade. These companies also employ huge numbers of people in an industry that is spread throughout many states of America, which makes the influence of the industry on state and federal politicians nearly impossible to counter. This situation is a curse both on America and on the rest of the world, because to market the technologies to the world, the industry needs conflicts. Thus, imperialistic America is always ready to create conflicts, especially in countries that can afford to purchase weapons, such as South Korea, Japan, Australia, the NATO countries, the oil-rich countries of the Middle East, and others. Further damage to the world is caused by the arms race that results when other developed countries compete with America or as a deterrent from feeling the threat of American expansionism.

These are some of the reasons why America currently places the military option as a priority when dealing with the world instead of engaging in trade and diplomacy and places politics ahead of American values without realizing that these actions are the main causes of its decline. Prioritizing its arms trade and hard power results in the following consequences: first, conflicts and warfare slow the world economy and lead to stagnation; second, doing so means that the United States is neglecting the other more profitable trade of American soft power related to globalization and free trade.

As for globalization and free trade, it is worth engaging in the following discussion.

The State University of New York's Levin Institute defines globalization as a process of interaction and integration among the people, companies, and governments of different nations; it is a process driven by international trade and investment and aided by information technology (IT). This process has effects on the environment, on culture, on political systems, on economic development and prosperity, and on human physical well-being in societies around the world. [72]

Immediately after World War II, the Western countries moved toward collective protection of their national industries by coordinating and combining them under one national umbrella to enable their economies to move forward. Under the current global conditions and free trade, however, these industries are becoming less national and more specialized through a global niche-market orientation. This encourages company innovation and to do things differently compared with others, which leads to better efficiency and higher productivity. In the general market, competition is very intense, as the general aim is to produce the same product at a cheaper price, which largely depends on the costs of material and labor. Accordingly, poorer countries with lower living standards can produce the same general products at a cheaper price.

Although globalization started centuries ago, it became prominent in the past fifty years, coinciding with the technical revolution in telecommunications, air travel, television, credit cards, the Internet, and other technologies. These and many other technological changes, accompanied by deregulation throughout the world, resulted in large-scale innovation and market volume, which made technology more affordable. Unfortunately, in many developed countries, lingering nationalism, protectionism, and the pressure brought to bear by various lobbying groups have all resulted in slow progress in free trade and globalization.

Poorer countries, especially in Africa and Asia, which depend mostly on trade of their agricultural products to earn income, are excluded from the process. Other poor countries that are rich in natural resources, like Nigeria, Namibia, Zambia, Congo, and Pakistan, among others, are generally exploited by affluent countries through their multinational companies or by installing corrupt puppet regimes to serve their own strategic interests without enriching the local populations. This is one reason why rich countries become richer while poor countries become poorer. It is a process that creates an underclass—desperate and hopeless people who have nothing left to lose—which constitutes a grave threat to the civilized world when religious fanatics recruit and brainwash these desperate people to fight for their cause. The civilized world is now fighting the consequences of these nations' greed instead of eliminating the causes of the problem.

Early in the twentieth century, poverty and the exploitation of disadvantaged people brought socialism to the world. In this century, history could repeat itself, as can now be observed in the revival of **socialism*** in several poor Latin American countries. An examination of the developed countries' behavior reinforces the poor countries' perception that they are being exploited. The perception is also reinforced by the practice of protectionism and the heavy subsidies of Western countries' products and their refusal to remove tariffs and quotas to allow poor countries to prosper. The exploitation generally does not stack up against the principle of globalization, which is based on science, innovation, rationalization, efficiency, universality, and free trade.

* **Socialism**: It took over seventy years for Western capitalism to subdue socialism and socialist ideology. The ideology has not been totally defeated following the collapse of the Soviet Union, but it is hibernating, to reincarnate itself once extreme capitalism, which makes the rich richer and the poor poorer, becomes unsustainable and reaches the boiling point, which will in turn lead to major upheavals and self-destruction. All the signs point to the reappearance of socialist ideology in a more benign form of a **social democracy**, where the fair distribution of wealth and a reasonable safety net apply as an alternative to the extreme form of capitalism that is practiced in America today. **Social democracy** is a political ideology defined as a policy regime involving a universal-welfare state and a collective-bargaining system within the framework of a capitalist economy. The ideology is based on evidence and pragmatic humanism, where individuals exist in a social context and where the government is just big enough to provide essential services and social necessities. It sits between the left and the right and regards neither socialism nor the extreme American model of capitalism as the best way to create social justice, promote individualism, and provide safety nets for the disadvantaged. The term "social democracy" often refers to the social model and economic policies, prominent in western and northern European countries, that sprang up after World War II and still exist today, especially in the Swedish model, which is widely regarded as a moderate form of capitalism.

Free trade provides many advantages to developing countries. In an online article by management consultant Angie Mohr entitled "The Advantages of Free Trade in Developing Countries," the author lists the following advantages. The first advantage is higher employment rates as new job opportunities open up for local workers, which then leads to a higher standard of living and more consumer purchasing, which in turn ultimately sparks a country's economy and helps develop locally owned business. Second, less child labor occurs once companies invest in equipment and pay higher wages to adult workers through the kinds of foreign investment that boost family income, thus enabling them to send their children to school rather than to work. Third, access to new markets allows native companies to sell to foreign markets, which expands their customer base and leads to new products and services and makes investing in innovation more viable. This situation is helped by companies no longer having to worry about absorbing the costs of tariffs and other barriers to market entry and by selling their products freely. Fourth, through free-trade agreements, restrictions on foreign investment are reduced, which helps stimulate the banking system, thus leading to more investment and consumer lending. All these factors, combined with those we discussed earlier, lead to increases in life expectancy from the alleviation of hunger, improved medical care, fewer infant deaths, and more children becoming educated. [73]

Globalization and free trade do admittedly have a few negative effects on developed countries—especially in job losses and the transfer of jobs to lower-cost countries, as well as the transfer of technologies to places like China—but globalization and free trade have overwhelming advantages in controlling inflation, especially in these economic systems' abilities to produce cheaper goods and in the positive impact they have on the world's growth, which benefits developed and developing countries alike. But this can happen only if multinational companies stop exploiting developing countries' labor forces with unfair and unsafe working conditions and the use of slave labor, stop causing environmental destruction, stop engaging in political interference, and above all stop using tax havens to avoid paying taxes in both their own countries and the countries in which they operate. [74]

Alongside modern advancements in technologies, especially in travel and telecommunications, the world has come closer together. Because the twentieth century's political barriers between countries are now much lower than they once were, free trade is very simple to pursue. This situation happened following the rapid industrialization of Japan, China, and much of South America and Europe, which helped these powers catch up with America's productivity, especially in agriculture and technology, which in turn spurred competition and improved the world's productivity. Competition in turn spurred innovation and countries' specialization to produce the best products at the lowest possible cost, which has helped workers learn new skills in order to produce products that are suitable for export markets and the global economy.

The principle of globalization and free trade, if allowed to flourish without the interference of excessive greed, could have a tangible benefit to all countries as a result of the world's economic growth. World growth could be generated by raising the living standards of poorer countries by their citizens becoming consumers instead of beggars or economic refugees. Another advantage would be the integration of all countries' economies, which could result in the softening of destructive nationalism around the world. The integration and synchronization of the world's economies could help bring the world closer together and make boundaries less relevant. The role of governments should gradually become less relevant because of the indirect loss of countries' economic sovereignty, as well as the loss of capacity for local economic and financial manipulation. [75]

The loss of economic sovereignty is the first step toward bringing the world together and acting against the current fragmentation and conflicts that afflict the globe. This is simply because genuine globalization and free trade are economic and geographical rather than political, thus reducing the need for military alliances and gradually developing the economic integration of the world. In this paradigm, America could still lead the world with its scientific talent, innovation, research and development, and its well-advanced technologies.

Unfortunately, America, in adopting its new populist platform of "America first," is hindering the process of globalization and free trade. In an April 2004 article on quora. com entitled "Globalization and Free Trade," Professor Richard Ebeling stated that "the path to this bright economic future is a policy of free trade. Governments—including the US government—do not have the wisdom or ability to guide or assist this process. They can only hinder it with controls and restrictions that slow down progress and serve special interests who don't want to face the future. The best way for mastering the global challenges and opportunities of our new century is to allow each individual to use his own knowledge and ability in the competitive market, free from the controlling hand of government. Freedom will enable us triumphantly to find our way in the new global economy." [76]

We should always remember that world growth is impossible without trade. I will conclude this chapter with several relevant quotes about America. [77]

Radical changes in world politics leave America with a heightened responsibility to be, for the world, an example of a genuinely free, democratic, just, and humane society.
—Pope John Paul II

There is nothing wrong with America that cannot be cured with what is right in America.
—Bill Clinton

Whatever America hopes to bring to pass in the world must first come to pass in the heart of America.
—Dwight D. Eisenhower

My dream is of a place and a time where America will once again be seen as the last best hope on earth.
—Abraham Lincoln

Terrorism and Conflicts

• • •

THE FOCUS IN THIS CHAPTER is on terrorism generally and more specifically on the current Islamic religious terrorism that is engulfing the world. The discussion is based on the idea of religious terrorism being an extension of the historical tribal terrorism. As stated in the introduction to this book, tribal terrorism refers to when a powerful and aggressive tribe (or its aggressive tribal or religious leader), for an economic, religious, or nationalistic purpose, finds a pretext to attack other tribes or other sects, which results in an opposite reaction (with an opposite pretext) or a fight for survival. In the old, uncivilized world, the conquering and subjugation of weaker groups meant the superior group was destined to rule all others. In the current state of international relations, religious terrorism has it causes, one of which is an opposite reaction to aggression from excessively powerful, religious, nationalistic, or economic groups in an attempt to dominate weaker groups that have the wealth and the resources the powerful groups need for their expansion and to become even more powerful. Such aggression could also be undertaken to enslave or to use the human resources of weaker nations as cheap labor, to the benefit of the powerful. Based on the principles of "human greed has no limit" and "power is addictive and corrosive," powerful nations will always be motivated to conquer weaker nations, which will then provoke a fight for survival. This situation also relates to the natural processes of "violence breeds violence" and "for every action, there is an equal and opposite reaction."

DEFINITION AND HISTORY

Terrorism has existed throughout human history; it was a common part of tribalism and tribal wars. It has expanded into sectarianism with the entrenchment of religion, nationalism, and idealism in the world's social culture.

In modern history, many events could be classified as state terrorism, including the nationalistic Napoleonic Wars, the Nazi war in Europe, the American war of ideology in Vietnam, the French economic war in Algeria, the Israeli apartheid subjugation of the Palestinians, the American invasion of Iraq, and so on.

Organizational terrorism is waged by religious, nationalistic, or idealistic terrorist organizations, some of which include the French Secret Army Organization (OAS, for Organisation armée secrète); the Irish Republican Army (IRA); Basque Homeland and Liberty (ETA, for Euskadi Ta Askatasuna, the group's Basque name); the Ku Klux Klan (KKK); Germany's Baader-Meinhof Gang (or Group);

various white supremacist and neo-Nazi groups; the Japanese Red Army; and al-Qaeda and other Islamic jihadi groups, especially the recently emerged and perhaps most barbaric group, the Islamic State (IS). [1]

Ironically, al-Qaeda originally flourished with the support of Saudi Arabia, Pakistan, Egypt, and the United States for the purpose of helping the Taliban in its fight against the Soviets in Afghanistan. Sunni-dominated Saudi Arabia and Turkey, together with a few other Sunni countries, supported other jihadist groups, including al-Nusra Front (which changed its name to Jabhet Fateh al-Sham in July 2016), the Free Syrian Army, the Islamist Salafi group Ahrar al-Sham, and many other groups in fighting Syria's Assad regime as part of these groups' sectarian war against Shiite Iran, which America and Israel stoked through their policy of regime change.

All the above events and organizations had reasons to happen or to exist, whether it was nationalism, religion, or a desire to dominate because of greed, or resistance against subjugation, or just to indoctrinate people who were ignorant and blindly followed charismatic leaders motivated by the desire for power and control. In all cases, the driving force behind the power play could be related to the historical tribalistic domination, the law of the jungle, the fight for survival, or simply resistance to subjugation.

The current organizational or state terrorism is taking place due to a combination of ignorance and lack of leadership or the ability of manipulative or fanatical leaders to brainwash and steer their followers into destructive action. The rise of various far-right movements in the world today is an indication the world is heading toward a catastrophe if the moderate voice continues to be drowned out by the voice of extremists or if the silent majority doesn't wake up in time to secure the future of the generations to follow. [2] (For more on the rise of the far right and the clash of civilizations, see the subsections below.)

As for the United States' actions in the Middle East, if the country had applied wisdom and directed its efforts toward creating a peaceful and harmonious region instead of a region constantly at war, then the United States would have benefited greatly from trade with the region's oil-rich countries and their growing middle-class consumers. Instead of taking sides and stoking conflicts that disturb the balance of power between various factions by using a divide-and-conquer policy, it could have brought Iran and Saudi Arabia together to avoid the current implosion of the Islamic world. Such a policy has resulted in abject poverty, major displacement of people, failed states, and a mass-refugee problem that will sooner or later cause a major global security problem—the next round of terrorism, acted out by people who have nothing left to lose and who turn to God and revenge out of desperation. Painting Iran as a threat to Saudi Arabia to make the Saudis dependent on and obedient to America was very shortsighted. This was the catalyst for the current sectarian war, which is going to be extremely difficult to live with. The problem is further aggravated by Israel's direct negative input in the region and its indirect influence on American foreign policy, which involves unconditional commitment to Israel.

In his book *They Dare to Speak Out: People and Institutions Confront Israel's Lobby* (2003), former congressman Paul

Findley wrote of America's unconditional commitment to Israel:

> In the aftermath of 9/11, the people of the United States and their institutions struggled against disruptive forces. The nation was suddenly at war. Muslims and people of Arab ancestry found themselves constantly on the defensive as racial and ethnic profiling became facts of life. So did long lines at airports and anxiety about where terrorists may strike next. Spending for military purposes soared, plunging government surpluses into red ink. Funds for education and social services were cut. Some people considered these disruptions to be byproducts of the US government's decades-long blind support of Israel, but most Americans were not even aware of the nature and extent of this support. [3]

More discussion on America and Israel will follow.

TRIBAL AND RELIGIOUS TERRORISM

Early in human history, the instilling of religion into the human psyche often moderated the impulses of domination and greed and had some degree of moral control over the tribal wars and terrorism of the time, which were generally characterized by economic and ethnic aspects. In the long run, however, religions have added new dimensions to human conflicts, including idealism and sectarianism, as exemplified by conflicts between Protestants and Catholics in Europe (and more recently in Northern Ireland), Sunnis versus Shiites in the Middle East, and the Christian Crusades against Muslims. Often the religious dimension of a conflict is set aside when the tribal factor of ethnicity or economics is the motivation. This can be illustrated by the civil war in South Sudan—where mostly Christian Catholic tribes fight one another—and with the continuous genocides and massacres between the Hutu and Tutsi ethnic groups in both Rwanda and Burundi, where the majority of both groups are Christians. In Rwanda, for example, in 1994 the Catholic Hutu government at the time was involved in genocidal attacks on the Tutsi minority, which resulted in the deaths of some eight hundred thousand people. Several Catholic priests, as well as nuns and brothers, were charged with participating in the genocide and were tried by the International Criminal Tribunal for Rwanda and by a Belgian court, which did lead to a few convictions. Following a meeting in March 2017 between Pope Francis and Rwandan president Paul Kagame, the pope pleaded for forgiveness for "the sins and failings of the Church and its members" implicated in the genocide.

Historically, despite the common claim that religion creates peace, religious conflicts were renowned for their brutality and their expansionist nature; the followers of one religious creed were most often intolerant of other creeds. Such people justify the killing of others in the name of God or for being on the side of the truth. They do so despite the fact that ideological truth is relative, and nobody has a monopoly over it. Religious or any other ideological truth means something to someone but means the opposite to others. This makes the claim of God being on the side of the truth very deceptive and leaves no room for compromise, which historically has caused numerous conflicts and genocides. Although many religions claim to worship the "one God" (and thus one would hope harmony would prevail among them), such propositions don't suit those religious leaders whose survival depends on creating sectarian conflict and bigotry to maintain their power and control. At the root of the problem is the use of ideology as an ultimate guide to human relationships, especially when one powerful ideological group sees itself as superior to others and thus as deserving of privileges. [4]

Religious ideologies are relevant to the current international state of affairs and to the following discussion, especially the discussion of the conflicts in the Middle East that have now spread throughout many parts of the world. The origin of these conflicts dates back to the times of the Jewish, Muslim, and Christian conquests during the periods of gradual transition from early tribal warfare toward more modern ideological and religious wars. [5]

In the majority of historical conflicts, groups form alliances for their mutual benefit to ensure a positive outcome for the conqueror. The psychological tribal reasons that drive alliances have to do with the human survival instinct and insecurity, especially when weaker people and groups subordinate themselves to stronger people and groups. This situation relates to the historical tribal system where the weaker group (tribe) subordinates itself to the stronger tribe. In modern society, an identical psychology can be observed when an aggressive, bullying, intimidating, and threatening football player (to pick one example) attracts cheerleaders who, for their part, seek the acceptance of the bully because of the insecurity of both the bully and the cheerleaders. [6] On a global scale, this phenomenon may be observed in a bullying major power attracting countries that seek its acceptance in the hope that the bullying power may protect them or throw a few crumbs their way from the looting and pillaging of weaker countries. This situation is demonstrated by the relationship between America and the NATO countries and by the relationship between Saudi Arabia and the other Gulf states.

Two key human psychological factors are behind this drive for domination. First, humans have the spirit of competition, which refers to getting more than others, getting ahead, and getting a better social status. People's survival instinct leads them to want more than their fair share. The fundamental problem is our underlying excessive greed, be it greed to have more wealth than others or greed for more power and control of others. The basic problem is that far too many people simply want more than their fair share. If and when they get more, this only stimulates the need to get even more. The only way this problem can be solved is by educating all children from early in life to understand that nobody is entitled to have more than a fair share. This education should be part of US national school curricula; other countries could also adopt such curricula to become part of a universal culture. In our analysis of human behavior, it is worth adding what political scientist

Samuel Huntington wrote in his 1996 book *The Clash of Civilizations and the Remaking of World Order*:

> It is human to hate. For self-definition and motivation people need enemies: competitors in business, rivals in achievement, and opponents in politics. They naturally distrust and see as threats those who are different and have the capability to harm them. The resolution of one conflict and the disappearance of one enemy generate personal, social, and political forces that give rise to new ones. "The 'us' versus 'them' tendency is," as Ali Mazrui said, "in the political arena, almost universal." In the contemporary world the "them" is more likely to be people from [a] different civilization. [7]

The second main psychological factor is the human drive to gain mutual benefit from collaboration with others in order to acquire more resources. In the same paragraph, Huntington adds that "the end of the Cold War has not ended conflict but has rather given rise to new identities rooted in culture and to new patterns of conflict among groups from different cultures which at the broadest level are civilizations. Simultaneously, common culture also encourages cooperation among states and groups which share that culture, which can be seen in the emerging patterns of regional association among countries, particularly in the economic area." [8]

Unfortunately, however, collaboration sometimes extends into the military arena, which can often go awry, especially when such actions are linked to excessive greed. This situation is what happened when various Western countries (which George W. Bush referred to as the "coalition of the willing") collaborated with America in attacking Iraq for the control of its oil reserves on false pretenses. Other bad examples of Western collaborations include the Vietnam War and the adventures in other tribal and sectarian countries, such as in Afghanistan, Libya, Yemen, and Syria, all of which caused poverty, further spreading of terrorism, major refugee problems, and the destruction of homes and infrastructures. [9]

Western countries' collaboration with America in waging proxy wars to achieve geopolitical advantage by removing secular dictators in Iraq, Libya, and Syria is a lesson the world should learn about how *not* to collaborate; it creates a vacuum for terrorism to be born into.

RELIGIOUS-NATIONALISTIC TERRORISM

Although nationalism is generally driven by the feeling of superiority of one nation over others, it is mainly founded on the feeling of human insecurity, which goes back to the evolutionary tendency of humans to organize into distinct groupings based on an affinity for one's birthplace that existed in the tribal eras before the inception of the first religion. Religious nationalism was the result of leaders who subjectively linked the strict interpretation of the written text of their religion with nationalism and were able to produce extremist sentiments by coupling religious traditions to the land and ethnicity. Because religious nationalism is ideologically driven, far-right leaders, who are often driven by the religious establishment, promote and enact stricter religious-adherence laws and act against secular nationalism. [10] (For more on far-right movements, see the subsection below.)

It is unfortunate that the cause of most conflicts is a combination of indoctrination and conditioning by religious and political leaders in their quest for power and control. The ignorance and insecurity of the average people and groups who become foot soldiers and constitute the power base of these leaders are at the heart of the problem. Leaders who use religion and nationalism as motivating factors to designate enemies are the main culprit for the current conflict that is engulfing the world. I consider such leaders to be sinister. In my book *Psyche and Personality* (2013), I wrote the following:

> A sinister leader refer[s] to a leader who promotes conflict and fragmentation for his or her own political, religious, and social survival. Such an individual is self-serving, dishonest, domineering, egotistical, divisive, manipulative, and destructive; he or she attracts condemnation. This sort of leader is usually afflicted with personality disorders, especially toxic narcissism, which stems from the feeling of insecurity or inferiority and manifests itself in compulsiveness, manipulation, fibbing, and distortion of facts [as well as] anxiety, depression, and stress. [11]

Political leaders who are afflicted with toxic narcissism usually distort reality and attack facts, as well as those who convey the facts. The above description and my earlier definition of narcissism in chapter 1 will likely remind readers of what did happen in America during and after the presidential election of 2016. In politics, alarm bells should sound when a political leader becomes more concerned about satisfying vocal minorities and the elite rather than the mainstream majority. It could be to the detriment of the country if people forget that political apathy, especially by the middle class, leads to surrendering the people's power to vested interests and vocal minorities who do not necessarily have the wider national interest as their top priority, especially when they place God or their race ahead of the interests of the country as a whole.

It is detrimental to Western democracy when people's political awareness doesn't extend beyond the biased information they hear from the right-wing media, far-right commentators, and politicians who manipulate mass psychology to meet their objectives. Politicians and religious leaders usually play on people's emotions, ignorance, and insecurity; they exploit people by promoting fear and uncertainty and by giving them false hopes now and in the afterlife.

In using their emotional intelligence and social intelligence (EI and SI), sinister leaders can skillfully mask their real intentions. They seek to establish social fears, prejudices, and stereotypes. To such leaders, however—whose only desire is to achieve specific results—EI and SI become less relevant when the leaders are exposed and become more vulnerable. When this occurs, they are widely perceived as being phony. Unfortunately, such leaders often have the ability to cause much social damage before they are exposed. To avoid a major catastrophe, it then becomes necessary for the moderate majorities from all sides to wake up before it's too late, shed their apathy, and take control of the political agenda. All that is required for social harmony and a peaceful world is to understand the destructiveness of religious nationalism. Religious nationalism can lead only to vendettas, hatred, and warfare. The world is now in the grip of a conflict that is driven by Christian, Jewish, and Islamic religious nationalism; we are in desperate need of wise leaders and moderate people to subdue the aggression and the feeling of hatred that is causing the fragmentation of society and the world.

ISRAEL'S ROLE IN THE MIDDLE EAST CONFLICT

As chapter 1 stated, far-right Zionists and other neoconservatives advocate the theory of "unilateral and assertive wars as an essential strategy in achieving world hegemony and in shaping the international environment to the advantage of the United States." The theory and the actions have dangerous and unintended built-in consequences and ignore the lessons of history—specifically, the rise of the Third Reich and World War II. The conducting of assertive wars that create a war machine to conquer the world is fraught with danger. It embodies the rise of nationalism, which develops into fascism and a government that becomes secretive by virtue of being controlled by its military elites, who gradually take the country into the path of a dictatorship. America, as it stands, appears to be following a similar course under the far-right leadership of Donald Trump, who is surrounded by military advisers and is supported by the theologically oriented Tea Party, which in turn is driven by the religious-right Evangelicals, who are themselves supported by the far-right Zionists.

In a February 2017 speech at the Conservative Political Action Conference (CPAC), President Trump outlined his plan to strengthen the military in both offensive and defensive capabilities, stating that it constitutes the greatest military build-up in American history. Earlier in the same week, he had said he wanted the country's nuclear arsenal to be at "the top of the pack," because he was concerned that America's atomic-weapons capacity had fallen behind. [12] Worse yet, to satisfy his **far-right Zionist*** constituency, President Trump falsely claimed he would be neutral on Israel and Palestine but then appointed his campaign advisers, the ultra-Zionists David Friedman and Jason Greenblatt, as diplomatic envoys to Israel and to the endless and fruitless peace talks with the Palestinians. It is worth noting that Friedman once served as a guard at an Israeli settlement, so his objectivity is questionable. For the sake of short-term gains for Israel, American far-right Zionists support the further militarization of America without taking into consideration the unintended consequences.

* **Far-right Zionists** are represented by various Israel lobby groups, especially the American Israel Public Affairs Committee (AIPAC), which has enormous power over the American political system; in using their wealth, they can make or break the career of any congressperson who doesn't toe their line. This is especially the case when the American elections are largely dependent on contributions of billions of dollars. The group is closely linked

to the neoconservative movement in their objective of benefitting Israel at the expense of the Palestinians.

Pro-Israel lobby groups direct their efforts to influence opinion and policy, most often focusing on national institutions, especially the federal government. The groups' various branches extend their influence to reach local political leaders, businesses, organizations, and private individuals who are involved in Middle East issues.

AIPAC and other Israel lobby groups should adopt the wisdom of Rabbi Michael Lerner, who in 1996 founded Beyt Tikkun, a Jewish renewal movement described as a pro-Israel alternative to AIPAC. Lerner's organization insists on the right of the Palestinian people to self-determination, an end to the Israeli occupation, and the dismantling of the Israeli settlements.

In his book *They Dare to Speak Out* (2003), Paul Findley wrote the following:

In an article in the Los Angeles Times on April 28, 2002, Lerner wrote: "[We should] affirm the equal value of all beings. Reject all anti-Semitism, as well as demeaning of Palestinians and Arabs. Let our elected officials and media know that you will no longer tolerate a political culture that prevents balanced and honest discussion of the Israeli-Palestinian conflict. But criticism of Israel must not slide into the denial of the validity of Israel's existence or anti-Semitic rhetoric...Jews are affirming the highest values of their culture and religion when they conclude that being pro-Israel today requires pushing Israel to end the occupation...All of us are outraged at the immoral acts of Palestinian terrorists...But many of us also understand the Israeli treatment of Palestinians has been immoral and outrageous. [13]

In his book *The Power of Israel in the United States* (2006), James Petras analyzes the power and influence of Israel through its Zionist and pro-Jewish lobby on America's foreign policy, especially its Middle East policy. The book raises serious questions about the policy's benefit to America. Petras details the Zionists' lobbying power to ensure America's unconditional backing of Israel's illegal colonization of Palestine, which has caused massive injustice in the uprooting of Palestinians and the confiscation of their land. By its unconditional backing of Israel, America has been pushed by the Jewish lobby into the costly invasion of Iraq and the threat to invade Syria and Iran, which in turn has fermented massive hostility against the United States in the Islamic world. Petras calls for America to review its Middle East policy to reclaim its independence of action based on its national interest. Its current Middle East policy, which has resulted in an invasion of a sovereign Arab state on false pretenses, has also allowed Israel to invade Lebanon, Syria, Gaza, and the West Bank with total disregard for America's strategic interests. Many enlightened and credible Americans are now seeing that America's foreign policy has been hijacked by a well-organized political lobby of religious-right Zionists and **Christian Zionists**.** The mission of these lobbies is to advance the strategic, political, and military interests of Israel. [14]

** **Christian Zionists**: This term refers to various far-right sociopolitical and religious groups—the Assemblies of God, Evangelicals, and born-again Christians, among others—who subscribe to an apocalyptic end-of-time theology. One of their fundamentalist beliefs is that Christians alone are biblically mandated to occupy all secular institutions until Christ returns. They gain political power by bringing Christians and Jews into the government on the basis that there will never be world peace until God's house and God's people are given their rightful place of leadership. Their support of Zionism stems from their belief that people of the Jewish religion will return to Israel in order to hasten the second coming of Christ, which will convert the Jews to Christianity. This belief is based on the Apocalypse of John in the New Testament. American Christian organizations such as the Christian Friends of Israeli Communities (CFOIC), Christians United for Israel (CUFI), the Hebron Fund (HF), and others not only raise funds for Israel but also actively support the illegal Jewish settlements in Palestine. [15]

In their book *The Israel Lobby and US Foreign Policy* (2007), John J. Mearsheimer and Stephen M. Walt, political scientists at the University of Chicago and Harvard University, respectively, describe the malign influence of the pro-Israel lobby on the US government. They explore the coalition of pro-Israel groups and individuals, including American Jewish organizations and political donors, Christian fundamentalists, neocon officials in the executive branch, and the media allies who smear critics of Israel as anti-Semites. Mearsheimer and Walt describe AIPAC as having an almost unchallenged hold on Congress and the power to pressure the US government into Middle East policies that are strategically and morally reprehensible and unjustifiable. The US government lavishes financial subsidies on Israel despite its illegal occupation of Palestinian territories. AIPAC pressures America into confrontations with Syria and Iran and achieved America's uncritical support of Israel's 2006 bombing of Lebanon and the war on Gaza that violated the laws of war, including the use of cluster bombs on civilians in Lebanon and phosphor bombs on civilians in Gaza. Without AIPAC, the Iraq War would not have occurred, and American support for the Israeli war against Lebanon and Gaza would have been unthinkable.

In the same book, Mearsheimer and Walt warn Jews about the consequences of dealing and trusting Christian Zionists:

Awareness of the Christian Zionists' agenda has made more moderate Israelis and Jewish Americans deeply wary of their embrace. "But for the need of Israel," observes the historian Naomi Cohen, "most American Jews would have rejected out of hand any dealing with the New Christian Right." They fear that converting Jews to Christianity is still a long-term goal of many evangelical groups, and they worry that Christian Zionists' uncompromising views will make it more difficult to reach a lasting peace with the Palestinians. Jo-Ann Mort of American Peace Now terms the collaboration between American Jews and the Christian Right an "unholy alliance," and the Israeli moderate Yossi Alpher warns that Christian support for continued settlement expansion is "leading us into a scenario of out-and-out disaster." As he told CBS News, "God save us from these people." Similarly, the Israeli American scholar Gershom Gorenberg notes that dispensationalist theology does not foresee a happy fate for Jews: in the end of times "the Jews die or convert." In particular, he warns, the Christian Zionists "don't love real Jewish people. They love us as characters in their story, in their play [and] it's a five act play in which the Jews disappear in the fourth act." How important is the Christian Zionist branch of the Israel lobby? By providing financial support to the settler movement and by publicly inveighing against territorial concession, the Christian Zionists have re-inforced hard-line attitudes in Israel and the United States and have made it more difficult for American leaders to put pressure on Israel. Absent their support, settlers would be less numerous in Israel, and the US and Israeli governments would be less constrained by their presence in the Occupied Territories as well as their political activities. [16]

The authors have boldly gone where many other academics fear to go; they have been accused of anti-Semitism for their efforts. Their message is that all moderates and secular people should stand up and be counted by not allowing a destructive, religious-right minority to highjack the agenda and gamble with their future and the future of the generations to follow. Jewish extremist leaders have no regard for the negative impact and the calamities their actions can have on all Jews around the world. [17]

The aforementioned former congressman Paul Findley wrote the following in an article in October 2007 on counterpunch.org:

> I know what it is like to be targeted in this way. In the last years of my long service in Congress, I spoke out, making many of the points now presented in the Mearsheimer-Walt book. In 1980, my opponent charged me with anti-Semitism, and money poured into his campaign fund from every state in the Union. I prevailed that year but two years later lost by a narrow margin. In 1984, Sen. Charles Percy, then chairman of the Foreign Relations Committee and an occasional critic of Israel, was defeated. Leaders of the Israel lobby claimed credit for defeating both Percy and me, claims that strengthened lobby influence in the years that followed.
>
> The result is that Members of Congress today loudly reward Israel as it violates international law and peace agreements, lures America into costly wars, and subjects millions of Palestinians under its rule to apartheid-like conditions because they are not Jewish.
>
> It is time to call politicians to account for their undying allegiance to a foreign state. Let the

Mearsheimer-Walt book be a clarion that bestirs the American people to political action and finally brings fundamental change to both Capitol Hill and the White House.

Citizen participation in public policy development is a hallmark of our proud democracy. But the pro-Israel groups subvert democracy when they engage in smear campaigns that intimidate and silence critics. America badly needs a civilized discussion of the damaging role of Israel in US policy formulation. [18]

The further evidence Findley presents in the same article is overwhelming and should make every free-thinking person angry. To criticize Israeli policy is not anti-Semitism; it is merely to hold Israel accountable for its actions and its behavior toward the Palestinians. Findley didn't deserve the insults and slurs he suffered for telling the truth. One of the truths is highlighted in his statement: "There is an open secret in Washington. I learned it well during my 22-year tenure as a member of the US House of Representatives. All members swear to serve the interests of the United States, but there is an unwritten and overwhelming exception: The interests of one small foreign country almost always trump US interests. That nation of course is Israel." He further states that "on several occasions, colleagues told [me] privately that they admired what [I] was trying to do in Middle East policy reform, but they could not risk the pro-Israel protest back home by supporting [my] positions. The pro-Israel lobby is not one organization orchestrating the US Middle East policy from a backroom in Washington, nor is it entirely Jewish. It consists of scores of groups, large and small, that work at various levels. The largest, most professional, and most effective is the American Israel Public Affairs Committee." [19]

Findley also wrote about AIPAC as a leading Jewish political force in America in *They Dare to Speak Out* (2003):

AIPAC's charter defines its mission as legislative action, but it now also represents the interests of Israel whenever there is [a] perceived challenge to that country's interests in the new media, the religious community, on US college campuses—anywhere. Because AIPAC's staff members are paid for contributions by American citizens, they need not register under [the] Foreign Agents Registration Act. In effect, however, they serve the same function as foreign agents.

Over the years the pro-Israel lobby has thoroughly penetrated this nation's governmental system, and the organization that has made the deepest impact is AIPAC, to whom even a president of the United States turned when he had a vexing political problem related to the Arab-Israeli dispute. [20]

Why is the Israel lobby so effective? One reason, according to Mearsheimer and Walt, is the wide-open nature of the American political system. The United States has a divided form of government, as well as an established tradition of free speech, and a system in which elections are very expensive to run and where campaign contributions are weakly regulated.

This environment gives different groups many different ways to gain access to influencing policy. Interest groups can direct campaign contributions to favored candidates and try to defeat candidates whose views are suspect. Interest groups can also mold public opinion in numerous ways. The lobby's effectiveness also reflects the basic dynamics of interest-group politics in a pluralistic society. In a democracy, even relatively small interest groups can exercise considerable influence if they are strongly committed to a particular issue while the rest of the population is largely indifferent. The disproportionate influence of small but focused interest groups increases even more when opposing groups are weak or nonexistent, because politicians have to accommodate only one set of interests, and the public is likely to hear only one side of the story. [21]

AIPAC's success is due in large part to its ability to reward legislators and congressional candidates who support its agenda and to punish those who do not, based mainly on its capacity to influence campaign contributions. Money is critical to US elections, which have become increasingly expensive to win, and AIPAC ensures that its friends get financial support so long as they do not stray from AIPAC's line. [22]

The Israel lobby groups have brought about a situation where it has become impossible for elected officials to question support for Israel, much less redirect foreign policy that would in any way be contrary to the perceived self-interest of Israel, including deceiving Americans about who was behind the disastrous invasion of Iraq.

In *They Dare to Speak Out*, Findley describes Senator Charles Mathias's frustration with the influence of AIPAC on the US Congress and on American presidents when Mathias cited the Israel lobby as the most powerful ethnic pressure group that didn't focus on the vital security of America. Findley quotes Mathias as saying that "with the exception of [the] Eisenhower administration, which virtually compelled Israel's withdrawal from the Sinai after [the] 1956 war, American presidents, and to an even greater degree Senators and Representatives, have been subjected to recurrent pressures from what has come to be known as the Israel lobby." [23] Under the heading of "Leave the Grandstanding to Others," Findley describes how some senators find it necessary to confer with AIPAC executives before introducing legislation related to the Middle East. Findley wrote, "One such politician is Senator Dianne Feinstein (D-CA), who in the 2000 elections won out over her challenger, former Representative and critic of Israel Tom Campbell. Feinstein went on to sponsor, along with Mitch McConnell (R-KY), every blatantly pro-Israel piece of legislation in the 107th Senate. These senators reportedly conferred with Howard Kohr, executive director of AIPAC, before drafting their legislation. Kohr claims to receive dozens of calls from lawmakers asking what they can do to help Israel." [24]

As for Israel spying on America and on having easy access to secret information from the US Defense and State Departments, especially with the assistance of a few committed Zionists who place Israel first, it is worth referring to the section in chapter 6 of *They Dare to Speak Out* titled "Penetrating the Defenses at Defense and State." [25] Sooner or later, Americans will wake up to the fact that America's interests conflict with Israel's and will decide to curtail the power of the various Israel lobby groups in America. This action, which should happen sooner rather than later, will likely be viewed positively throughout the world as a first step toward world peace.

Israel's utilization of America's military strength to destroy a helpless nation contradicts all human-rights principles. By enlisting America's backing to sideline international laws, and by expanding Jewish settlements in the Israel-occupied territories, Israel is seriously miscalculating the final outcome, especially by not taking into consideration the rapid decline of America. America's rapid decline relates to its lack of understanding that the radical Islamic terrorism toward it is fueled mainly by American leaders' failure to resolve the Israeli-Palestinian conflict and its lack of understanding that poverty, unemployment, injustice, and ignorance are the main drivers of terrorism.

The destruction of the Palestinian nation that commenced before and continued after the end of the British mandate over Palestine was accompanied by systematic Zionist atrocities against the civilian population, including a plan that was decided on in March 1948 that resulted in the destruction of over 530 villages and the uprooting and deportation of close to eight hundred thousand people.

In his book *The Ethnic Cleansing of Palestine* (2007), Ilan Pappe, an Israeli historian at Britain's University of Exeter, wrote the following:

> After the Holocaust, it has become almost impossible to conceal [large-scale] crimes against humanity. Our modern communication-driven world, especially since the upsurge of electronic media, no longer allows human-made catastrophes to remain hidden from the public eye or to be denied. And yet, one such crime has been erased almost totally from the global public memory: the dispossession of the Palestinians in 1948 by Israel. This, the most formative event in the modern history of the land of Palestine, has ever since been systematically denied, and is still today not recognized as an historical fact, let alone acknowledged as a crime that needs to be confronted politically as well as morally...[26]

For Palestinians, and anyone else who refused to buy into the Zionist narrative, it was clear long before this book was written that these people were perpetrators of crimes, but that they had successfully evaded justice and would probably never be brought to trial for what they had done. Besides their trauma, the deepest form of frustration for Palestinians has been that the criminal act these men were responsible for has been so thoroughly denied, and that Palestinian suffering has been so totally ignored since 1948. [27]

The stalemate in establishing a Palestinian state carries grave risks for both the Israelis and the Palestinians of a continuation of the deadly wave of terrorism and killings that have afflicted the region. The United States and the European Union—Israel's closest allies—have expressed unusually stern criticism of Israel in recent times; this criticism reflects their frustrations with Israel's far-right governments, yet they have failed to take action that could achieve positive results for the Palestinians. It is not good enough for America and Israel's other allies to decry Israel's illegal settlement, ethnic cleansing, collective punishment of the Palestinian population, and land-confiscation policy when they know that the far-right Zionists will take no notice but will instead continue with the **Zionist project***** of colonizing Palestine, supported by the American pro-Israel lobby groups who control the US Congress.

*** The **Zionist project**: In May 1948, Israel's first ethno-nationalist prime minister, David Ben-Gurion, proclaimed the founding of the state of Israel. Immediately after, Jewish commandos in Palestine launched what Israel called its war of independence. By the time Israel had struck an armistice with the armies of Egypt, Transjordan, and Syria in 1949, more than 750,000 Palestinians had been forced to flee their homes. They became refugees from their own country, which the Jewish Zionist armies now controlled. Rather than seeking to break free from imperialism, Israel actively courted patronage from imperialist powers. Rather than promising self-determination to the people of Palestine—the vast majority of whom were Arab—it expelled them. It should be noted that some ultraorthodox Jews oppose the establishment of an Israeli state because they believe the true Jewish state will only be established on the coming of the Messiah. [28]

Other than the illegal settlements and the collective punishment of the Palestinian population, the Israeli government also produced laws to ensure that Palestinians would not be allowed to buy or lease their own land that had been confiscated. Under the notion of guarding the nation's land, the government enabled the Jewish National Fund (JNF) and the Israel Land Authority (ILA) to reinforce this position.

In the same book, Pappe wrote the following:

The legislative takeover of the land and the process of turning it into JNF property was completed in 1967 when the Knesset [Israel's legislative branch] passed a final law, the law of Agricultural Settlement, that also prohibited the sub-letting of the Jewish-owned land of the JNF to non-Jews (until then only sale and direct lease were prohibited). The law furthermore ensured that water quotas set aside for the JNF lands could not be transferred to non-JNF lands (water is scarce in Israel and hence sufficient quotas are vital for agriculture).

The bottom line of this almost two-decades-long bureaucratic process (1949–1967) was that the legislation regarding the JNF, barring the selling, leasing and sub-letting of land to non-Jews, was put into effect for most of the state lands (more than ninety per cent of Israel's land, seven per cent having been declared as private land). The primary objective of this legislation was to prevent Palestinians in Israel from regaining ownership through purchase of their own land or that of their people. [29]

It is estimated that seventy percent of the land belonging to the Palestinians in Israel has been either confiscated or made inaccessible to them...[30]

As the owner of lands in general, along with other agencies that possess state land in Israel such as the Israeli Land Authority, the army and the governments, the Jewish National Fund was also involved in establishing new Jewish settlements on the lands of destroyed Palestinian villages. Here, dispossession was accompanied by the renaming of the places it had seized, destroyed and now recreated. This mission was accomplished with the help of archaeologists and biblical experts who volunteered to serve on an official Naming Committee whose job it was to Hebraize Palestine's geography. [31]

While the Middle East is in a state of flux, the far-right Israeli government is busy expanding Jewish settlements in Palestine, in a hurry to illegally colonize the country. The Zionist project usually becomes most active during the American presidential nominations and congressional elections, when nominees generally avoid making any negative remarks about Israel because of Israel's power in America and the financial power of the Jewish lobby groups who can elect or unseat any candidate. The far-right Zionists usually prefer Republicans over Democrats in getting a free hand for building illegal settlements in the Israel-occupied territories and in colonizing Palestine. Israel's actions are adding fuel to the fire and must be stopped, but they cannot be stopped by a weak American leader who cannot get elected without pledging loyalty and total commitment to Israel. It is worth reminding the world of what General David Petraeus told a congressional committee in March 2010: "the perception of US favoritism for Israel in the Israeli-Palestinian conflict [is] sparking anti-American sentiment in the Arab world."

In April 2016, the far-right Israeli government used the turmoil in the Middle East, especially during the civil war in Syria, as an excuse to declare that Israel would annex the Golan Heights after fifty years of illegal occupation. The international community had never accepted Israel's annexation of the Golan Heights. In accordance with the UN Security Council resolution of 1981, which the council reconfirmed in April 2016, Israel's imposition of its laws, jurisdiction, and administration in the occupied Syrian Golan Heights was null and void and lacked international legal status. The council agreed that the status of the Golan Heights, which Israel had seized from Syria in 1967, would remain unchanged.

Adding fuel to the fire is Trump's recognition in December 2017 of Jerusalem as Israel's capital, overturning seven decades of US policy in the Middle East, which effectively ending hopes of a two-state solution.

EVANGELICALS, THE TEA PARTY, AND ISRAEL

Most moderate people feel that the Tea Party is a negative thing for America and the rest of the world. The grassroots of this dogmatic group are among Evangelicals, who have succeeded in converting the Republican Party into a theocracy-oriented party. Through the Republican Party, they seek to control American politics by using God as a justification for almost every issue: crime and punishment, foreign policy, health care, abortions, taxation, energy, regulations in general, social services, and so on. Their greatest enemy is a secular government and anybody who advocates for a secular government. This theocracy is indistinguishable from an Islamic fundamentalism in which religion and politics are inseparable. The Evangelicals' support of Zionism stems from their belief that people of the Jewish religion will return to Israel to hasten the second coming of Christ, which will convert the Jews to Christianity. As noted earlier, this is why the term "Christian Zionism" is now often used to describe Christians who support Israel. The beliefs of these Christian fundamentalists come from their interpretation of the Book of Revelation, the last book of the New Testament, which is also called the Apocalypse of John. [32]

It was not long ago that George W. Bush, who has identified himself as a born-again Christian, brought Paul Wolfowitz, Douglas Feith, and other far-right Jewish religious nationalists into his administration knowing full well what their agenda was. Before hiring anyone who might deal with sensitive, national-security areas, federal agencies typically perform exhaustive security-clearance checks on these potential employees. This means the administration had to know exactly what these men's agenda was before hiring them. Christian Zionists' belief in supporting Israel's expansionist policies on biblical grounds is exactly what American Jewish Zionists needed to advance Israel's cause. As a result, the world has witnessed the invasion of Iraq; as a result of that war, Americans and the rest of the Western world now suffer from increased terrorism. And as desired by Israel, the regime change in Syria that is being implemented by Saudi Arabia, Jordan, Turkey, and America (which plunged the country into a civil war). Also demanded by Israel, is the destruction of Iran (which is in the planning stages). The damage to their country will gradually lead Americans to discover the reason behind their country's decline and what constitutes the biggest threat to America.

It is amazing to see Evangelicals at Tea Party gatherings call for the support of the military and a return to God by asking their followers to get on their knees and pray for redemption in order to rebuild America's sacred honor. This is ironic, because they themselves have destroyed America's honor and its economy by pushing the nation into wars that stand no chance of being won and that result in the killing of many innocent people, including women and children, which provokes a desire for revenge among the invaded peoples. Instead, America's honor can be restored by respecting other countries' sovereignty and by dealing with the world on a win-win basis, rather than on a winner-takes-all basis. America's honor can also be restored by reigning in Israeli aggression and its expansionism at the expense of the Palestinians.

It is worth noting that many evangelical churches were pacifistic until the Arab-Israeli War of 1967 (also known as the Six-Day War), when these churches decided to adopt a new position of affirming their loyalty to the government of the United States in war or peace. Before 1967, the Assemblies of God, along with the majority of other Pentecostal denominations, officially opposed Christian participation in war and considered themselves for peace and nonviolence. Their participation in many elections, including the election of George W. Bush, and their commitment to the Republican Party have proved that many of these denominations now support violence. They currently lead the way, together with far-right Zionists, in their campaign against Islam under the slogan of the "clash of civilizations."

Their interpretation of the prophecies in the Apocalypse of John about the second coming of Christ and the catastrophic end-time events will likely have destructive consequences. This ideology—of the clash of Christianity against the secular governments as part of God's intervention to save mankind from self-destruction, which will lead to the establishment of God's government and an end to man's self-rule—could lead the world to catastrophe. The dangerous aspect of the prophecy is the killing of billions of people to save them from self-destruction. Clearly, this contradiction doesn't add up, especially when we consider that humans have proved over millennia that we are rational thinkers who are equipped with the natural instincts of survival and self-preservation. These people's religious delusions should not be allowed to drive American politics, especially when America is meant to be a secular country where, constitutionally, religion and state are separated. To be guided by religious dogma based on conjecture is dangerous to both America and humanity.

In *The Israel Lobby and US Foreign Policy* (2007), Mearsheimer and Walt wrote the following:

Convincing hard-line Christian Zionists to abandon their commitment to a greater Israel is less likely, given the central role that prophecies about the end-time play in dispensationalist theology, and given the apparent willingness to see the Middle East engulfed in a highly destructive "apocalyptic" war. Hope may be found in the tendency for evangelicals' agenda to shift in the perennial quest for new members and in the general tendency for these movements to fluctuate in strength over time. The next president is unlikely to be as sympathetic to these groups as George W. Bush has been, especially given the disastrous results that [Bush's] Middle East policies have produced. Jews in Israel and America may also realize that Christian Zionism is a dubious ally—especially when they consider the unappealing role they are expected to play in the end-time—and begin to distance themselves from the evangelicals' embrace. For their part, Christian evangelicals should be encouraged to reflect on the human tragedy that Israel continues to inflict on the

Palestinians and to consider whether their own commitment to a "greater Israel" is truly consistent with Christ's message of love and brotherhood. [33]

Evangelical groups achieve their religious objectives by combining their fundamentalism with their charisma to manipulate the less aware section of society, especially in their ability to employ mass psychology on the unaware through their megachurches. The survival of their religious leaders largely depends on entangling religion with politics, thus allowing these leaders to use religion for lobbying purposes. They engage in political activity in a variety of ways, including through national media campaigns and grassroots organizations aimed at supporting particular candidates in elections and by using mail and phone calls to reach officeholders. They are now heavily involved in presidential elections and national politics while continuing to pursue specific issues at lower levels of government. Nationally, they encourage electoral participation among their members and use registration drives to enroll churchgoers to vote for their endorsed candidates.

Their action became lethal when they joined forces with far-right Zionists to elect George W. Bush as president, which was arguably an awful part of America's history. The Bush administration left behind a history of conflict and destruction that the world will rue for many years to come. In linking America's future to that of Israel's, these Christian Zionists are risking their country's future by their contributions to a clash of civilizations that can produce no winner. Christian Zionists often overlook the fact that Israel's far-right governments, for many decades, have shaped biblical mythology to fit politically expedient ends. They do this even when this theology contradicts modern international laws, such as the claim that Jerusalem was always the capital of Israel. The European Union, for example—in accordance with international law—does not recognize Israeli sovereignty over the territories it captured in the 1967 Arab-Israeli War, including the West Bank and East Jerusalem, where the Palestinians hope to establish a state. Other biblical mythology, like the idea that God promised that the land would belong to the Israelites, contradicts all historical facts. After over fifteen hundred years of Canaanite rule over Palestine, the land between the Jordan River and the Mediterranean Sea fell under the rule of numerous invaders, including the Philistines, the Israelites, the Phoenicians, the Assyrians, the Babylonians, the Persians, the Macedonians, the Romans, the Arabs, and the Crusaders, and then it was ruled by various Islamic caliphates from 1291 until the British mandate in 1922. The Israelites' control barely lasted for seventy-seven years, and much evidence contests the notion that Israeli Jews of today are even blood relatives of the groups who inhabited Palestine two thousand years ago. Yet that notion was enough for the modern Israeli national myth, which far-right religious extremists in both America and Israel now champion. [34]

WHERE DO AMERICA AND ISRAEL GO FROM HERE?

First, it should be emphasized that America and its Western allies have a choice: whether to treat other religious and ethnic groups as equals, which would make them fight for peace and harmony, or to treat them as despised peoples and make them fight for their dignity and survival. The West knows well that survival and human dignity are the most valuable things in the world. The West also knows well that all humans are born equals and atheists until they are brainwashed into becoming religious fanatics, good citizens, criminals, bigots, or terrorists. Fanaticism and terrorism—closely associated with prejudice, racism, and bigotry—are common in all nations and are usually fueled by extremist leaders who are trained in mind control. The success of these leaders is directly related to the level of entrenched ignorance and to the power and charisma of such leaders in political, religious, and social manipulation.

The Jews' suffering before and during World War II should be a lesson that no nation should suffer the consequences of fascism. Israel's policy of segregation, ethnic cleansing, and the entrenchment of apartheid are no different from what happened in South Africa. In the process of implementing the Zionist project, Israel has tried to destroy the Palestinian nation, which is causing a massive Islamic backlash. Israel is acting with impunity and is supported by imperialist America on the grounds of self-defense when in fact it is the provocateur, the aggressor, and the occupier of Palestinian land. The self-defense argument is a powerful piece of propaganda, one that America has become comfortable in hiding behind while maintaining its unconditional commitment to Israel.

In his book *Palestine: Peace Not Apartheid* (2007), former president Jimmy Carter describes the forced segregation in the West Bank and the terrible oppression of the Palestinians as a violation of human decency. The book is about the Israel-occupied territories and the desire of a minority of Israelis to confiscate and colonize Palestinian land, and it is about the violation of basic human rights. This is the main cause of the conflict and of Arab animosity toward Israel and America—a conflict that is threatening the whole region. Carter points out that, based on a Hebrew University poll, the majority of Israelis and Palestinians are in favor of a comprehensive settlement similar to the "Roadmap for Peace" that was proposed by the Quartet of the United States, the European Union, Russia, and the United Nations, or the Saudi proposal adopted by all Arab countries. The Saudi-sponsored 2002 Arab Peace Plan offered Israel full normalization in return for full withdrawal from Arab lands occupied in 1967.

Carter describes a system of apartheid, with two peoples occupying the same land but completely separated from each other, with Israelis totally dominant and suppressing resistance by depriving Palestinians of their basic human rights. [35] He adds, "The bottom line is this: Peace will come to Israel and the Middle East only when the Israeli government is willing to comply with international law, with the Roadmap for Peace, with official American policy, with the wishes of a majority of its own citizens—and honor its own previous commitments—by accepting its legal borders." [36]

A Nobel Peace Prize winner in 2002 for his decades of work for peace, human rights, and international development, Carter sees that Israeli sovereignty and security can coexist permanently and peacefully alongside a Palestinian state. The lack of goodwill from the Israelis, however, has resulted in a bloody struggle often interrupted by negotiations that turn out to be anything but honest. Carter assigns ultimate blame to Israel, arguing that the country's leadership has routinely undermined the peace process through its obstinate, aggressive, and illegal occupation of the territories it seized in 1967. He is decidedly less critical of Arab leaders; he accepts their concern for the Palestinian cause at face value and includes their anti-Israel rhetoric as a matter of course. But Carter also treats the Israelis gently, considering the massive human-rights abuses they have committed.

President Carter and a few other presidents before and after him, along with American public opinion, have been manipulated by the Zionists. These Zionists have exploited the fear that a second Holocaust and the potential destruction of the Jewish state are imminent. The Zionists' propaganda, while demonizing the Arabs as a threat to Israel's survival, has helped Israel secure massive American military and financial support at the same time when the Palestinians face ethnic cleansing and oppression. The Zionists' propaganda conceals the fact—as stated in chapter 1—that Zionism is not the same as Judaism.

I should mention that Carter has learned, like Gerald Ford before him and all the following presidents, to make Israel a beneficiary of America's Middle East policy. Furthermore, these administrations have learned that no politician can withhold funds for Israel, even if these payments contravene international law and human decency. During George W. Bush's term in office, Findley wrote in *They Dare to Speak Out* (2003) that "it was a lesson well learned by American politicians, as no US president since has openly threatened to withhold funds to ensure Israeli compliance with international law. Indeed, according to *USA Today*, current President George W. Bush says his father, the first President Bush, made a political mistake that helped cost him re-election when he threatened to withhold some US aid from Israel." [37]

This is one reason why America's leadership role in the world is diminishing: America is incapable of controlling a small minority of influential lobby groups who are causing it to lose face in the eyes of the world, especially because the nation applies a double standard when dealing with the world. It is incapable of reconciling the opposing ethnic and religious groups in Israel and elsewhere. For this reason, a simple solution that would avoid mutually assured destruction would be for all sides to adopt a more moderate stance. America can easily influence its allies, especially the religious-right Israeli government, to observe human-rights principles in dealing with a nation under its occupation. All that is needed is to apply the principles of coexistence and tolerance as a guide in human relationships. Wisdom and moderation can make Israel the most prosperous country in the world if it sets aside its religious nationalism and embraces a reasonable two-state solution, which would make it an acceptable neighbor that would have access to huge markets throughout the Arab and Islamic worlds. As many world leaders and academics say, Israel's expansion into Palestinian land is in violation of international laws and in contradiction of the peace process Israel pretends to be engaged in, although a negotiated agreement revolves around the total evacuation of Jewish settlements from Palestinian territories to the 1967 borders.

Religious-right groups, with their fundamentalist interpretations of religion, are behind the unfair American and Israeli policies toward the Middle East. These groups ignore the fact that revolutions and religions generally come about as a consequence of the resentment and resistance engendered by conflicts and injustices inflicted on people. "Live and let live," instead of "Live and let die," is the best solution to many human conflicts. The application of true justice for everyone is a prerequisite for peace and harmony in the world. It is common sense; America and Israel should know by now that to avoid a major upheaval, people who live in the shadows must be given a chance. Above all, the world is to remember that the recent phenomenon of terrorism and suicide bombings has been exasperated as a violent reaction to America's military interventions and to Israel's aggression against the Palestinians. The violence and terrorism in the Middle East originated as a reaction to Israel's unjust treatment of the Palestinians; as is always the case, when there is no justice, there can be no peace.

Now it is time for America and its allies to ensure that Israel abandons its occupation and the apartheid-type treatment of the Palestinians, in the same way that the Western world succeeded in forcing South Africa to abandon its apartheid regime. By spreading fear in the hearts of the Palestinians by committing atrocities, Israel has condemned its population to continuous revenge from people who are left with no hope. And when people are left with no hope, the worst outcome for all should be expected. Although millions of Jews oppose far-right Zionism, millions of Christians oppose Christian fundamentalism, and millions of Muslims oppose Islamic extremism, extremists speak louder through their control of media resources and religious establishments. The religious-right groups' hate has spread across the globe like a plague on humanity and can bring only conflict and misery to the world.

Moderate Jews should be vigilant against the zeal of some of their far-right Zionist leaders, who place too much emphasis on short-term gains while ignoring the ultimate consequences, especially in terms of America's rapid decline. One of the main dangers for Israel stems from the linking of its strategic interests with those of America without taking into consideration the fact that America, for its own strategic interests, uses Israel to spearhead control over the fragmented oil-rich Arab countries and to cement its presence in the Middle East. Israel, in turn, uses America in its short-term quest to expand and colonize Palestine, but when America becomes comfortable with its control of the Middle East, it will require stability. Israel will then become a major liability because of its provocative actions against the Palestinians and its other Arab neighbors. To achieve their common short-term strategic interests in the Middle East, America and Israel have come to the conclusion that Arab nationalism is the primary stumbling block in the way of meeting their objectives and therefore must be fought by all means possible. In the process, they overlooked the fact that Arab nationalism is directly related to the Islamic religion; hence, the war on Arabs is widely perceived as a war on Islam, dressed up as a war on terrorism. It is in fact a religious-nationalistic war that nobody can win, and its ultimate unintended consequence will be mutually assured destruction. [38]

Despite various human-rights groups' rejection of Israel's collective punishment of Palestinians, the nation has revived the policy while America has remained silent. It is an arbitrary policy that affects every Palestinian indiscriminately, for example by demolishing the homes of parents for their children's resistance against the Israeli occupation. What is the fault of the parents, one may ask? If the Palestinians were Europeans or Americans, how would the world have reacted? Is the world waiting for Israel to commit an all-out genocide before it steps in to stop the repeat of Nazi Germany's and South African's fascism? The world has turned a blind eye to Israel's atrocities in Gaza and the West Bank, which still continue without respite. What is the civilized world waiting for?

To highlight the plight of the Palestinians under Israeli occupation, it is worth referring to the United Nations report of March 2017 by the Economic and Social Commission for Western Asia (ESCWA) entitled "Israeli Practices toward the Palestinian People and the Question of Apartheid" (2017). The full report can be found at www.unescwa.org.

The report is based on the principle that no nation or state is immune to the norms and rules enshrined in the International Convention on the Elimination of All Forms of Racial Discrimination, which must be applied impartially. The prohibition of apartheid, which, as a crime against humanity, can admit no exceptions, flows from the convention. Strengthening that body of international law can only benefit all groups who have historically endured discrimination, domination, and persecution, including Jews. The report set out to determine whether specific acts constitute evidence of apartheid and to examine whether they contribute to the overarching purpose of sustaining an institutionalized regime of racial oppression and domination.

The studies in the report point to the assertion that Israel has applied numerous policies, practices, and measures to enforce a system of racial discrimination, all of which threaten regional peace and security. UN resolutions have long recognized that danger and have called for resolution of the conflict so as to restore and maintain peace and stability in the region. To assert that the policies and practices of a sovereign state amount to apartheid constitutes a grave charge. A study aimed at making such a determination should be undertaken and submitted for consideration only when supporting evidence clearly exceeds reasonable doubt. The authors of the report believe that the evidence for suspecting a system of apartheid has been imposed on the Palestinian people meets such a demanding criterion. Given the protracted suffering of the Palestinian people, the authors of the report assert that it would be irresponsible not to present the evidence and legal arguments regarding whether Israel has established an apartheid regime that oppresses the Palestinian people as a whole and not to make recommendations for appropriate further action by international and civil society actors.

In sum, the study was motivated by the desire to promote compliance with international human-rights law, to uphold and strengthen international criminal law, and to ensure that the collective responsibilities of the United Nations and its member states are fulfilled regarding crimes against humanity. More concretely, it aims to see the international community's core commitments to upholding international law applied to the case of the Palestinian people in defense of their rights under international law, including the right of self-determination. [39] The authors of the report conclude that the weight of the evidence supports, beyond a reasonable doubt, the contention that Israel is guilty of imposing an apartheid regime on the Palestinian people and that the United Nations and its agencies, and all member states, have a legal obligation to act within their capabilities to prevent and punish any instances of apartheid brought to their attention.

Civil-society institutions and individuals also have a moral duty to use the instruments at their disposal to raise awareness of this ongoing criminal enterprise. They must also exert pressure on Israel to dismantle apartheid structures and to negotiate in good faith for a lasting peace that would acknowledge the rights of Palestinians under international law and would allow the two peoples to live together on the basis of real equality.

Apartheid in South Africa was brought to an end, in part, by the cumulative impact of a variety of measures (including economic sanctions and sporting-event boycotts), undertaken with the blessing of various United Nations bodies and of many member states and with grassroots support in nations with strong strategic and economic ties to South Africa. The effectiveness of the antiapartheid campaign was in large part due to the transnational activism of civil society, which reinforced the intergovernmental consensus that took shape in the United Nations. [40] The authors of the report make several recommendations, some of which are general and others of which apply to United Nations bodies, to national governments, to private-sector actors, and to civil society, including religious organizations. [41]

To secure the future of the Israelis and of the Palestinians, it is worth taking Pappe's words into consideration from *The Ethnic Cleansing of Palestine* (2006):

> Still, the solution would appear simple: as the last postcolonial European enclave in the Arab world, Israel has no choice but willingly to transform itself one day into a civic and democratic state.
>
> That [this] is possible we see from the close social relationships that Palestinians and Jews have created between themselves over these long and troubled years and against all odds, both inside and outside Israel. That we can put an end to the conflict in the torn land of Palestine also becomes obvious if we look at those sections of Jewish society in Israel that have chosen to let themselves be shaped by human considerations rather than Zionist social engineering. That peace is within reach we know, above all, from the majority of the Palestinians who have refused to let themselves be de-humanised by decades of brutal Israeli occupation and who, despite years of expulsion and oppression, still hope for reconciliation.

But the window of opportunity will not stay open forever. Israel may still be doomed to remain a country full of anger, its actions and behaviour dictated by racism and religious fanaticism, the features of its people permanently distorted by the quest for retribution. How long can we go on asking, let alone expecting, our Palestinian brothers and sisters to keep the faith with us, and not to succumb totally to despair and sorrow into which their lives [were] transformed the year Israel erected its Fortress over their destroyed villages and towns? [42]

To conclude this subsection, it is worth highlighting American political scientist, professor Norman Finkelstein's warning to Jewish elites in his book *The Holocaust Industry: Reflection on the Exploitation of Jewish Suffering* (2000):

If Israel fell out of favor with the United States, many of those leaders who now stoutly defend Israel would courageously divulge their disaffection from the Jewish state and would excoriate American Jews for turning Israel into a religion. And if US ruling circles decided to scapegoat Jews, we should not be surprised if American Jewish leaders acted exactly as their predecessors did during the Nazi holocaust. "We didn't figure that the Germans would put in the Jewish element," Yitzhak Zuckerman, an organizer of the Warsaw Ghetto Uprising recalled, "that Jews would lead Jews to death." [43]

A Brief History of Neoconservatism

In *The Israel Lobby and US Foreign Policy* (2007), Mearsheimer and Walt define neoconservatism as a political ideology with distinct views on both domestic and foreign policy:

> Most neoconservatives extol the virtues of American hegemony—and sometimes even the idea of an American empire—and they believe US power should be used to encourage the spread of democracy and discourage potential rivals from trying even to compete with the United States...
>
> They tend to be skeptical of international institutions (especially the UN, which they regard as both anti-Israel and as a constraint on America's freedom of action) and wary of many allies (especially the Europeans, whom they see as idealistic pacifists free-riding on the Pax Americana). The neoconservatives generally favor the unilateral exercise of American power. They believe that military force is an extremely useful tool for shaping the world in ways that will benefit America...[44]
>
> But not all neoconservatives are Jewish, which reminds us that the lobby is defined not by ethnicity or religion but by political agenda. There are a number of prominent gentiles who have adopted most if not all of the basic tenets of neoconservatism, to include vigorous support for Israel and a tendency to favor its more hard-line elements. Their ranks include the *Wall Street Journal* editor Robert Bartley, former Secretary of

Education William Bennett, former UN Ambassadors John Bolton and Jeane Kirkpatrick, and former CIA director James Woolsey. Although these non-Jews have played an important role in pushing forward the neoconservative agenda, Jews nonetheless comprise the core of the larger pro-Israel movement. Jewish Americans are central to the neoconservative movement, just as they form the bulk of the lobby, but non-Jews are active in both. Neoconservatives are also emblematic insofar as much of their political agenda is at odds with the traditional views of most American Jews. [45]

Ironically, the neoconservatism (or "neocon") movement was started in the 1970s by a group of left-wing students who included Irving Kristol at City College in New York (CCNY). The group adopted the views of the 1930s by German Jewish philosopher **Leo Strauss*** from the University of Chicago. Kristol, a far-right Zionist, was an American columnist, journalist, and writer who has been dubbed the godfather of neoconservatism. Following World War II, in the 1960s and 1970s, the group turned to the far right and against the left-wing and other Marxist sympathizers who opposed the Vietnam War. The Israel lobby groups also moved to the right at this time, especially following Israel's victory in the 1967 Six-Day War against its Arab neighbors.

*** Leo Strauss (1899–1973)** was a German American political philosopher who specialized in classical political philosophy. He was born in Germany to Jewish parents and later emigrated from Germany to the United States. He spent most of his career as a professor of political science at the University of Chicago. Strauss was often depicted as an influential figure in neoconservative policy circles, notably in connection with US foreign policy during the George W. Bush administration (2001–09), which was guided by neoconservatives such as Paul Wolfowitz. [46] His philosophy originated from the works of Plato and Aristotle, from whose ideas Strauss established the idea of "regime," which became a central dogma of conservativism. In this concept, a regime is not a visible set of formal institutions but a system whereby formal political institutions and informal habits are constantly shaped by one another. Alternatively, the form and structure of a society determine the behavior and outlook of its citizens, and vice versa. Therefore, the regime concept became the anchor of neoconservative philosophy and domestic policy. They believed that by fixing the regime and changing public perceptions, crime and disorder could be eradicated. By the time the neoconservatives gained control of Washington, however, they started to apply the concept of regime change to American foreign policy. [47]

In *The Israel Lobby and US Foreign Policy* (2007), Mearsheimer and Walt wrote the following:

> Most American Jews have long supported liberal causes and the Democratic Party, and a majority of them favor a two-state solution to the Israeli-Palestinian conflict. Nevertheless, some of the most important groups in the lobby—including AIPAC and the Conference

of Presidents—have become increasingly conservative over time and are now led by hard-liners who support the positions of their hawkish counterparts in Israel. As J. J. Goldberg chronicles in his important book, *Jewish Power*, the Six-Day War and its aftermath brought into prominence a group of "New Jews" drawn disproportionately from hard-line Zionists, Orthodox, and neo-conservative circles. "Their defiance was so strident, and their anger was so intense," he writes, "that the rest of the Jewish community respectfully stood back and let the New Jews take the lead. The minority was permitted to speak for the mass and become the dominant voice of Jewish politics." [48]

In *The Holocaust Industry* (2000), Finkelstein elaborates on the above:

Everything changed with the June 1967 Arab-Israeli war. By virtually all accounts, it was only after this conflict that the Holocaust became a fixture in American Jewish life. The standard explanation of this transformation is that Israel's extreme isolation and vulnerability during [the] June war revived memories of the Nazi extermination. In fact, this analysis misrepresents both the reality of Mideast power relations at the time and the nature of the evolving relationship between American Jewish elites and Israel...

From its founding in 1948 through the June 1967 war, Israel did not figure centrally in American strategic planning. As the Palestinian Jewish leadership prepared to declare statehood, President Truman waffled, weighing domestic consideration (the Jewish vote) against State Department alarm (support for a Jewish state would alienate the Arab world). To secure US interests in the Middle East, the Eisenhower Administration balanced support for Israel and for Arab nations, favouring, however, the Arabs...

Paradoxically, after June 1967, Israel facilitated assimilation in the United States: Jews now stood on the front lines defending America—indeed "Western civilization"—against the retrograde Arab hordes. Whereas before 1967 Israel conjured the bogy of dual loyalty, it now connoted super-loyalty...

Accordingly, American Jewish elites suddenly discovered Israel. After the 1967 war, Israel's military clan could be celebrated because its guns pointed in the right direction—against America's enemies. [49]

Israel's victory in the 1967 war became the catalyst for consolidating the neoconservatives' power and their influence on America's aggressive foreign relations. In the 1970s, the CCNY group joined forces with other believers in Strauss's philosophy, including political analyst William Kristol (son of Irving Kristol), political scientist Francis Fukuyama, and Paul Wolfowitz, to form the neoconservative movement. They formed the idealistic views of opposing liberalism and guiding society to share these same beliefs and purpose, especially to spread democracy throughout the world. They became influential by convincing people in power—such as Ronald Reagan, Donald Rumsfeld, Dick Cheney, and others—of their theory of regime changes around the world to achieve American hegemony.

In *America at the Crossroad: Democracy, Power, and the Neoconservative Legacy* (2006), Fukuyama wrote the following:

The Kristol-Kagan effort to refine neoconservative foreign policy was first laid out systematically in [a] 1996 article they wrote for *Foreign Affairs* (expanded into a book entitled *Present Dangers* [2000]), defining a "neo-Reaganite" agenda for the Republican Party. They took issue with Jeane Kirkpatrick's brief for a return to American "normalcy" after the end of Cold War and called instead for "benevolent hegemony" under American leadership, a policy that entailed "resisting, and where possible undermining rising dictators and hostile ideologies…supporting American interests and liberal democratic principles; and providing assistance to those struggling against the more extreme manifestations of human evil." [50]

The neoconservatives reached their peak during the George W. Bush presidency, especially after the 9/11 attacks, which were followed by the war on terror, where America sought to topple regimes hostile to it and to spread democracy by force in the belief that spreading democracy around the world would bring peace and benefit America. The problem of spreading democracy, especially in the Middle East, is that doing so overlooks a few important facts. First, American democracy is not a true democracy; it is corrupted by money, which means that America is governed by a dictatorship of the dollar. Second, America is often a bullying and intimidating country that is run by special-interest groups. Third, America cannot be believed, because it contradicts itself by supporting autocratic and oppressive regimes such as Saudi Arabia, Egypt, and now Turkey, which proves to the world that its foreign policy is interest based rather than value based. Fourth, as an imperialistic power that uses its hard power and military interventions to destroy nations and human lives because of their disobedient governments, America often displays no concern for morality and justice, which has resulted in the destruction of its credibility. The people of the world became aware of America's hypocrisy in human-rights issues when they observed the abuse of prisoners at Abu Ghraib prison in Iraq; the torture of others at Guantanamo Bay, Cuba; and America's tactic of shuttling other prisoners to puppet countries to be tortured.

In *Israel vs. America vs. the World* (2011), I wrote the following:

The CIA's torture of prisoners or the shuffling of prisoners around the world to countries where torturing people is common and was intensified following the September 11 attacks...The McClatchy Press [the second-largest American newspaper company] reported that a former senior intelligence official familiar with the interrogation issue added that the Bush administration applied relentless pressure on interrogators to use harsh methods on detainees, in part to find evidence of cooperation between Al-Qaeda and Saddam Hussein's regime. There was constant pressure on the intelligence agencies and the interrogators to do whatever it took to get that information out of the detainees, especially the few high-value ones; and when people kept coming up empty, they were told to push harder. [51]

The neoconservatives' advocacy of regime change to American domestic institutions to achieve social change has progressed to an advocacy of changing the characters and cultures of other nations by manipulation or by forcing changes to foreign-governmental structures and institutions. When they were in control of Reagan's and G. W. Bush's administrations, the neoconservatives argued it was imperative that America liberate countries from the tyranny of dictatorships and promote democracy to prevent any threat to America from undemocratic regimes. Reagan and Bush came to the conclusion that the internal character of regimes defines their external behavior and that American security depended on the promotion of regime change in other societies. The target for Reagan was Central America, while for Bush it was the Middle East. [52, 53]

During the Reagan presidency, the neoconservatives were able to pursue one of their first implementations of the regime-change program. Reagan's concern with the regimes of Central America bordered on obsession, and the majority of his attention in this region was focused on putting an end to the communist government of Nicaragua. In March 1983, he put the regime-change policy into practice when CIA-trained and CIA-supported counterrevolutionaries called Contras began an insurgency operation against the Sandinista government. The US Congress had banned America from aiding the Contras, but Reagan and the CIA continued to assist them in secret. Despite this secret help, the Contras failed to overthrow the Sandinista regime. [54]

During the presidency of G. W. Bush, the neoconservatives were able to convince the administration to adopt a preemptive and unilateral approach to foreign policy that set America above international law. Accordingly, they pursued a military invasion of Iraq by convincing the administration that destroying the dictatorship of Saddam Hussein would open the floodgates for other regime changes in the region. At times like this, military invasion is generally a form of colonization. The invasion was implemented with the help of the coalition of the willing under false pretenses, without United Nations approval, and without any plan for nation building or Iraq's reconstruction as it transitioned to the post-Saddam era. It became clear that the rationale for the security justification for the war in Iraq was a cover-up for the real objective of securing the oil resources and the protection of Israel, and not for democracy and human rights. The removal of Saddam Hussein has proved ever since then to be a catastrophe, not only for Iraq but for the whole Middle East and beyond. It also proved that the neoconservatives' assertion that America and its allies would be welcomed as liberators was intentionally misleading, as the civil wars in the region and the war on terror are still raging, with no winner in sight. (For more on the invasion of Iraq, see the subsection below.)

The end of the G. W. Bush presidency did not end the war on terror or the attempt to topple regimes hostile to America and Israel, because America's foreign policy is still in progress and still produces ever more religious and nationalistic radicalization and more anti-American and anti-Israeli sentiment. America's foreign policy still entails sidelining the United Nations and acting unilaterally, when the only way to fight terrorism—which was created by America's unilateralism—is through multilateralism. The end of the G. W. Bush presidency also did not stop the policy of regime change in the Middle East. To achieve its hegemony over the world, America has extended the same foreign policy to other parts of the world, including Russia and China, which could bring the world closer to a nuclear holocaust. Finally, it should be said that subsequent presidents—including Barack Obama and Donald Trump—have persisted with the same foreign-relations policy that is interest based rather than value based, which is not helping America become "great again," as Trump has put it.

THE NEOCON ZIONISTS AND AMERICA'S FOREIGN POLICY

As stated above, the neoconservative movement is an ultra-conservative group that advocates the assertive promotion of democracy and US national interests in international affairs, including through military means. Many of its adherents became politically famous during the Republican presidential administrations of the 1970s, 1980s, 1990s, and 2000s. Neoconservatives peaked in influence during the administrations of G. W. Bush, when they played a major role in promoting and planning the 2003 invasion of Iraq. Prominent neoconservatives in the Bush administration included Paul Wolfowitz, John Bolton, Elliott Abrams, Richard Perle, Robert Kagan (who prefers to be called a "liberal interventionist"), William Kristol, Douglas Feith, and Paul Bremer. Although Vice President Dick Cheney and Secretary of Defense Donald Rumsfeld didn't identify themselves as neocons, they surrounded themselves with neoconservative Zionist advisers. [55]

The neoconservative movement became dominated by the far-right Zionists following the invasion of Afghanistan. The original Zionists' push for regime changes around the world was illustrated a week after the invasion of Afghanistan in October 2001 by the publication of William Kristol's *Weekly Standard* article in which Rich Lowry, editor in chief of the conservative *National Review*, wrote under the headline "The Case for American Empire," thus advocating a kind of low-grade colonialism to topple dangerous regimes beyond Afghanistan. Later on, as Zionist columnist Charles Krauthammer put it, given complete US domination "culturally, economically, technologically, and militarily," people were now coming out of the closet about the word "empire." The *New York Times Magazine* cover for Sunday, January 5, 2003, read "American Empire: Get Used to It." [56]

I should note that the greater targets of the neoconservative Zionists beyond Afghanistan were regime changes in Iraq and Iran. Some even advocated a regime change in Iran ahead of the invasion of Iraq; they considered Iran a bigger threat to Israel because of Iran's military capacity.

In *The Israel Lobby and US Foreign Policy*, Mearsheimer and Walt wrote the following:

As usual there was a bevy of articles by prominent neoconservatives—essentially the same people who had helped push the war in Iraq—making the case for going after Iran. William Kristol wrote in the *Weekly Standard* on May 12 that "the liberation of Iraq was the first great battle for the future of the Middle East... But the next great battle—not, we hope, a military battle—will be for Iran. Michael Ledeen, one of the leading hawks on Iran, wrote in the *National Review Online* on April 4, "There is no more time for diplomatic 'solution.' We will have to deal with the terror masters, here and now. Iran, at least, offers us the possibility of a memorable victory, because the Iranian people openly loath the regime, and will be enthusiastically combat it, if only the United States supports them in their just struggle." [57]

In their quest for regime change in Iran, the far-right Zionists pushed the Bush administration to support the Mujahedeen al-Khalq, a group based in Iraq at the time that was committed to overthrowing the regime in Tehran. [58] Contrary to the far-right Zionists' push for regime-change policy was the opinion advanced by Mearsheimer and earlier by Hans Morgenthau, who argued that the internal structure of states should be of no concern to foreign policy makers and that the flaw with democratization is that it erroneously assumes the desire for democracy is stronger than the pride of nationalism—a pride that sparked the foreign intervention in Iraq. In an article in *Open Democracy* in May 2005 on Morgenthau's book *The Iraq War: Realism versus Neo-Conservatism*, Mearsheimer wrote the following:

Hans Joachim Morgenthau was one of the most important political thinkers of the 20th century and one of the great realist thinkers of all time. Morgenthau, along with almost all realists in the United States—except for Henry Kissinger—opposed the Vietnam War. Their opposition came early, long before it became clear that the war was a lost cause; in fact Morgenthau was warning against American military involvement in Vietnam in the late 1950s.

Equally, almost all realists in the United States—except for Henry Kissinger—opposed the war against Iraq. Many supporters of that war are now having second thoughts, since it is becoming increasingly clear that American troops are stuck in an open-ended conflict from which there seems to be no exit. The realists, however, anticipated big problems before the war began; in this, they have been proved largely correct.

Taken together, these facts raise the obvious question: would Hans Morgenthau, the realist who opposed going to war in Vietnam, also have opposed the war on Iraq? We can never know for sure and it would be foolish to say with total certainty that Morgenthau would have opposed the Iraq war. Nevertheless, given his theory of international politics, his opposition to the Vietnam War and the parallels between the two conflicts, it is highly likely...

Critics of the Iraq war would also say to the neoconservatives that it would make sense to solve the Israeli-Palestinian conflict before invading Iraq. Neoconservatives would answer that an American victory in Iraq would compel Yasser Arafat to sign a peace treaty with Israel. The road to Jerusalem, they would argue, runs through Baghdad. If the mighty United States got tough with troublemakers in the Arab world, the Palestinians would read the writing on the wall...

Some forty years later, the Bush administration thought that it could turn the domino theory to its advantage. Knocking off Saddam, the war party thought, would have a cascading effect in the Middle East, if not the wider world. The Iranians, the North Koreans, the Palestinians, and the Syrians, after seeing the United States win a stunning victory in Iraq, would all throw up their hands and dance to Uncle Sam's tune. [59]

On the topic of imposing Western-style democracy in other countries, Samuel Huntington further argued that democracy is a product of Western culture and may not be as suitable in other nations as it is in the West because of cultural differences that make democracy incompatible in some places. [60] Despite such realistic opinions—which the failure to impose democracy in Afghanistan and Iraq proved to be true—the neoconservatives persisted in advocating the policy of regime change. William Kristol and Robert Kagan, in their book *Present Dangers: Crisis and Opportunity in American Foreign and Defense Policy* (2000), wrote that "to many the idea of America using its power to promote changes of regime in nations ruled by dictators rings of utopianism. But in fact it is eminently realistic. There is something perverse in declaring the impossibility of promoting democratic change abroad in light of the record of the past three decades. After we have already seen dictatorships toppled by democratic forces in such unlikely places as the Philippines, Indonesia, Chile, Nicaragua, Paraguay, Taiwan and South Korea, how utopian is it to imagine a change of regime in a place like Iraq?" [61]

And in *Israel vs. America vs. the World*, I wrote the following:

A large number of committed Jewish nationalists [worked] in the Pentagon under Paul Wolfowitz and elsewhere within the Bush administration and... were the driving force behind the Iraq war. Paul Wolfowitz, Douglas Feith, Elliot Abrams, Richard Perle and Barry Rubin were the major promoters of the war against Iraq. They worked closely with other Zionist ideologues, like Bush speechwriter David Frum to promote the "Axis of Evil" declaration to facilitate wars against other regimes hostile to Israel and America. Wolfowitz and Feith set up the Office of Special [Plans], run by fellow Zionist Abram Shulsky, who used the Iraqi politician Ahmed Chalabi to provide phony intelligence on Iraq to justify that war and a regional war aimed at destroying any regime that is critical of Israeli expansionism. [62]

The problem was that G. W. Bush was pushed by the neoconservatives and the Israel lobby groups to declare war on Iraq, with the total backing of the Christian Zionist movement—which has a huge power base in the Republican Party, as discussed earlier.

In *Empire for Liberty* (2010), Richard Immerman describes how America's efforts to expand its empire gradually caused it to lose its humanity and the ideals the nation was built on. The United States became obsessed with the national interest, which caused it to fail in designing a morally based foreign policy. Following 9/11, its foreign policy of intervention in the Middle East—a policy mainly influenced by Wolfowitz—has caused the decline of the empire. Immerman also describes the neoconservatives' role in identifying the United States with the "politics of liberty," in which the neocons advanced the idea that no tension should exist between a human-rights agenda, the imperatives of geopolitics, and the internal character of a regime. From these premises, the neoconservatives advanced the concept of regime change and of molding the international environment to benefit the United States, which instead turned out to be the greatest strategic blunder in US history. [63]

It is worth adding that the main objective of Wolfowitz and his fellow far-right Zionists in the neoconservative movement was the Israeli colonization of Palestine; they saw no other option but to push Christians into a war with Muslims under the banner of the clash of civilizations. This was simply because the Jewish population in the world is so small—approximately seventeen million—so it has no capacity to fight 1.7 billion Muslims in the world, or for Israel to fight its immediate Arab neighbors of over 350 million. This is when the Jewish population in Israel is approximately six million, with the same number of Jews living in America, while the other five million are scattered across various countries around the world. [64]

Based on the outcome of the advocacy of Wolfowitz and the Israel lobby groups for America's militarily unilateralist and preemptive approach to its foreign policy (as well as the sidelining of the United Nations), several things should be stated. First, America has suffered massive financial and human costs without tangible returns. Second, it has suffered a loss of prestige and credibility, not only among many of the countries of the world but also among its allies. Third, it has created more enemies against the empire, which is contributing to its decline. Fourth, it has destabilized the world, especially the Middle East, which has resulted in millions of civilian casualties and numerous displaced people and refugees. Fifth, it has commenced the religious clash of civilizations as a result of fueling Islamic terrorism. This strategy will not result in anyone winning; instead, the whole world will lose. Above all, the United States has proved to the world that the far-right Zionists' influence on US foreign policy is increasing America's and its Western allies' vulnerability to terrorism and is contributing to its decline, which should in turn prove to the Americans that Israel is a liability; it is no longer an asset.

On the aspect of Israel being a liability and no longer an asset, Mearsheimer and Walt wrote the following:

Steadfast US support might also make sense if the United States received substantial benefits in return, and if the value of these benefits exceeded the economic and political cost of US support. If Israel possessed vital natural resources (such as oil or natural gas), or if it occupied a critical geographic location, then the United States might want to provide support in order to maintain good relations and keep it out of unfriendly hands. In short, aid to Israel would be easy to explain if it helped make Americans more secure or more prosperous. Israel's strategic value to the United States would be further enhanced if backing it won America additional friends around the world and did not undermine US relations with other strategically important countries...[65]

Backing Israel may have yielded strategic benefits in the past, but the benefits have declined sharply in recent years while the economic and diplomatic costs have increased. Instead of being a strategic asset, in fact, Israel has become a strategic liability for the United States. Backing Israel so strongly is making America more vulnerable—not less—and making [it] harder for the United States to achieve important and urgent foreign policy goals. Although there are compelling reasons for the United States to support Israel's existence and to remain committed to its survival, the current level of US support and its largely unconditional nature cannot be justified on strategic ground...[66]

Today, America's intimate embrace of Israel—and especially its willingness to subsidize it no matter what its policies are—is not making Americans safer or more prosperous. To the contrary: unconditional support for Israel is undermining relations with other US allies, casting doubt on America's wisdom and moral vision, helping inspire a generation of anti-American extremists, and complicating US efforts to deal with a volatile but vital region. In short, the largely unconditional "special relationship" between the United States and Israel is no longer defensible on strategic ground. [67]

America's and its Western allies' vulnerability to international terrorism has been inflamed by Israel's atrocities against the Palestinian people and because of the absence of a decisive action to establish a viable Palestinian state. While Israel and its American lobby groups convince the United States that Israel is a partner against terror, the fuse of Islamic terrorism will keep burning. This is because America's and Israel's combined actions in the Middle East lit the fuse. People who still believe that Israel is an asset are denying there is a direct connection between Islamic terrorism and the United States' unconditional support for Israel. They deny that the Israeli policy of domination, injustice, and suffering imposed on the Palestinians is hurting America, which has become a hated country in the Middle East and in other Islamic countries for its unconditional support for Israel.

The only achievement for America, however, is the militarization of the world, especially the Middle East, which is helping it sell arms and keep its arms-manufacturing industry going for more years to come. As often happens, some of these American-supplied weapons inevitably fall into the hands of terrorists, which further complicates the unintended consequences.

THE INVASION OF IRAQ

In 2003, the United States made Iraq—the home of the earliest civilization of Mesopotamia—a war zone by ousting its secular Sunni president, Saddam Hussein, and installing a religiously oriented Shiite-led government headed by the American-chosen and sectarian prime minister Nouri al-Maliki. Since then, Iraq has descended into chaos and has become embroiled in a power struggle between the Sunni and Shiite sects, the outcome of which was the emergence of insurgency groups that have culminated in the formation of the most violent group to date, the Islamic State. (For more on the IS, see the "Islamic Terrorism" subsection below.) The formation of the IS, along with its ideology, was a counteraction to the violent American action in Iraq, which created a war of ideas—a war that is much harder to fight than battling an army with bombs and missiles.

Sectarianism in Iraq started soon after the American invasion, when the Americans dissolved the government institutions and the Iraqi army and created a governing council on a sectarian basis among Shiites, Sunnis, and Kurds. This situation has developed into a sectarian war and has turned Iraq into a failed state.

The war in Iraq was part of a plan for forced regime change in any Middle Eastern country that was critical of America and Israel. To allow the economic expansion of America and the territorial expansion of Israel, it became necessary to install new regimes that were loyal and willing to serve these nations' interests. History shows that this cannot be achieved without installing corrupt governments that operate on the basis of mutual benefit with their masters. In the process, these corrupt governments—assuming their existence in power will be short lived—enrich themselves as fast as they can, at the expense of impoverishing their nations. The outcome of this is disenfranchised and desperate people who react violently against whoever is causing their plight. These people, who have nothing left to lose, are then recruited to fight for a cause, often for religious and nationalistic causes.

This situation is what the Iraq War has achieved, and the same outcome is happening in Libya, Syria, and Afghanistan. The Iraq War was one of those wars designed to allow America to have direct control over an oil-rich country while at the same time protecting Israel and allowing it to expand.

Declassified documents and documents released following a request under the Freedom of Information Act show that former president G. W. Bush's advisers focused on toppling Saddam Hussein's regime as soon as he took office; they discussed how to justify a war in Iraq shortly after invading Afghanistan in 2001. A few hours after the September 11 attacks in 2001, according to the minutes of a meeting on that day, Defense Secretary Rumsfeld spoke of attacking Iraq, as well as Osama bin Laden. Furthermore, according to the papers posted by the Washington-based National Security Archive (an independent research institute), Rumsfeld told a Pentagon lawyer to go to his deputy to get support for a supposed link between the Iraqi regime and al-Qaeda's founder. [68]

Mearsheimer and Walt wrote of the role that Mossad (the Israeli intelligence agency) played in convincing Wolfowitz to bypass the CIA and to create the Policy Counterterrorism Evaluation Group:

The Office of Special Plans (OSP) was directed to find evidence that could be used to sell the war against Iraq. The OSP was headed by Abram Shulsky, a neo-conservative Zionist long associated with Wolfowitz, and its ranks included several recruits from pro-Israel think tanks, like Michael Rubin from the American Enterprise Institute and Michael Makovsky, who had worked for then Prime Minister Shimon Peres after graduating from college. OSP relied heavily on information from Chalabi and other Iraqi exiles, and it had close connection to various Israeli sources. Indeed, the *Guardian* reported that it "forged close to a parallel, ad hoc intelligence operation inside Ariel Sharon's office in Israel specifically to bypass Mossad and provide the Bush administration with more alarmist reports on Saddam's Iraq than Mossad was prepared to authorize." The Department of Defense's inspector general released a report in February 2007 that was critical of OSP for disseminating "alternative intelligence assessments" that "were in our opinion, inappropriate given that the intelligence assessments were intelligence products and did not clearly show the variance with the consensus of the Intelligence Community." [69]

Confronting Iraq was also the focus of a July 2001 memo to the national security adviser at the time, Condoleezza Rice, with Rumsfeld urging a high-level meeting on policy toward Baghdad. Forecasting an optimistic outcome far from the result the Iraq War actually produced, Rumsfeld said that Washington's image in the region and the world would benefit from toppling Saddam. Another document shows Rumsfeld discussing war plans for Iraq just two months after the 2001 US invasion of Afghanistan. In a meeting with

General Tommy Franks (head of US Central Command at the time), Rumsfeld told the general to ready the armed forces for the decapitation of the Iraqi regime. [70]

The rest is history. Saddam's regime was decapitated, and the horror of Islamic backlash and radicalization was underway. Following its "shock and awe" slogan, America pursued the delusion of winning the war with Bush's premature declaration of "Mission accomplished."

The Iraq War is anything but "won," as we may see by the fact that violence has escalated to a level where society is not functioning, and bombings and large-scale outbreaks of ethnic and sectarian violence are becoming the norm rather than the exception. Much of the violence in Iraq has an ethnic and sectarian character to it, entrenched by the new American-designed Iraqi constitution, which is aimed at dividing Iraqis along ethnic and sectarian lines—a division that makes national security impossible to achieve. Sunni activists, together with the previous Baathist regime, see Iran orchestrating the political environment in the country. The Iranian intervention and the American manipulation provoke feelings of conspiracy within the Sunni population. Adding fuel to the fire is America's support to the Kurds to take control of Kirkuk, in northern Iraq, where large oil reserves exist. A coalition of Shiites and Kurds has left Sunnis in a weaker position. Because of the disenfranchisement of Sunnis and the feeling that an American conspiracy has occurred, the stage is set for a never-ending sectarian conflict and concomitant hatred toward America, all of which will make Iraq an ungovernable state for many years to come. Iraq's constitution, written by the Americans, has sown the seeds of permanent social and political division and is backfiring against its creator.

The world is now witnessing that Iraq is a state that resembles Lebanon, Somalia, and Nigeria combined. Lebanon's similarity is reflected in its sectarian constitution, which is a source of constant conflict and civil wars. Somalia's similarity is its constant suicide bombing and other terrorist activities. Nigeria's similarity is reflected in the constant blowing up of oil pipelines because of the disenfranchisement of segments of the Nigerian population.

In his book *The Gamble: General Petraeus and the American Military Adventure in Iraq* (2010), *Washington Post* reporter for military affairs Thomas Ricks focuses on the military surge in Iraq and what lay beyond it for the Obama administration. He warns that the gains of the surge could easily unravel and that the administration would face some very tough choices, including a confrontation with the generals. He warns that this would be extremely tough and that the United States would be fighting in Iraq for many years to come. In the book, Ricks paints a gloomy picture of the scenario in Iraq, especially for the gradual withdrawal of troops from areas that aren't secure, that aren't safe, and that the army is worried about. He further argues that the basic problems the surge was meant to solve had not been solved, including the friction between Sunnis and Shiites and between Shiites and Kurds. His prediction became a reality, as the withdrawal of troops resulted in the IS gaining control of Anbar province and Mosul—the outcome of which was thousands of civilian casualties and millions of displaced people.

Since then, the world has also witnessed the occasional coordinated attacks and suicide bombing of buildings and civilian targets, including oil installations, bridges, and other strategic targets as part of destabilization campaigns. The disenfranchisement of Sunnis became a haven for al-Qaeda and other jihadist recruiters for Arab and Islamist causes. The main jihadist organizations active at the time were Jaish al-Mohammad, the Salaheddin Army, and the Islamic Army of Iraq. These jihadist organizations have since morphed into the more savage jihadist group, the IS. [71]

America's adoption of a divide-and-conquer policy is no longer applicable in the globalized world, when the world economy dictates harmonious human and international relations. The current policy of stoking sectarian warfare between Sunnis and Shiites in the Middle East will cause tremendous damage to the world (and especially the West) from economic stagnation and the unintended consequences of bringing the threat of terrorism to new heights with biological, chemical, and dirty bombs. Bringing Saudi Arabia and Iran together, instead of encouraging them to fight, would be much more beneficial to the world. They could then use their oil wealth, both in their own countries and in other Islamic countries, toward solving problems such as poverty, unemployment, poor health, and lack of education; rebuilding infrastructures and institutions that have been destroyed; and solving the refugee problem. Furthermore, selling arms and encouraging conflicts in the world may help America in the short term, but in the long term, armed conflicts and civil wars cause stagnation of the world economy, create world recessions, devastate many countries' infrastructures, spread poverty, and create more enemies for the empire instead of creating prosperity and more consumers in the world who could then stimulate economic growth, to the benefit of both the world and the empire. [72]

An all-out sectarian war in Iraq is not far away, as we may easily see from the Shiite religious and theocratic parties, encouraged by Iran, that are sidelining the majority of the disfranchised Sunni groups, who have suffered the most from the American invasion of Iraq. The unintended consequences of the internal conflict in Iraq have not remained within its borders but have spread to its neighboring countries and reached the world at large through the civil wars in Syria and Libya.

Iran is playing a major role in uniting the pro-Tehran factions for control of the Iraqi government under the Shiite sect. Iran's influence involves not only Iraqi Shiites but also the Syrian and Lebanese group Hezbollah. Iran's idea is to create a buffer to counter America's and Israel's interests, especially since America intends to change its relationship with Iraq from military occupier to civilian partner to gain the benefit of Iraqi petrodollars to rebuild the devastated country. Some analysts say Iran's activities behind the scenes began to intensify as soon as America decided to withdraw its combat troops from Iraq.

Iran's move to control the political agenda in Iraq is becoming a recipe for endless conflict, not only in Iraq but throughout the Middle East. The signs of what lies ahead can be seen in the WikiLeaks diplomatic cables published in November 2010. In one of the documents, King Abdullah of Saudi Arabia urged the United States to attack Iran to destroy its nuclear program.

But for Iraq, no government at this stage is capable of serving either American or Iranian interests, despite the fact that America has occupied Iraq indirectly while Iran has gained control of Iraq at many levels of the Iraqi government. The disenfranchisement of the Sunnis will sooner or later culminate in an all-out civil war that will be even worse than what is happening in Libya, Yemen, and Syria.

This situation is the result of the misuse of America's military power in the Middle East, which has caused chaos and violent conflicts, which in turn have resulted in the United States' main imperialistic objectives being doomed to failure, especially following the creation of failed or near-failed states in the region. The main reason for America's failure is that it took advice from the neoconservative elements in government—discussed earlier—and from the army generals. The army generals, because of military culture and its history, are set on attacking other nations rather than defending America; the army knows one thing only: war. The army, being the core of the American military complex, is designed to fight on many fronts around the world, which goes far beyond the country's military and financial capacity. Although the military complex is making money for America by militarizing and selling arms to the world, the nation's military wing is becoming a huge financial imposition on the American economy and is one cause of America's decline. Using force to subjugate other nations—instead of employing diplomacy—to establish American hegemony is an outdated method that creates many enemies and makes America vulnerable. [73]

Under international law, any illegitimate attack on a sovereign state is a crime. The invasion of Iraq and the ensuing bloodbath was the most horrible crime of the twenty-first century. It was carried out by the civilized nations of America and Britain under the disguise of ridding the world of nonexistent weapons of mass destruction (WMD). The assault on the defenseless civilian population to give them an unwanted democracy has resulted in the deaths of many innocent people. The motive for America and Britain was the control of Iraq's oil reserves, which are the second largest in the world after those of Saudi Arabia. [74]

Chomsky wrote in *Hegemony or Survival* (2004) on the WMD propaganda and the exploitation of a possible rise in terrorism:

In the present case, the administration was surely aware, even without warnings from respected authorities, that its planned war against Iraq and other related actions were likely to increase the risks of proliferation of WMD and terror against the US and its allies. But evidently it assigns low priority to such threats compared with other goals. Furthermore, though planners of course do not welcome the proliferation of WMD and terrorism, they know that they can exploit such developments for their own purposes, both global and domestic. Even the fear they elicit throughout the world is quite acceptable: they are not trying to be loved, but obeyed, and if this is achieved by fear, that is fine—another contribution to "maintaining credibility." [75]

It is worth further exposing America's propaganda and its double standard regarding WMD in not only tolerating but assisting Israel in developing its nuclear arsenal and WMD program. Mearsheimer and Walt in *The Israel Lobby* wrote the following:

> In addition to its nuclear arsenal, Israel maintains active chemical and biological weapons programs and has yet to ratify either the Chemical or Biological Weapons Convention. The irony is hard to miss: the United States has pressured many other states to join the NPT [The Nuclear Non-Proliferation Treaty, 1968], imposed sanctions on countries that have defied US wishes and acquired nuclear weapons anyway, gone to war in 2003 to prevent Iraq from pursuing WMD and contemplated attacking Iran and North Korea for the same reason. Yet Washington has long subsidized an ally whose clandestine WMD activities are well known and whose nuclear arsenal has given several of its neighbors a powerful incentive to seek WMD themselves. [76]

It became obvious that the invasion of Iraq had nothing to do with WMD but rather was about oil. In a September 2007 interview with Peter Beaumont and Joanna Walters following the publication of his book *The Age of Turbulence: Adventures in a New World* (2007), former chairman of the US Federal Reserve Alan Greenspan admitted the Iraq War was about oil. Greenspan's damning comments about the war came a week after a survey of Iraqis claimed that up to 1.2 million people may have died because of the conflict in Iraq—lending weight to a 2006 survey in the medical journal the *Lancet* that reported similarly high levels. [77]

The legacy of oil was clear from the start when America hurriedly decided to abandon the war in Afghanistan in order to invade Iraq when it had the upper hand in the fight against the Taliban and the remnants of al-Qaeda. It was in a hurry to prevent Russia, Germany, and France from establishing a foothold in Iraq's oil industry when Saddam Hussein's government was in the process of signing oil-exploration and production contracts. For the Russians, losing Russia's foothold in Iraq was a turning point in driving it closer toward Iran, which became the catalyst for the increased competition and tension in the Middle East. In the absence of multipolar superpowers, Russia's approach to weakening America's expansionism has been to encourage the resistance of as many regional powers as it can against America—one of which happens to be Iran. I should point out that, following the invasion of Iraq, by pressing the advantage, America initially succeeded in signing lucrative, long-term oil contracts with the al-Maliki government, which it had installed through the barrel of a gun. But in the long run, as we can see from the ensuing chaos and the civil wars in the region, America's Middle East strategy is flawed: no winner has emerged, and none is expected to emerge anytime soon. America's interventions for the sake of controlling the oil supply and the oil reserves have resulted in many failed states and a shattered Middle East that is morphing into the site of a religious war that will have tragic consequences for many years to come.

In abandoning the war in Afghanistan for the war in Iraq, America lost on several fronts:

1. It lost the initiative in pursuing al-Qaeda in Afghanistan and Pakistan.
2. In widening the war on terror under false pretenses, it provided an opportunity for Middle Eastern jihadists and other jihadists around the Islamic world to join the fight and to make Iraq, Afghanistan, Pakistan, Yemen, Libya, Somalia, and other Muslim countries their training venues.
3. Many moderate Muslims saw the war in Iraq as a war on Islam, which encouraged them to join al-Qaeda and other Islamic jihadi organizations. This was happening at a time when America was giving Israel the green light to destroy Palestinians' dreams of their own state.
4. Many moderate Muslims have interpreted America's actions in the Middle East as a new crusade and new religious-oriented expansionist nationalism through which Christian enemies once again invade Muslim lands.

5. Above all, moderate Muslims are losing their influence over and control of the extremist elements within their ranks in the same way that American and Israeli moderates are losing their control over their own fanatics: the Christian Zionists and the extremist Jewish Zionists. The extremist minorities from all sides have gained the momentum to create a euphoric atmosphere for their ideologies to rapidly spin out of control and to become a major threat to world peace. [78]

In his book *Against All Enemies: Inside America's War on Terror* (2004), former chief counterterrorism adviser Richard A. Clarke clearly demonstrates that G. W. Bush had decided to invade Iraq long before the September 11 terrorist attacks; in effect, the invasion was no more than a political marketing opportunity. Clarke's claim was supported later by Tony Blair's secret letters to Bush in which he backed military action against Iraq the year before the two nations ordered an invasion, as was also disclosed in January 2010 in the British government's Iraq Inquiry (unofficially known as the Chilcot inquiry). Earlier evidence in the inquiry suggested that Tony Blair had decided to back Bush after the two leaders met at the president's Texas ranch in April 2002—eleven months before the British Parliament gave the go-ahead for the March 2003 invasion. [79] It became clearer after the invasion that the proinvasion hawks were the Zionists and the Israel lobby groups. In his book *A Pretext for War: 9/11, Iraq, and the Abuse of America's Intelligence Agencies* (2005), James Bamford, a former *ABC News* producer and a US intelligence expert, provides more details about the lies and deception the Bush administration employed. [80]

Following Fukuyama's defection from the neoconservative movement as a result of the war in Iraq, the author criticizes the war that had put him at odds with his earlier neoconservative friends both within and outside the Bush administration in *America at the Crossroad: Democracy, Power, and the Neoconservative Legacy* (2006). He explains how, in the Bush administration's decision to invade Iraq, the administration failed in its stewardship of American foreign policy. First, the administration wrongly made preventive war the central tenet of its foreign policy. Second, it badly misjudged the global reaction to its exercise of "benevolent hegemony." Third, it failed to appreciate the difficulties involved in large-scale social engineering and grossly underestimated the difficulties involved in establishing a successful democratic government in Iraq. Fukuyama explores various Bush administration critics' contention that the administration had a neoconservative agenda in dictating its foreign policy during the president's first term; he provides a fascinating history of the varied strands of neoconservative thought since the 1930s. Fukuyama argues that the movement's legacy was a complex one that may be interpreted quite differently from what was the case after the end of the Cold War. Analyzing the Bush administration's miscalculations in responding to the post-9/11 challenge, Fukuyama proposes a new approach to American foreign policy through which such mistakes might be turned around—one in which the positive aspects of the neoconservative legacy were joined with a more realistic view of the way American power can be used around the world. [81]

In the same book, the author wrote of the change in America's adoption of the new and illusionary strategic approach to military interventions:

From the first Gulf war on, Americans became familiar with video footage of American bombs streaking toward their targets and blowing up individual buildings or vehicles. Aging B-52 bombers with JDAMs (the Joint Direct Attack Munition that turned "dumb" bombs into precisely targeted ones) became a staple of Afghan war, where they could be called forth from the sky by Special Forces troops riding horses with Northern Alliance fighters. These developments, plus a parallel revolution in information and communications technology, made possible [a] vast transformation in the way that warfare could be conducted.

This shift toward a lighter, faster, and…more mobile form of combat, strongly promoted by Secretary of Defense Donald Rumsfeld as a military "transformation," also made American interventions more likely. It created a sense that war would be low-cost from the standpoint of American casualties. The 1991 Gulf War produced fewer than two hundred combat deaths; the numerous small interventions of [the] Clinton administration in places like Haiti and Bosnia culminated in the 1999 Kosovo war, in which not a single American died. Rumsfeld seemed to want to invade Iraq with [the] smallest possible force structure to demonstrate the feasibility of this kind of warfare.

It is of course, better for the United States if fewer Americans die in war. On the other hand, the success of American military technology during the 1990s created the illusion that military intervention would always be as clean or cheap as the Gulf or Kosovo wars. The Iraq war has clearly demonstrated the limits of this form of light, mobile warfare: it provides no special advantages in fighting prolonged insurgency. [82]

The war in Iraq was also carried out without the authorization of the Security Council; in fighting the trillion-dollar war, thousands of allied soldiers died, including more than forty-two hundred American soldiers. Millions of Iraqis became refugees, and about half a million defenseless Iraqis died as a result of an illegal invasion of a helpless nation. As a result of Iraq's occupation, America has left the nation in a state of devastation and with a chronically corrupt government. The invasion has left Iraq not only a decimated society, divided along sectarian lines, but with a destroyed infrastructure and a devastated middle class. The final outcome of America's war in Iraq has been the destruction of one nation followed by the destruction of other nations in the region, with no end in sight.

The genesis of the crisis in the Middle East has its roots in the twentieth century, when the Western world was preoccupied with acquiring a cheap oil supply and looting the riches of the Arab world. In the process, they ignored the social and cultural development of the region, at the same time implementing a divide-and-conquer policy, which had been one of the anchors of British imperialism. As a result, the West is now witnessing an upheaval with enormous potential. The upheaval and the anarchy took an Islamic religious direction that has been provoked by American imperialistic ambitions and Israel's oppression of the Palestinians. Historically, in a backward country, when anarchy and rioting take place, the military often uses the opportunity to step in and establish a military dictatorship as an excuse for maintaining law and order and for saving the country. The dictators dismiss the government, abolish the country's constitution, and become the absolute rulers, all with the prompting and backing of Western powers.

After many decades of ruling by military and monarchical dictatorships, a huge political vacuum has been created, which has made the emergence of well-structured secular democracies extremely difficult. Even when an underground secular political party has existed, it could not match the power and influence of the existing religious groups and parties. Religious establishments own and control the infrastructure of mosques and Islamic schools, which enables them to dictate religious and political messages. Islamist religious leaders thus will eventually become the rulers and dictators of the future Arab world if the militaries and their Western masters decide to stay on the sidelines. The Western world, in the meantime, should plan for the worst, since the secular middle class and other disenfranchised people will not be ready or able to counter the power of entrenched Islam. The first pillar of democracy is the separation of religion and state, which the Arab world is far from ready for, mainly because of the absence of effective secular political leaders and secular education.

The plotting against secular leaders in the Middle East and North Africa has resulted in a vacuum created by America, Israel, France, and Britain when they actively eliminated many of the more democratic and nationalistic leaders of the 1950s, 1960s, and 1970s, including Gamal Abdel Nasser of Egypt, Abdul Karim Qasim of Iraq, Hafez al-Assad of Syria, Ahmed Ben Bella of Algeria, and Mohammad Mussadegh of Iran. Since then, these imperialistic powers have prevented any secular nationalistic leaders from emerging. [83]

The upheaval has only gotten worse since the elimination of the secular leaders Saddam Hussein in Iraq and Muammar Gaddafi in Libya, which has also extended to eliminating the secular regime of Bashar al-Assad in Syria. The vacuum that was created from the elimination of these secular leaders, who were in control of the religious dimension in their countries, is the genesis of the current Islamic terrorism.

In *Axis of Evil*, I wrote of the secular regimes of the Middle East and North Africa:

> To control the oil supply and to protect Israel, Western imperialistic powers and Israel, from the 1950s to date, have been continuously plotting to destroy any secular or nationalistic regime in the Middle East and North Africa that was perceived to be a threat to

their interests. The outcome is that the new regimes are fragmented, corrupted, and mostly Islamic fundamentalists, which are the cause of the turmoil in the region. The secular regimes of Egypt, Iraq, Syria, Algeria, Iran, and Libya, under which citizens had been living in peace, provided with free education and health care and with unemployment at unnoticeable levels, were destroyed or are being destroyed. And most importantly, Islamist fundamentalists would be kept under control to the benefit of the whole world if it wasn't for the shortsightedness of regime-change policies. [84]

In the political climate of today's Middle East, America's attempt to control the Middle East's resources through regime change with the help of Saudi Arabia—especially in pursuing a dangerous strategy of arming Islamic groups to fight other Islamic groups—will most likely end in disaster. As is often the case, America's allies of today can disappear and be replaced by hostile ones tomorrow, or the same allies can turn into enemies, especially when Islamic civilization was and will always be in conflict with Western civilization. The weapons in the hands of Muslims will sooner or later be used against Christians and Jews. America arms Saudi Arabia with heavy weapons to kill opposing sects, clans, tribes, and ethnic groups, without considering that the Saudi regime is one of the most hated and vulnerable regimes in the Middle East and that its weapons will be equally vulnerable from within and externally. America's attempts to form coalitions with

Islamist organizations often ignore the fact that these organizations promote Islam against non-Muslim forces. The unintended consequences of arming and financing Islamist fighters for America's short-term objectives, and of providing them with camps, training grounds, and logistical facilities, have been the legacy of producing Islamist terrorists who started in Afghanistan while fighting the Soviets.

In *The Clash of Civilizations and the Remaking of World Order* (1996), Samuel P. Huntington wrote the following:

American dollars and missiles were indispensable to the defeat of the Soviets. Also indispensable, however, was the collective effort of Islam, in which a wide variety of governments and groups competed with each other in attempting to defeat the Soviets and to produce a victory that would serve their interests. Muslim financial support for war came primarily from Saudi Arabia. Between 1984 and 1986 the Saudis gave $525 million to the resistance; in 1989 they agreed to supply 61 percent of a total of $715 million, or $436 million, with the remainder coming from the United States. In 1993 they provided $193 million to the Afghan government. The total amount they contributed during the course of the war was at least as much as and probably more than the $3 billion to $3.3 billion spent by the United States. During the war about 25,000 volunteers from other Islamic, primarily Arab, countries participated in the war. Recruited in large part in Jordan, these volunteers were trained by

Pakistan's Inter-Service Intelligence agency. Pakistan also provided the indispensable external base for the resistance as well as logistical and other support. In addition, Pakistan was the agent and the conduit for disbursement of American money, and purposefully directed 75 percent of those funds to the more fundamentalist Islamic groups with 50 percent of the total going to the most extreme Sunni fundamentalist faction led by Gulbuddin Hekmatyar. Although fighting the Soviets, the Arab participants in the war were overwhelmingly anti-Western and denounced Western humanitarian aid agencies as immoral and subversive of Islam. In the end, the Soviets were defeated by three factors they could not effectively equal or counter: American technology, Saudi money, and Muslim demographics and zeal. [85]

Under American imperialism, civil wars and lawlessness and the creation of corrupt governments have condemned many countries in the Middle East, Africa, and parts of Asia to decades of impoverishment and entrenched anarchy. This situation contradicts what America preaches about free trade and helping poor countries stand on their own feet. Instead, these countries are producing people without hope who will become lawless and a threat to Western civilization. This situation is in contrast with the earlier British philosophy—during the first British Empire—of acting as an agency for encouraging free markets, the rule of law, and investor protection and installing relatively incorrupt governments within most British colonies. [86]

Islamic Terrorism

To provide a balanced perspective before discussing Islamic terrorism, it is worth reminding Christians of their historical religious terrorism against one another and against other faiths, as highlighted by the recent Irish conflict. [87] The Catholic terrorism against Muslims and Jews, exemplified by the Spanish Inquisition, was established in the fifteenth century and not abolished until the nineteenth century. It was a dark period of Spanish Catholic history characterized by severe censorship, paranoia, torture, death, and the general persecution of heretics and anybody else who disagreed with the tenets of the Catholic Church. [88] Later, in the eighteenth century, when the British Protestant heritage came to the fore, Britain defined itself through a series of wars against a hostile Catholic France. Religion was part of many smaller colonial conflicts of the era. Britain's imperial expansion came to be intimately linked with Protestant evangelism. Missionary groups grew enormously from the end of the eighteenth century, when they gained widespread currency in response to the conflicts of the Napoleonic era. [89]

Religion played a key role in colonial expansion, the killing of innocent people, and the destruction of their countries as part of British imperial power. Religious nationalism often plays a major role in many forms of violence throughout the world. Today, Jewish Zionism and Christian Zionism are playing an active role in the clash of Western civilization with Islamic fundamentalism, especially in their push for an aggressive militaristic American foreign policy. (For more on

Religion and Conflicts, see chapter 2 of my book *Axis of Evil: Imperialism – Religion – Nationalism* [2016].)

Islamic terrorism is carried out by groups who believe that violence and terrorism are justified in the interests of realizing political objectives. Violent Islamic jihad is part of the rejection of any non-Islamic teachings and the adherence to a strict interpretation of the written text of the Koran in its most literal form, which advocates absolute commitment to jihad. Islamic jihadists consider America and its puppet regimes to be the greatest enemy of Islam. The IS in Syria and Iraq came into being as a result of the military interventions and destruction of those countries' institutions and infrastructures, the destruction of the middle class, the installation of corrupt regimes, the displacement of large numbers of people, a general lack of secular education, high unemployment, and extreme poverty. Furthermore, the removal in a military coup in 2013, by General el-Sisi of mainstream Islamic movements of the Muslim Brotherhood in Egypt, has contributed to more Muslims becoming radicalized. Under the leadership of Dr. Mohammad Morsi, the Muslim Brotherhood government, which attempted to work within the democratic process, was forcibly removed in July 2013. The removal and the jailing of its leaders have convinced more Muslims to use brute force to achieve better results rather than wait for the kindness of their enemies—that is, the Christian fundamentalists, the far-right Zionists, and their puppet regimes. Additionally, the atrocities and terrorist acts committed by various Israeli governments against Palestinian civilians since 1948 were equally as bad as the current Islamic terrorism. For detailed proof of Israeli atrocities, ethnic cleansing, and terrorism against the Palestinian people, it is essential to refer to the informative book *The Ethnic Cleansing of Palestine* (2006) by professor Ilan Pappe, who is an Israeli historian and the chair in history at the University of Exeter in the United Kingdom.

The terrorist group the **Islamic State (IS)*** did not emerge out of nowhere; it emerged as a consequence of America's military interventions in the Middle East and the ongoing Israeli atrocities against the Palestinians, conducted with America's unconditional support. The group also emerged out of frustration from the marginalization of the Sunnis by empowering the Shiites as a result of the Iraq War. The constant American use of the military option has resulted in the destruction of people's lives, their homes, and their countries' infrastructures and institutions. Western and Israeli eagerness to topple Saddam Hussein's and Bashar al-Assad's regimes in Iraq and Syria (respectively), including the total American support of the Israeli apartheid regime in Palestine, provided the perfect conditions for the IS to launch itself and helped the group recruit other Sunni radicals from around the world.

*** Islamic State (IS)**: In March 2016, America declared the IS a genocidal organization on the basis of self-proclamation, by ideology, and by actions. The declaration is correctly based on article II of the 1948 UN Genocide Convention, which classifies as genocide those acts committed "with intent to destroy, in whole or in part, a national, ethnical, racial or religious group." In the case of the IS, this declaration is because of the group's targeting of Christians, Shiites, and **Yazidis** and also because the IS was responsible for crimes against humanity and ethnic cleansing in areas it controlled in Syria and Iraq. (**Yazidis** is a small persecuted religious minority who are often unjustly referred to as "devil worshippers" for their worshipping of the Peacock Angel. The Yazidis are estimated between eight hundred thousand and one and a half million, scattered mostly across northwest Iraq, northwest Syria, and southeast Turkey.)

For convenience and to suit its strategic interests, America glossed over the fact that Saudi Arabia's Wahhabi school of Islam and its ideology were behind the genocide of Christians, Shiites, and Yazidis. Above all, the collaboration between Saudi Arabia, Turkey, Israel, and the CIA is behind the financing and arming of extremist Sunni terrorists as part of the conspiracy for regime change in the Middle East. The American declaration, however, did not show that the United States had any intention of changing its policy in the region to justify it's pointing the finger at others. [90]

Failure to ignite a rational international debate about America's foreign policy and Israel's assault on the Palestinians has aggravated the problem of terrorism. Worse yet, terrorism has become a tool in the hands of the Western elites to diminish the democratic and civil rights of their citizens, in the name of national security, in order to deflect any opinion that might expose their own contributions to the problem. This lack of debate also helps powerful countries such as the United States use terrorism as a brand to achieve their political and strategic objectives, especially in demonizing leaders of disobedient countries, declaring economic embargos and sanctions, and declaring war if necessary without having to provide proper evidence, as the United States did in its war on Iraq. It is most likely the United States will employ similar approach when it decides to declare war on Iran. The national-security banner and the promotion of war propaganda have resulted in a stifling of the discussion on the elementary causes of terrorism. Furthermore, America's war propaganda has helped many oppressive regimes in the Middle East avoid the scrutiny of their roles in exasperating terrorism. To suit these regimes, the United States decides which groups represent the "good" terrorists and which ones are the "bad" terrorists. Guided by propaganda to serve its own national interests, the United States uses the good terrorists to justify the arming and financing of these groups, the main purposes of which are regime changes in the Middle East and to fight the Shiites for being a threat to Israel. From there, the good terrorists' fight against the bad terrorists has expanded to include any group who might become a threat to arguably the most backward and oppressive regime in the Middle East—the Saudi regime—which not only uses sectarian propaganda in the region but also funds terrorism while accusing others of doing the same. (For more on Saudi Arabia's role in terrorism, see the subsection below.)

America and Israel also stifle the debate over their role in provoking Islamic terrorism by deflecting any criticism against their actions and policies with accusations of anti-Americanism or anti-Semitism, despite ample evidence that America's military interventions and Israel's atrocities against the Palestinians are the main causes of Islamic terrorism, provoked as it has been by injustice, destruction, poverty, death, and misery. American and Israeli policies in the Middle East have created a haven for all regional Middle Eastern fundamentalists, which have become a major threat to Western civilization. They are creating a distinguishable new group of radical Islamic insurgents who originally were not motivated by Islamist-supremacy fundamentalism but are now more fanatical about Islam. These new fundamentalist groups want to turn back the clock and force everyone to live in the long-past era of the caliphs of some fourteen hundred years ago.

The Western countries' attempts to destroy an ideology that is based on an extreme interpretation of Islamic religion is a futile exercise; instead, their focus should be on secular education and on fighting poverty and unemployment in those countries where economic disparity and social inequality are making hopeless, marginalized, and impoverished people an easy target for recruitment to fight for a violent religious ideology. The process of destroying the cancer of extremist Islamic ideology could take many decades and should be accompanied by correcting earlier British, Israeli, and American policies toward Islamic countries and by dealing positively with these nations' legitimate grievances. Massive effort will be required to correct some of the problems created by earlier policies, especially the reconstruction of homes and infrastructures destroyed earlier by Israeli, British, Russian, and American interventions; the reestablishment of proper state institutions and nation building; and the resettling of millions of displaced people and refugees. These problems were the result of the war on terror in countries such as Iraq, Libya, Syria, Afghanistan, Lebanon, Somalia, Yemen, and Pakistan, and later on in Egypt, Jordan, and Iran. As it stands, Iraq, Libya, Yemen, Syria, Afghanistan, Pakistan, Egypt, and Lebanon are heading the way of Somalia, soon to be failed states. Judging by their track record, the imperialistic powers have always shown themselves to be more capable of destroying than of building. The problem is aggravated by the current American adoption of the old British divide-and-conquer policy in the Middle East in its attempt to control the region's resources. This policy has caused major chaos that has now spun out of control. Uniting Muslims instead of stoking sectarian violence that leads to extremism and further destruction could prove to be a wiser policy, especially if it is coupled with the persistent encouragement of secular education, not only in Islamic countries but all over the world.

As it stands, the divide-and-conquer policy has set the stage for the opponents' mutually assured destruction, especially for the element of religious nationalism that is behind the conflict, which is evolving into major hostility between Muslims on the one hand and Christians and Jews on the other—a hostility that will have no winner. But if the moderate silent majorities from all sides wake up in time, shed their apathy, and take control of the political and social agendas, then they could prevent a major catastrophe. All that is needed for peace and harmony in the region and the world is the adoption of the concepts of respect and equality and the entrenchment of secularism instead of imposing sectarian or corrupt puppet regimes in the region to serve Western interests. The Western and Islamic moderate majorities, by neglecting their responsibilities, have created a vacuum that has instantly been filled by extremist minorities on all sides who pursue conflicts to solve their differences.

In the Middle East, the problem is aggravated by foreign influence, which is driven by the national interests of the sponsoring countries who are in control of running expansionist or religious-nationalistic agendas. As we have seen, the foreign influence involves the clash of competing geopolitics and national interests of the sponsoring countries, which makes reaching compromises extremely difficult and often results in grave consequences when every power wants to have total control of the outcome. This situation generally ends with no winners—only mutual destruction. In Syria, for example, America and its coalition have conflicting goals and strategies; Turkey and Saudi Arabia are financing and arming groups that are opposite and different from those the Americans, the British, and the French are arming and financing. Even if the Assad regime is toppled, these conflicting groups will turn against one another in a continuous civil war, as happened in Libya and may be worse. Above all, the objectives of the Russians and the Americans are diametrically opposed. Syria is stuck in the middle of a regional control, which includes a conflict between Sunnis and Shiites that has displaced millions of people, while far-right Zionists are dictating America's foreign policies to suit Israel's strategic interests.

Israel is a key player in the region's geopolitics. It considers Iran, Syria, and Hezbollah (supported by Russia) as a threat to its security, while it considers Turkey, Egypt, Jordan, Saudi Arabia, and other Gulf states (supported by America) to be friends and allies that will cause no threat to its security. Therefore, the focus was on the destruction of the Assad regime of Syria first, followed by an Israeli-American-coordinated military attack on Iran; eventually, Hezbollah will become the final and easiest target to eliminate. In the meantime, Syria's civil war became the catalyst for establishing the IS insurgency group by Abu Bakr al-Baghdadi, who considered al-Qaeda to be a timid group. From there, al-Baghdadi expanded his state building to include Iraq by establishing ISIL, which refers to the Islamic State of Iraq and the Levant, whose latest and shorter version is the Islamic State (IS). In June 2014, al-Baghdadi declared himself a caliph and started to expand the IS insurgency across the Middle East and Africa; he even received pledges from loyal Islamic groups in Southeast Asia, including Indonesia and the Philippines. Other jihadi groups emerged that also evolved from al-Qaeda, including al-Nusra Front, Jund al-Aqsa, Tahrir al-Sham, and dozens of other factions, some of which America considers good terrorists who are worthy of being armed and financed in their fight to bring down the Assad regime.

The success of the IS in mobilizing Islamic jihadists stems from the general perception that Christians and Jews are willing to kill Muslims, which has attracted and galvanized other Muslims from around the world to join in the fight as a religious duty. The situation is aggravated by the disaffection among Iraqi Sunnis, especially members of the previous Baathist Saddam regime and various Sunni tribes, who were placed at a great disadvantage by their country's American-written constitution and a democracy that was imposed through the barrel of a gun.

THE PROBLEM WITH AMERICA'S WAR ON TERROR

In the over seventeen years (as of this writing) since the American declaration of war on terror—a declaration supported by a Western and Middle Eastern multinational coalition—the Islamic insurgency is still decentralizing, expanding, and generally going strong. This is happening because the strategy of combating the problem is inappropriate, especially for the collateral civilian casualties and the destruction of infrastructure it causes, which multiplies the number of enemies against America and its coalition. For propaganda purposes to show that the nation is making progress in the fight against terrorism, America often loudly broadcasts the elimination of various terrorist masterminds as a great achievement. In fact, the outcome of eliminating one terrorist mastermind is that many masterminds are created. It is the nature of the Islamic religious war that makes every fighter a martyr and every fighter dispensable—not only dispensable, but death becomes a badge of honor to carry on one's way to paradise. America is unable to understand that the Islamic insurgency, despite its primitiveness, does have some military and political direction (especially in succession planning), which makes replacing terrorist leaders an easy task.

The war on terror's problems are further aggravated by the lack of a proper approach to factionalism and to finding the right balance between the region's tribal, social, religious, and political structures, all of which are relevant to Middle Eastern geopolitics. This is especially so with the disturbance of the balance of power between the various groups, sects, and tribes, which is getting out of hand and proving to be one of the main reasons for America's failure. It could take America many decades of pain in the Middle East before it comes to the conclusion that the original balance of power—where the secular Sunni minority was in control of Iraq and the secular Shiite minority was in control of Syria—was and may still be the best solution for all concerned. It should follow this path instead of imposing what it believes to be the more civilized Western democratic culture and values on backward or developing countries without allowing for a natural evolutionary process to reach the desired outcome of peaceful and gradual transition into more harmonious societies, which can be helped by encouraging and contributing to secular education in these countries.

In tribal, sectarian, and poor countries, secular dictatorships should be tolerated until the nations are ready for locally evolved democracies. Imposing Western-style democracy through the barrel of guns that install corrupt puppet governments is a shortsighted propaganda idea designed to mislead the world by hiding the US imperialistic agenda. The installed puppet governments can survive only through political affiliation and systematic patronage, which leads to corruption and the impoverishment of the majority. In the process, imperialism produces failed states afflicted with entrenched anarchy, to the detriment of the world. Some of the unintended consequences of this created regional conflict include the destruction of countries such as Afghanistan, Iraq, Syria, Libya, Yemen, Somalia, and many more to follow. It is the destruction of infrastructure, the countries' institutions, and the spirit of coexistence between communities that will take many decades to restore. Other major problems that will have long-term detrimental effects include the entrenched poverty, illiteracy, and unemployment that cannot be resolved without contributions from the major Western countries. The destruction is usually accompanied by the destruction of the middle class, the mover of these countries and the anchor of evolving democracies in the region, which is the hardest commodity to replace. If, however, the West is unwise and decides to leave these problems behind without pursuing nation building, then the instability in the region and beyond will linger for many decades, much to the detriment of the world, as more terrorists with nothing to lose will emerge from the wreckage. The most important task is to restore the coexistence between communities that existed before the imperialistic interventions that have stoked the sectarian divide.

Islamic fundamentalism is generally a by-product of indoctrination by madrassas and mosques. ("Madrassas" in Arabic means schools or any place of learning. In Islamic religious context, however, madrassas offer religious-based instruction and focus on Islamic theology as dictated by the

Koran. In the Western world, madrassas are perceived as places where fundamentalist, Islamic instruction is combined with anti-Western ideology.) These institutions, with their widespread organizational structures, can easily mobilize people to fill a political vacuum, especially when Islamic religion and politics are inseparable. A secular dictatorship cannot be replaced by a secular political party, because political parties in a dictatorship are not allowed to exist and—as stated earlier—cannot match the religious establishments that own and control the infrastructure of mosques and Islamic schools, which enables them to dictate social and political messages. Accordingly, Islamist religious leaders sooner or later become the new rulers and dictators in the region, to the detriment of their nations and beyond, especially the Sunni Salafists, who live in many parts of the world. (Please see the "Saudi Arabia's Role in Terrorism" subsection below for a discussion on the Salafists.) To visualize the point, imagine that America's two major parties, the Republicans and the Democrats, are under the absolute control of the ultraconservative theological religious-right Evangelicals. What is worse in the Middle East is that regime changes to serve imperialistic interests are usually followed by corruption, unemployment, brutality, and poverty; the region's history shows that these are a recipe for instability and continuous conflict.

To prevent mutually assured destruction, the United States and its allies must abandon aggression, the desire for domination and control, and the winner-takes-all approach and replace them with compromise: the give-and-take and win-win principles. America and its allies also need to consider that wars lead to destruction, homelessness, injustice, refugees, and poverty and will result in more enemies, resentment, and revolt. When poor and ignorant people lose hope, they often turn to guns and religion for salvation; in the Islamic case, this is martyrdom. There is a better way: the adoption of moderation, mutually beneficial actions, and a diplomatic approach to achieve desired outcomes rather than domination by intimidation and the use of force.

America's aggression in the Middle East and elsewhere—driven by its unlimited and undefined strategic interests—has weakened the power and influence of its own moderates and the moderates throughout the Islamic world. This in turn has empowered and emboldened its own far-right elements and its military, as well as Islamic fundamentalists, which has had a detrimental impact on the stability of the whole region and the world. The radical Islamic movement is on a growth path, especially considering that more Islamic youth (mostly those who are unemployed and poorly educated) are being attracted to the idea of jihad as a result of American and Israeli aggression against Muslims. For their strategic interests, America and Israel appear to be purposefully ignoring the root causes of the Islamic revolt. I should repeat that some of the main causes of the radicalization and revolt of Muslims stem from American military interventions; the Israeli atrocities against the Palestinians; and the poverty, killings, destruction, injustice, high unemployment, and widespread ignorance and illiteracy in the region. The problem is further aggravated by the West's far-right movements in their bigotry and discrimination against Muslims, which boosts the process of radicalization and makes them easy targets for recruitment by terrorist organizations such as the IS. The marginalization and stereotyping of Muslims has also driven their moderate intellectuals into isolation and on to the defensive or, at worst, has made them participants in terrorism. Their marginalization and stereotyping has prevented the intellectuals from having much input in a long-overdue reformation of Islam that would allow for a moderate reinterpretation of Islam in the same way that happened in Christianity during the Martin Luther era of the sixteenth century. At that time, Islam was not exposed to modernity and contemporary science and often justified fanaticism, since all other religions had fanatics as well. [91] It is worth noting that Luther is often credited with the rise of secular democracy, among other things.

As for Muslims living in Western countries, especially those who are exposed to hard-line radical Islamic teaching, they are often people who are brainwashed into believing that fighting and dying for "Allah" will take them to paradise. Such an ideology is to be confronted by secular education and reasoning, but not by force, especially when dealing with susceptible marginalized youths who are struggling to find their identity in a society that despises them. If the silent majority maintains its apathy and allows far-right politicians and far-right commentators to run populist political and social agendas, then the future of the generations to follow will be bleak. Although far-right Western politicians and commentators become more popular by exaggerating and overreacting to terrorist attacks, at the same time, they are playing into the hands of the terrorists. They reward these fanatics by treating them as celebrities, and in the process they enhance and promote terrorist activities because terrorism is about terrorizing people and by making their targets feel that their lives are under constant threat, which results in advancing the terrorist agenda.

In the case of Islamic terrorist groups, it isn't the religion that motivates people but the politicized form of the religion. Islamic terrorist groups inspire marginalized Muslims by their charisma and by winning a few battles. By understanding that they must be denied winning in any battlefield and by stopping the marginalization of Muslims and the spread of **Islamophobia****, these groups' main source of recruitment would then be cut.

** **Islamophobia** is defined as unfounded hostility toward Muslims because of fear or general dislike. Islamophobes believe that Islam is inferior to the West and that Islam is a violent ideology. Islamophobia has a similar meaning to "xenophobia," which is a contrived prejudice fomented by Eurocentric and orientalist global power structures that reaffirms a global racial structure with built-in discrimination and bigotry. Islamophobia is the irrational hatred of Muslims and the Islamic religion. Its main promoters are ultraright white supremacists, who believe they are self-entitled because of being white. They also believe they are privileged to do and say what they want and to discriminate against Muslims and any others whom they consider inferior. The same goes for those of different color or who do not look or sound like them. [92]

Opportunistic Western populist politicians and right-wing media commentators have promoted the marginalization of Muslims in an attempt to appeal to the ignorant and vocally racist section of the community through intemperate comments and the purposeful spread of hatred. The impact of their agitation—if analyzed sensibly—amounts to an unpatriotic act for the division it causes within their own society and in provoking terrorists' counteractions, both locally and internationally. Any sensible person can conclude from suicide bombings and the slaughter of innocent people that these events make all citizens of any country sitting ducks who are burdened with fear and insecurity, which is the primary aim of the terrorists.

International relations are currently in an explosive mode, poisoned with religious hostility that leaves the world in desperate need of moderation and the emergence of moderate leaders. This is the time for the silent majority to wake up before it is too late. The world doesn't need sinister leaders who promote the politics of identity, which encourages people to define themselves in a narrow and subjective way by ethnic, religious, and cultural terms. Doing so leads to disengagement between social groups and increases the chances of polarization and hostility between individuals and groups. Taken to the extreme, as in the current state of affairs, polarization and hostility can have devastating consequences, both locally and internationally. The devastation is mainly the result of the radicalization of people who are divided through discrimination and bigotry on the grounds of race, religion, and ethnicity. At times like this, radicalism is generally proportional to the degree of discrimination and bigotry. Radicalism operates in accordance with Newton's third law of physics: "For every action, there is an equal and opposite reaction." Radicalism is often a form of revolt against people's miserable social and economic conditions and the conditions of others around them. This revolt often has nothing to do with religion; it is often the sense of disaffection and disenchantment from perceived bigotry and injustice that can make an individual or group susceptible to radicalization.

Therefore, to solve the problem of radicalism, one must examine the causes before deciding on a solution. For example, for the sake of protecting Israel, American far-right Zionists' control over American foreign policy is driving the United States into continuous military interventions in the Middle East that are causing massive losses of life and property and infrastructural destruction in the targeted countries, which in turn results in an opposite reaction, a consequence of which is the radicalization of Islamists. This radicalization culminates in the formation of vengeful terrorist cells to counter the Christian and Jewish assault on Islam. Looking deeper into Islamic terrorism can help in dealing with the problem constructively, especially by understanding the potent mix behind the problem of terrorism: the core articles of faith embedded in Islamic tradition and culture, which often result in blood feuds and other acts of vengeance. We should look into the abuses behind these acts, which are embedded in the American military interventions and Israeli atrocities against the Palestinians.

It is worth noting that the blood feuds and the revenge elements in Islamic tradition are not restricted to Islam. These things are universal, as we may see in the reaction of besieged countries, which are often inclined to develop WMD, including nuclear weapons, as a deterrent or for revenge. This is visible in the case of Iraq before the invasion, currently in the case of North Korea, and earlier in the case of Iran, before the lifting of sanctions.

In *Hegemony or Survival* (2004), Chomsky wrote the following:

Mainstream experts agreed that an attack by the most powerful military force in history against a defenseless enemy might well stimulate the quest for revenge or deterrence. Prominent international relations scholars have pointed out that potential targets of US adventurism "know that the United States can be held at bay only by deterrence," primarily by WMD (Kenneth Waltz). In this way, "American policies stimulate the vertical proliferation of nuclear weapons and promote their spreading from one country to another." The same policies stimulate terrorism: "Unsurprisingly... weak states and disaffected people...lash out at the United States as the agent or symbol of their suffering," and if no efforts are made to address the grievances, they are likely to react with the means available to them, including terror. US intelligence added that the "deepening economic stagnation" caused by

Washington's version of globalization was likely to have similar effects. [93]

As for the current relentless wave of discrimination and bigotry against Muslims in the Western world (fueled by far-right politicians and vested interests), this wave will ultimately destroy the social fabric of the Western countries and will have a devastating effect on international relations. Creating 1.7 billion despised people, targeted as the enemy, will never lead to world peace but to a protracted war for many generations to come. Discrimination and bigotry against Muslims is now the norm rather than the exception. The constant barrage of bullies, media messages, and personalities of authority who demean Muslims because of their faith has had a negative effect on the morale of this social group. Islamophobia is a form of racism that is characterized by social profiling, stereotyping, hostility, and intolerance against Muslims in their exclusion from mainstream political and social life. The world is in desperate need of winning over all moderate Muslims to control the extremists within instead of pushing the moderates to become extremists by despising them.

History is littered with examples of nations that have not benefited from fragmentation. Promoting irrational fear and hatred against a group of people because of an aspect of their identity or their beliefs is a recipe for bullying and institutionalized discrimination. Politicians and religious leaders who engage in spreading fear and hatred for temporary popularity gains are guilty of bringing long-term harm to the social harmony that future generations should enjoy. The fragmentation of society will lead to a country's decline and eventual demise.

America and its Western allies are reaping the fruits of their past conspiracies to remove any moderate secular (but less democratic) leaders in the Middle East and North Africa—leaders who were capable of controlling the political, religious, and social agendas in their countries. During the reign of past moderate and secular leaders, the economic health of their countries was generally good, sectarian problems were under control, and terrorism didn't exist. As discussed in the previous subsection, the removal of the moderate secular leaders in the region has created a social and political vacuum, which is proving to be one of the main causes for the current chaos. Above all, America and its allies have always ignored the fact that Islamic terrorism stems from extremism and radicalization, which starts in religious schools and results in religion and politics becoming inseparable. Instead of countries spending trillions of dollars on escalating religious wars, the money should have been spent on encouraging and persisting with secular education in backward countries. By the same token, America and its Western allies—to avoid the stigma of applying a double standard—should set a good example by entrenching secular education in their own countries rather than subsidizing religious schools that also result in religion influencing politics. A shining example of this is the huge influence the Jewish Zionists and the Christian Evangelicals have on American policies, especially on US foreign policy, which is one of the main sources of religious conflict and the clash of civilizations. (More on secular education is discussed in the upcoming subsection "Far-Right Movements and the Clash of Civilizations" and in chapter 3.)

In conclusion, that which has been created by military intervention cannot be solved by more interventions; violence cannot be solved with more violence. It is delusional for America and its allies to think that defeating the IS on the battlefield will rid the world of Islamic terrorism, because America's leaders have no plan for the next stage of Islamic radicalization or the consequences of the further decentralization of Islamic terrorism. Furthermore, America and its Western allies have no plan to deal with nation building following the destruction of so many Islamic countries. There is no doubt that, given their firepower and the help of their financed and equipped local foot soldiers, America and its allies will prevail in destroying the IS's fighters and the cities they occupy, but the next stage will be the hardest fight to win. Without solving the underlying problems and addressing the grievances that originally escalated terrorism, the West will continue to suffer from the war of ideologies for many decades to come.

Having a feeling of "mission accomplished" in winning Mosul and Raqqa can provide a sense of security that can result in several things. First is ignoring that Islamic State is linked to the tribal system of the Middle East and has the capacity to target many more towns and villages. Second is ignoring that the remaining IS fighters will scatter to many parts of the Middle East and the West, where many of their sympathizers live—the many despised Muslims of the world. Couple this with the possibility that terrorists will acquire

WMD such as dirty bombs, and the end result is disaster. Third is ignoring the fact that there are competing voices within various American administrations, whereas the military's one and only mission is to defeat the IS. This is the easiest short-term goal: bombarding the hell out of their cities despite the presence of "human shields." The other voice is of the far-right Zionists, who are calling for widening the conflict to target Iran and Iran's proxies in Syria and Lebanon—a very dangerous goal, especially when Russia is committed to protecting its own interests in the region. Above all, these options result in killing and displacing more Muslims, which will result only in widening the conflict into a real clash of civilizations as more Muslims in other Islamic countries will react according to the Islamic duty for revenge. The escalation of the conflict since the invasion of Afghanistan has been the main reason for the failing American foreign policy, guided by Israel lobby groups. America, in hiding its ambition of dominating the world, has always been prepared to sacrifice other countries' civilians to protect its own, without moral accountability.

Saudi Arabia's Role in Terrorism

What is missing in the debate about Islamic terrorism is the role of Saudi Arabia in cultivating and financing the various aspects of terrorism, starting from the time of the establishment of al-Qaeda, with the help of the CIA, to fight the Soviets in Afghanistan. Because America is a close ally of Saudi Arabia, for convenience and to suit America's strategic interests, it has glossed over the fact that Saudi Arabia's Wahhabi school of Islam and its ideology are behind the genocide of Christians, Shiites, and Yazidis. Above all, the collaboration between Saudi Arabia, Jordan, Turkey, Israel, and the CIA is behind the financing and arming of fundamentalist Sunni terrorists. Saudi Arabia and its Sunni allies have adopted a similar policy of regime change in the Middle East to suit their sectarian strategic interests, which then became an extension of America's and Israel's strategy that the neoconservatives had designed and advocated (as discussed earlier).

At this point, to understand the current sectarian violence between the Sunnis and the Shiites, it is necessary to examine the Saudi Wahhabi fundamentalist school of Islam. I should first note that Sunnis make up 87–90 percent of the estimated 1.7 billion Muslims in the world, while Shiites make up 10–13 percent. The majority of Shiites live in Iran, Iraq, Syria, Yemen, Bahrain, Afghanistan, and Lebanon, while Sunnis live in these same countries and in the rest of the Islamic world. As an overwhelming majority of all Muslims in the world, the Sunnis tend to look down on and discriminate against (and, if possible, eliminate) the minority, which is a common problem where the feeling of domination by the majority is in play. [94]

Soon after the death in 632 AD of the Prophet Muhammad, the dispute between the two sects originated over who was entitled to become the next leader of Islam. Although the two sects have coexisted for centuries through intermarriage and other cultural and economic factors, during the recent history of British and American imperialistic influence through these nations' divide-and-conquer policies, the sectarian divide has developed into a conflict that it is now culminating in open hostility. This hostility is fueled by America's attempt to control the oil reserves in the Middle East and to allow Israel to colonize Palestine.

The differences between the Sunni and Shiite sects, which are generally similar to those found in other nations of different religions, extend to rituals, laws, theology, and religious organizational structure. Sunnis believe that a Muslim leader controls the state, while Shiites believe that a Muslim leader is under the control of the state. Shiites believe that Ali (the son-in-law of the Prophet Muhammad) and his descendants were entitled to lead the Islamic community; instead, Ali was killed as a result of the intrigues, violence, and civil wars that marred his caliphate. His sons, Hassan and Hussein, were denied what they thought was their legitimate right of accession to the caliphate. Hassan is believed to have been poisoned by Muawiyah, the first Sunni caliph of the Umayyad dynasty, while his brother, Hussein, was killed on the battlefield along with members of his family.

For centuries, some fundamentalist Sunnis, especially the Wahhabis of Saudi Arabia (who consider Shiites to be heretics), have preached hatred of Shiites. This developed into a conflict following the Iranian revolution of 1979, which launched a radical Shiite Islamist agenda. The new agenda was widely perceived to be a challenge to the ultraconservative and autocratic Sunni regimes in the region, especially to Saudi Arabia and the Gulf states. As part of American strategic interests in the Middle East, the United States encouraged and amplified the religious dimension of the conflict, which has culminated in the current open hostilities. These hostilities will benefit no one except for a short-term benefit to America from supplying arms to the region and from the temporary import of cheap oil. This strategy will sooner or later backfire when arms fall into the hands of terrorists and when the oil supply becomes limited and threatened.

Historically, sectarian conflict has always been part of all religions, including Islam. The genesis of the Islamic conflict between Sunnis and Shiites dates back to the years of the founding of the Salafist movement (780–855 AD), which advocated a return to the ways of the first Muslim ancestors, the Salaf al-Salih ("righteous ancestors"). Later on, the Salafist movement inspired devout Islamic scholar Muhammad ibn Abdel Wahhab (b. 1703) to form the Wahhabi sect in the Arabian Peninsula. He developed a strict version of Islam that he thought reflected the original faith and set out to spread his version with the help of political and military power. From its inception, Wahhabism has always justified violence in spreading Islam. In 1744, Abdel Wahhab made a critical alliance with the Saudi ruler at the time, Muhammad ibn Saud. It was a pact whereby Wahhabism provided the spiritual and ideological dimension for Saudi political and military expansion, to the benefit of both. The entrenchment of Wahhabi Salafism in Saudi Arabia, and the billions of petrodollars the nation gained access to, provided critical resources for jihadist militancy to wage the modern jihad (holy war) in the region and elsewhere. [95, 96]

Egyptian thinker Sayyid Qutb, who formed the Muslim Brotherhood (MB) organization, spread Salafism in the twentieth century. Qutb was born in Egypt in 1906 and hanged in 1966 on charges of involvement in a plot to assassinate President Gamal Abdel Nasser of Egypt. (For more on the MB, see the report in note 97.) During his life, Qutb provided a direct bridge from the thought and heritage of Abdel Wahhab and his predecessors to a new generation of jihadist militants; the culmination of his efforts was the development of al-Qaeda, followed by al-Nusra Front and the IS terrorist groups. Therefore, the ideological lineage of the IS goes back to Wahhabism, which Saudi Arabia has promoted. These fanatical groups consider all other Muslims who don't follow their interpretation of the Koran as apostates (infidels) whose killing is justified. Qutb had personal contact with al-Qaeda leader Ayman al-Zawahiri and inspired al-Qaeda founder Osama bin Laden. More than thirty-five years after Qutb was hanged, the official commission of inquiry into al-Qaeda's 9/11 attacks on the World Trade Center and the Pentagon in 2001 concluded that Bin Laden shared Qutb's stark view, permitting him and his followers to rationalize even unprovoked mass murder as righteous defense of an embattled faith. It must be said, however, that although most Salafists are radical, not all are violent, except for their promotion of ideas that can inspire people to commit violence for religious and political reasons. Thus, the MB is often considered to be in this category of Salafism.

It is worth noting that the MB of Dr. Mohammed Morsi's government in Egypt was democratically elected but was overthrown in 2013 by Abdel Fattah el-Sisi in a military coup with the backing of Saudi Arabia. The MB's ideology mostly revolves around the establishment of an authoritarian Islamic regime. Its ideology became popular during the Arab Spring uprising that toppled several Arab dictatorships with sweeping success in elections in 2011 and 2012. The Arab Spring brought fear to other authoritarian regimes, especially to those of Saudi Arabia and other Gulf states, which prompted these regimes to spearhead the anti-MB campaign by declaring it a terrorist organization so that they could justify its destruction and curtail its influence from spreading. But because these powers tagged the MB as a terrorist organization and then banned it and jailed its leaders, the MB was left with no choice but to abandon its more benign and peaceful approach to political Islam and to gradually adopt the violent approach of the Salafi jihadists, which will bring it closer to real terrorism. The impact of transforming over five million members from pursuing a benign form of political Islam to pursuing a violent one will gradually be felt throughout the Arab world, especially from the alignment of Egypt's and the Gulf states' policies with America's and Israel's policies against Hamas and Iran. (For more on Salafi jihadists, see note 98.)

Since the killing of Osama bin Laden in May 2011 by US forces in Pakistan, al-Qaeda has morphed into a franchise operation rather than a central-command organization. While America was declaring euphoric victory about his killing as a turning point against terrorism, many experts viewed his death as only a symbolic triumph—and they have been proved correct. As it turned out, his death caused a drastic shift in terrorist activities by creating subsidiaries of al-Qaeda with more fanatically minded Islamic groups, especially following the invasion of Iraq. The American war in Iraq and the nation's switching sides from the Sunnis to the Shiites (especially in sidelining the Sunnis in favor of the Shiites) have disturbed the balance of power between the sects, not only in Iraq but also in the Middle East generally, which changed the religious dispute into a power struggle. The power struggle has culminated in Iran backing various Shiite militias in Iraq, Syria, Yemen, and Lebanon, while Saudi Arabia's financing and arming of the Sunnis has culminated in the formation of the Gulf Cooperation Council (GCC)—which is composed of Bahrain, Kuwait, Oman, Qatar, the United Arab Emirates (UAE), and Saudi Arabia—as part of an undeclared war on the Shiites. The crunch will come when and if America and Israel unwisely decide to pull the trigger for a final showdown between the two camps, which will have many unpleasant and unintended consequences, especially now that Russia has flexed its muscles in the region because its interests in the Mediterranean are under threat.

The open hostilities between Sunnis and Shiites in Iraq, Yemen, and Syria were stoked, financed, and armed by external forces working in collaboration—namely, between Saudi Arabia, the UAE, Turkey, Jordan, Israel, Britain, America, and **Qatar*****—as part of a regime-change strategy in the Middle East and North Africa.

***** Qatar**: The current conflict between Saudi Arabia and its closest allies (the UAE, Egypt, and Bahrain) against Qatar is because of Qatar's support and financing of the Muslim Brotherhood movement (especially in Egypt and Gaza), which Saudi Arabia had earlier declared a terrorist organization. Saudi Arabia, the UAE, Bahrain, and Egypt cut ties with Qatar in June 2017 and imposed a land, air, and sea blockade of the country. The quartet has accused Qatar of funding terrorism, an accusation Qatar rejects as baseless. According to US Senator Bob Corker (chair of the US Senate Foreign Relations Committee and who has recently came out against Donald Trump), the Saudis are the real sponsor of terrorism. In his criticism of the Saudi crown prince over the blockade of Qatar, Corker stated in July 2017 that "the amount of support for terrorism by Saudi Arabia dwarfs what Qatar is doing." [99]

To emphasize the role of Wahhabism in the conflict, we should remember the top Saudi imam's declaration in a May 2009 interview with BBC Arabic in which the Saudi-appointed imam of Mecca, Sheikh Adel al-Kalbani, said that "all Shiite religious scholars are apostates. And because all Shiites deny the status of Abu Bakr, they are apostates." According to Wahhabism, all apostates are nonbelievers and, as such, should be hunted down and killed. On the topic of Jews and Christians living in the Arabian Peninsula, the Sheikh is guided by the Prophet's guidance that dictates driving the Jews and Christians out of the Arabian Peninsula, since they should be allowed to live there only if their presence is essential. [100]

Saudi Arabia—the main ally of the United States in the Middle East—is behind the exporting of Wahhabist fundamentalist ideology and terrorism to other parts of the world. Although Saudi Arabia is on its way to ruin, the nation has caused tremendous damage to the stability of the Middle East and the world on its way there. We should not forget that the Saudis' long-term promotion of an extreme interpretation of Islam is the version that Sunni terrorists have adopted. And, besides the Saudis' indirect involvement in arming and financing various Sunni groups in their fight against Shiites, they are also directly involved in terrorism against the Yemeni people, on whom they have used weapons happily supplied by the Americans and the British.

America and its Western allies appear to be encouraging the Saudis to use their wealth to create political and religious conflict in other countries, especially in its fellow Islamic countries. Their wealth and power are waning, however, because of the following truths:

1. In using their common anti-Iranian stance, America and Israel were able to manipulate Saudi Arabia into surrendering its economic and political sovereignty to their strategic and economic interests.

2. The United States tricked Saudi Arabia into a costly militarization to carry out and achieve America's objectives in the region while at the same time making billions of dollars from arm deals, despite the Syrian and Yemeni blood on the Saudi royals' hands from

arming and financing Sunni terrorist groups in a war of attrition against the Shiites.

3. The increasing power of Iran, with the help of Russia, has had a major impact on the region's geopolitics. Saudi Arabia will be affected negatively, especially after its defeat in Syria.

4. Saudi Arabia has a sizable oppressed Shiite minority who are becoming a threat to the nation's internal stability and security.

5. Sooner or later, the IS and other jihadi groups will combine with internal Saudi opposition forces in a revolt to bring the corrupted and deeply divided Saudi royal family to a violent end.

6. Saudi Arabia is hated by many Islamic and other nations around the world, which makes its government's existence unsustainable.

7. Above all, the collapse of oil prices that it engineered in 2015–16 to create an oil glut, which was designed by conspiring with the United States to intentionally or unintentionally destroy the Russian and Iranian economies, has backfired on the nation's own economy and budget.

We should remember that fifteen of the nineteen terrorists involved in the 9/11 attacks were Saudis, yet Saudi Arabia remains the United States' closest ally in the region. America—to satisfy the Saudis—has falsely declared Iran to be the major terrorist sponsor in the world, when Shiites generally do not commit terrorist acts.

In his 2014 article "Foundation of the US Empire," Petras wrote the following:

The second most important axis of power in the Middle East is the US-Saudi alliance. From the perspective of the US Empire, the Saudi connection has many advantages, as well as costs. Saudi financing, in collaboration with the US, was instrumental in recruiting, arming and financing the Islamist guerrillas, which overthrew the secular pro-Soviet government in Afghanistan. Saudi links to the Pakistani intelligence services and military has ensured Pakistan will remain a client-state of the US Empire. Saudi intervention in Yemen and Bahrain propped up the pro-empire, anti-democratic puppet regimes while ensuring US access to its strategic military bases.

Saudi Arabia is the principle backer of US sanctions and confrontation with Iran. It provides air bases, military intelligence operations and the funding of anti-Iranian terrorists, like the Mujahedeen al-Khalq terrorists in Iran. Saudi Arabia is the biggest market for US military exports. Saudi [Arabia] increased its oil output to compensate for a decline of oil in world markets due to the US embargo against and the destruction of oil production following the US attacks and devastation of Iraq and Libya. In exchange Saudi Arabia's absolutist monarchy obtains US protection, security and assistance in repressing its domestic unrest. Saudi billionaires, no matter how brutal and corrupt, have full access to lucrative financial markets in the US. The Saudi theocratic-monarchic dictatorship has clearly benefited from the US destruction of secular nationalist Arab regimes in the region. Indeed, secular nationalism has been the [Saudis'] primary target since its monarchy was set up by the British.

Nevertheless, the Saudi-US axis is fraught with tensions. The Saudi regime actively promotes Sunni extremist jihadi movements in Iraq, Syria and Lebanon undermining Washington-backed neo-liberal clients. The Saudi-backed terrorists in Libya have destabilized the US proxies. The Saudis promoted and financed the bloody military coup in Egypt of General Sisi. The Saudi Royals support the brutal military overthrow of the elected President Morsi and the suppression of the Egyptian Muslim Brotherhood because of Morsi's rapprochement with Iran. This has ruined Obama's more moderate goal of setting up a Muslim Brotherhood-Egyptian military power sharing arrangement in Cairo.

In other words, the US and Saudi axis converges in opposition to secular-nationalist regimes but diverges on the alternatives. The Saudis tend to choose the most retrograde Islamic extremist groups excluding and antagonizing all other tendencies, from conservative-secular neo-liberals to democratic, nationalist and socialist parties and movements. They end up with political polarizations unfavorable to US long-term imperial interests.

The Saudi choice of political alternatives tends to be minorities incapable of sustaining or overtly hostile to the US imperial order. Moreover, Saudi Arabia opposes Israel on religious grounds, the principle US political partner in the region, even as it works with the Jewish state against the secular or nationalist governments Syria, Iran and Lebanon.

Like its alliance with Israel, the US-Saudi axis comes at a very high cost. Saudi financing of the Taliban and other Islamic groups has cost the US empire builders hundreds of billions of dollars, thousands of military casualties and a humiliating retreat after a thirteen-year war.

Saudi funding for Sunni terrorists in Syria has decimated US-backed neo-liberal armed groups. Equally damaging, the same Saudi-backed jihadi groups have severely destabilized the US-imposed regime in Iraq. Saudi attacks on the US-Iranian nuclear negotiations have strengthened the Zionist-led opposition in the US Congress.

In other words the US-Saudi axis has buttressed the US Empire in the short run, but has become a strategic liability. Saudi's overseas projection of its most reactionary internal politics undermines the US effort to create stable imperial clients. Not to be overlooked is the Saudi role in financing Al-Qaeda and its operatives in the attack on the US on September 11, 2001. [101]

There are hopeful signs that some leaders in the West are starting to wake up to Saudi Arabia's role in spreading terrorist ideology. In a June 2017 speech delivered in northern England to his constituency before the upcoming general election, UK Labour Party leader Jeremy Corbyn said that "we must resist Islamophobia and division and turn out on June 8 united in our determination to show our democracy is strong…And yes, we do need to have some difficult conversations starting with Saudi Arabia and other Gulf states that have funded and fuelled extremist ideology." [102]

As a double down on Corbyn's suggestion that the UK foreign policy was related to repeated terrorism attacks in the West, Inderjeet Parmar, a professor of international politics at the City University of London, said, "For the first time, there has been a recognition right across the political spectrum, except within the Government, that there is actually a foreign policy connection in regard to these kinds of attacks that have occurred very recently." In criticism of the ruling conservative government, he added, "For example, the Conservative government during the Coalition period had commissioned a report on foreign funding of Jihadi groups and Jihadi terrorism…that has been put on hold." In relation to the UK and the US supply of arms to Saudi Arabia, he added, "That apparently shows a great deal of sensitive material about some of the powers in the Middle East to which the United Kingdom, and the United States, has been selling arms to for a long time and have been shown to be backing some of the forces which are now behind terror attacks in this country as well." [103]

Far-Right Movements and the Clash of Civilizations

In response to Islamic terrorism, the rise of far-right movements in the West is gathering momentum. This situation could lead to a global clash between Muslims on one side and Christians and Jews on the other. The "far-right movements versus Islamic terrorism" battle falls in the same category as "For every action, there is an equal and opposite reaction." These movements could be the outcome of the promotion of religious nationalism by all sides. These movements are fueled by ultranationalist and religious-nationalist leaders who use their social intelligence to promote themselves by asserting that cultures are not equal and that their countries have racial, religious, and cultural superiority. For far-right white supremacists, Western civilization means white Christian people versus others.

Similar assertions in the past were the cause of earlier tribal and sectarian wars and genocides. The purpose of promoting aspects of cultural superiority by some of the current far-right movements in the West can relate to Islamic terrorism, which has culminated in the current Western feeling of bigotry against Muslims and Islamic culture. The far-rightists, using fiery rhetoric, have made political discussion of issues related to Islam almost impossible. Their prejudices are not challenged but are merely further reinforced by the rhetoric of the prevailing and opportunistic far-right Western politicians, right-wing media, and far-right commentators.

We should remember that the far-right and religious-right movements of the West tend to forget, either intentionally or unintentionally, that the Catholic Church fought both the Reformation and the Enlightenment that followed it, both of which drew the church into burning, torturing, and imprisoning people who dared to challenge the notion of the presence of heaven and the sale of indulgences. They also forget the Spanish Inquisition; instead, they focus only on Islamic extremism, which was originally provoked by Western military interventions, especially the invasion of Iraq under false pretenses. [104] President G. W. Bush signaled this focus on Islam, for strategic interests, during his State of the Union address of January 2002 in which he singled out North Korea, Iran, and Iraq as countries that sponsor terrorism. The declaration, as part of the clash of civilizations, was written by the far-right Zionist speechwriter David Frum to facilitate wars against other regimes hostile to Israel and America. Although Bush mentioned the three countries—for immediate American strategic interest at that time—his main focus was on oil-rich Iraq as the plot for regime change started to thicken. What followed was the false American accusation that the Iraqi regime was armed with missiles and other WMD and was harboring and supporting terrorists, which culminated in the invasion of Iraq and the removal of Saddam Hussein's government in 2003. That war was where the oil reserves of Iraq entered into the calculation of America's messy, hypocritical, and contradictory imperialistic international relations. I should emphasize that America and other imperialistic powers must learn a lesson: removing Muslim dictators such as Mussadegh,

Qasim, Hussein, Gaddafi, and Assad will only create vacuums from which Islamist terrorists will be born.

It is also worth emphasizing that the American and Israeli assumption that the war in the Middle East and North Africa would result in the eventual surrender of the dispossessed people and the defeat of terrorism did not consider that population displacement; poverty; ignorance; and lack of access to education, employment, and health care have devastating effects on current and following generations, which will produce more people with no hope, who will then be ready to explode. The destruction of people's livelihoods has been the result of the indiscriminate bombardment of Islamic countries that were earmarked for regime change or the elimination of certain religious sects by vested interests. This destruction is coupled with the current Western resentment of the millions of refugees pouring into Western countries and the lack of UN funding to feed people and educate their children huddled in refugee camps throughout the Middle East and elsewhere. The outcome of having millions of destitute, hungry, ignorant, illiterate, and homeless people in the next generation is unpredictable; the West should expect the worst rather than assume these people will have no option but to accept their destinies as second- or third-class citizens. It is common sense. America and Israel should know by now that for them to avoid a major upheaval, people who live in the shadows must be given a chance.

The messy Middle East and North Africa of today, which the whole world is suffering from, is the result of America's military interventions in Iraq and in the whole region. The rulers of the region's countries, who face threats both from within their borders and from beyond, have been unable to stem the tide of the growing revolt against America's erratic foreign policies. America's erratic approach can be seen in its role in Syria's civil war, which was aimed at toppling the Assad regime. Through Turkey, Saudi Arabia, and Jordan, America supplied arms to people whom it calls the legitimate opposition to the Assad regime; these "good" terrorists amounted to fragments of several uncoordinated and sometimes opposing factions. Turkey, meanwhile, supplied the manpower, including training camps and arms to all terrorists—both the good and the bad. Often, the good terrorists have joined forces with the bad terrorists to achieve the same goal; at other times, all terrorists—the good, the bad, and the ugly—have fought one another for domination. The resulting situation is even worse than what has happened in Libya.

Through this cocktail and because America is serving its undefined and unlimited strategic interests, we must raise the following questions: Who is the legitimate opposition, and who is the brutal dictator who must be eliminated? Who is the good terrorist, and who is the bad one, when all the terrorists are Sunni Salafist jihadists? Who is the moderate, and who is the extremist, when all are Sunni fanatics fighting to destroy all Shiites in Yemen, Iraq, Syria, Lebanon, and ultimately in Iran? Who deserves to be armed and financed, and who doesn't? Who deserves to live, and who deserves to die? American drones and missiles take care of the rest.

American propaganda and its twisted logic can be summarized with what George Orwell wrote in his classic dystopian novel, *1984*: "War is peace. Freedom is slavery. Ignorance is strength." He also characterizes the new world government as the one that had brainwashed its population. Through all the mess, American strategists of the clash of civilizations, headed by far-right Zionists, are helping the terrorist organizations recruit ever more foot soldiers to become an even bigger threat to Western civilization. [105]

In *Hegemony or Survival* (2004), Chomsky wrote the following:

Nothing can appease those "who believe a 'clash of civilizations' with the West will restore Islam as a world power," the editors of the *Financial Times* write. But to "crush them…successfully they must be separated from the widening constituency." They add: "Put another way, while only might can destroy Al-Qaeda, its expanding support base can be eroded only by policies Arabs and Muslims see as just." Even destruction of Al-Qaeda will do little if "the underlying conditions that facilitated the group's emergence and popularity—political oppression and economic marginalization—will persist." Correspondingly, continuation of Washington's backing for "solid governments" can only bolster Al-Qaeda's claims that the US supports the oppression of Muslims and props up brutal governments. That is quite aside from specific policies regarding Palestine and Iraq and others, which have converted "a generation of Arabs wooed by the United States and persuaded by its principles [to] among the most vociferous critics of America's world view, [including] affluent businessmen with ties to the West, US-educated intellectuals and liberal activists." [106]

While America's focus is on dealing with the mess it has created, which has contributed to the rise of Islamic fundamentalist nationalism in the Middle East and North Africa, North Korea continues to experiment and build its nuclear capacity, which is now becoming an even bigger threat to America, it allies, and the world. According to former US intelligence chief James Clapper, North Korea, after restarting one of its reactors, could soon have enough plutonium for nuclear weapons. Meanwhile, the country is making progress in developing its intercontinental ballistic missile (ICBM) system. In February 2016, Clapper told the Senate Armed Services Committee that North Korea was committed to developing a long-range, nuclear-armed missile "capable of posing a direct threat to the United States." [107] At the April 2016 Nuclear Security Summit in Washington, former US president Barack Obama warned the world of the possibility of nuclear weapons and that the IS could acquire material for a dirty bomb. [108] This is when the clash of Western and Islamic civilizations could become a reality—namely, when North Korea or any other rogue state decides to sell nuclear material to Muslim terrorists as an act of desperation, for animosity against America, or for financial reward to overcome crippling economic sanctions.

The clash of civilizations could also become a reality when a powerful nation follows a sinister leader who uses religious-nationalistic slogans as motivation for designating enemies and justifying their destruction. We should remember that, throughout history, the clash of civilizations has always been one of the primary causes of the rise and fall of empires. Religion, nationalism, and economic expansion are behind past and current empires, and religious nationalism is a major cause of killing and destruction. [109]

The silent majority desperately needs to awaken in order to avoid a major conflict that could engulf entire societies of the world as a consequence of the rise of far-right movements, especially because of their promotion of bigotry and hatred against minority groups because of their race, religion, and color of their skin. As always happens, the grounds for bigotry and hatred are ignorance and lack of compassion, both of which engender a feeling of resentment and retaliation across society and the world. At an individual level, such bigotry denies people their civil rights and dignity and the chance to reach their full potential. The world should be able to conclude that equality for all as a foundation of human relationships is better than division that is engendered by the backwardness of religious nationalism and ethnic nationalism. Evolutionary social diversity is a reality and is here to stay. The alternative is ethnic cleansing or, ultimately, the genocide of minority groups.

We should remember that far-rightists—as has happened before—typically categorize ethnic and religious groups within their own society and the world in descending order, in which their focus is first on the lowest end of the scale, then on the second lowest, and so on. The world has rejected this concept before and should do the same again. We should also remember that far-rightists often use fear tactics, character assassinations of opponents, and the promotion of hate. They promote ethnic nationalism and religious nationalism at the expense of others, which is a recipe for conflict. Under well-crafted banners, they promote the political idea that the origin and the faith of the group is privileged at the expense of others, which leads to the rejection of others and the spread of bigotry. This ultimately leads to dividing society by setting citizens against one another rather than uniting people for common causes. Far-right leaders pretend to have a monopoly over patriotism, good values, and good causes, when in fact their actions lead to conflicts and fragmentation of people, which retards society. With their populism, they are able to tap into worries about jobs, housing, and national identity—insecurities that have ironically emerged from the same forces that were once widely celebrated as being able to draw people together, including globalization and the digital era.

In the current state of affairs, far-rightists promote the ideas of "us versus them" and the "West versus the others." These ideas are expressed well in Michael Dibdin's 1994 novel, *Dead Lagoon*: "There can be no true friends without true enemies. Unless we hate what we are not, we cannot love what we are. There are the old truths we are painfully rediscovering after a century and more of sentimental cant. Those who deny them deny their family, their heritage, their culture, their birthrights, their very selves! They will not [be] lightly forgiven." According to Samuel Huntington, statesmen and scholars cannot ignore the unfortunate truth in these old truths. For people who seek identity and to reinvent ethnicity, enemies are essential, and most dangerous enmities occur across the fault lines between the world's major civilizations. [110]

Huntington's book *The Clash of Civilizations and the Remaking of World Order* is essential reading for every civilized person who is interested in saving humanity from the destructive fragmentation of the world. Zbigniew Brzezinski, the former national security adviser in the Carter administration, wrote in the book's foreword:

In truth, *The Clash of Civilizations and the Remaking of World Order* represented in its policy implications a grand warning. Almost a decade before 9/11, Huntington's message was that in today's politically awakened world, our consciousness of several civilizations' mandates requires—as nuclear weapons with their unprecedented scale of danger already require—that we rely on cross civilizational coalitions based on reciprocal rationality, respect, and restraint in order to manage the relations between nations. Thus Huntington's work is not only intellectually pioneering; it dares to be politically wise. [111]

In promoting Western civilization as superior to other civilizations, far-right religious nationalists ignore the fact that the cultures and values of Europe and North America—being immigrant or imperialistic countries—have absorbed other cultures and other cultures' values in their own cultures through numerous exchanges. Far-right religious nationalists also ignore the fact that Western civilization is fragmented and is now in decline while others, especially many Asian civilizations, are in a state of revival. People who identify themselves by ancestry, language, and customs are looking backward into the narrow tribal system of identity by ethnic and cultural groupings. It is understandable that the resurgence of far-right religious nationalists was a response to Islamic terrorism, but the world, I hope, is now more aware that Islamic terrorism wasn't born in a vacuum. Rather, it is a consequence of imperialistic input, which can be solved when both sides become more tolerant and adopt secularism as a guide to their societies instead of fueling each other's reactions. When both sides, Christians and Muslims, adopt religious education that conditions their populations from childhood onward, antagonistic societies are created, together with the associated conflicts. When children are growing up, they should be mentally equipped with a wide perspective of knowledge to enable them to make appropriate and objective judgments about many aspects of life. Instilling religion in the mind of a child is a form of brainwashing and indoctrination that can cloud the child's thinking for the rest of his or her life.

In my book *Death by Choice versus Religious Dogma* (2012), I wrote the following:

Religion traps people in the box of subjectivity at an early age. This makes it difficult for the less-informed people to become free thinkers. Setting oneself free from something one didn't choose in the first place requires deep thinking. It is ultimately the individual's knowledge, self-analysis, and critical thinking that can get him or her out of the box to freedom.

To achieve their objectives, religious leaders employ mass psychology and brainwashing techniques on their constituency. They indoctrinate children early, when they are most susceptible, especially through the taxpayer-subsidized religious schools, which enjoy tax-exempt status. This is how the leaders ensure the continuity of their enterprise. Their strategy of indoctrinating children can be highlighted by the remarks attributed to Ignatius Loyola, the founder of the Jesuits, five hundred years ago, who said, "Give me the child for seven years and I will give [you] the man." [112]

To avoid the consequences of the clash of civilizations and to provide a chance for a **universal civilization*** to emerge—or at least for multiple civilizations to live in peace with one another—a starting point should be the adoption of secular education throughout the world. This may sound overly idealistic at present, but in a world that is flush with nuclear weapons capable of the total destruction of the planet, what chance does humanity have other than to adopt wisdom as a guide to survival? The other aspect that should be examined to soften world conflicts includes making a genuine commitment to the principles of free trade and globalization, which would diminish the need for militarism and imperialism and would reduce the impact of nationalism. The three elements of imperialism, religion, and nationalism are the main causes of conflict in the world; the way to reduce their combined impact is to consider them the axis of evil that is destroying the world and threatening the survival of humanity.

*** Universal civilization**: The West developed the idea of Western civilization as an extension of its military, political, and economic domination during the nineteenth and twentieth centuries. In the twenty-first century, however, the imposition of Western civilization on other civilizations has become unacceptable, especially with the adoption of free-trade and globalization principles, which have made the world a global village and individuals world citizens. All societies in the world share certain common basic values and ideas—morality, good and evil, social structure, and giving everyone a fair shot—that have existed in various human civilizations throughout history, even when not in contact with one another. The idea of a universal civilization implies the cultural coming together of humanity and an increased acceptance of common values, beliefs, practices, institutions, and schools of thoughts by people all over the world. The idea of the "citizen of the world" is a consequence of the astounding impact of technological advancement and changes in social attitudes that have made the people of the world come together regardless of religion, cultures, or beliefs. [113, 114]

The world is well aware that Western values can also be measured by the killing and displacing of millions of civilians throughout the Middle East and elsewhere while the West hides its real motives for promoting its hard power in adopting the clash of civilizations as a motto in dealing with others. The use of hard power is counterproductive to the needs of humanity, who can survive only by embracing the soft power of all civilized countries to elevate the developing and the less developed countries to a standard befitting human progress and dignity rather than to a standard that leads to killings and destruction. Western countries can achieve such a world by embracing and promoting the abandonment of religious nationalism and by spreading the idea of secular education to all parts of the world. This cannot succeed without the Western world setting the example by avoiding double standards and becoming a model for other countries to follow. A starting point should be enforcing the idea of free education for every child as a human-rights issue. Western countries should also stop subsidizing religious schools at the expense of public schools, a situation that results in negative outcomes for their own countries, partly by entrenching religious dogmas and **metaphysics.****

** **Metaphysics** is a type of philosophy that attempts to use a broad concept to define reality and our understanding of it. Generally, metaphysics seeks to explain those elements and features of reality that are not easily discovered or experienced in our daily lives and that are beyond the physical world and our immediate senses. It uses arguments based on human terms rather than logic, which is tied to human sensory perception of the objective world. It contradicts the laws of physics, which have been proved and are widely understood. [115]

In my book *Psyche and Personality* (2013), I wrote on the subject of subsidizing religious schools and the negative outcomes this has:

In pursuit of better schools, many researchers suggest the need for a major correction of the way funding is distributed. Because of the religious industry's influence on and control over politicians, Western countries are subsidizing private and religious schools at the expense of public and disadvantaged schools. As a consequence, the poor and disadvantaged schools produce less-fortunate youth [who] become unemployable and, in some instances, antisocial and criminal.

It is common that the funding system generates large differences between wealthy and impoverished groups. Private and religious schools in different countries are subsidized by taxpayers' money by different methods that are in addition to the high fees paid to schools by the wealthy parents (parents who, in many instances, claim the incurred cost against their income in their tax returns). In addition, wealthy parents use many loopholes to minimize their taxes when the rest of the population doesn't have the resources or the knowledge to do so. The wealthy also have the resources to hire private tutors, which will always give their children an educational advantage. Above all, the wealthy can nourish their children much better than the poor can nourish theirs, and nourishment is an essential element for the brain's proper development and functioning. No matter what, there will always be advantages and distinction for the rich over the poor, and this is acceptable in a capitalist system, provided that the adopted capitalist system is moderate, with a fair distribution of wealth.

In some countries, subsidy is provided by vouchers or tax credit; in other countries, all schools receive equal-per-student funding from general tax revenues. In all cases, private and religious schools are given the privilege of siphoning desperately needed funds from the public school system without offering the equal access that is the hallmark of public education...

Depriving public and disadvantaged schools proper funding makes the religious schools more attractive to wealthy parents. In the process, religion triumphs over secularism and conformism over individualism; as a result, the kids are exposed to brainwashing. Ultimately, the country ends up inhibiting children's creativity and enlightenment, especially by promoting creationism over science. At the heart of the problem is the violation of the secular system of government, in which the church and state are to be separate. [116]

Civilized countries, in applying their soft power and without being perceived as hypocritical, can influence backward-looking countries, especially in those countries where politics and religion are inseparable, through foreign aid that can be used as a prerequisite for secular education. Donor countries can achieve this by taking direct control of the money and resources they donate, instead of donating to corrupt governments. The biggest help Western countries can give to poor and developing countries is to build schools, supply teachers, and build infrastructure. Most of the foreign aid that is currently provided is government-to-government aid, which is mainly aimed at domination, goodwill, and the promotion of trade ties for the eventual benefit of the donor country. Often the donor country doesn't take into consideration whether the aid is directed toward military purposes or to prop up a corrupt regime. [117]

Removing the direct influence that dogmatic religious leaders have in conditioning children with mythology and superstition rather than reasoning and analysis, especially at an early age, is an essential step toward lessening the possibility of producing a religiously fanatic generation. It is inevitable that secular education, civilization, and the sophistication of people can sufficiently increase the level of political awareness to enable society to counter and prevent the political system from being exploited and influenced by these divisive religious interests. [118] Unfortunately, this is not what has happened, since the world has moved from being multipolar to bipolar and then to having a single superpower (the United States). This has created the false feeling that Christian America now dominates the world and can, through its military might, reach whatever goals it wants to reach.

In reality, however, America as a single superpower is only a temporary situation that has stimulated other countries to form other alliances as a countermeasure for their own survival. We can see this on the world stage by the evolving alliance between Russia and China, which is a direct reaction to the American strategic policies of encircling Russia and containing China. I should mention that during the bipolar-world era, the globe was divided by politics and economics rather than by the civilizational aspect. It was a conflict between capitalism and socialism and was laced with religious flavor. In contrast, in the post–Cold War world, the conflict still revolves around politics and economics, especially the control of the world and its resources, and is laced with cultural and religious flavors. This situation is likely what prompted the United States to create the slogan of the clash of civilizations. To promote Western civilization as superior to other civilizations is to lay the foundation for a never-ending war of civilizations, especially against Islamic civilization, that will have no winner but rather may end with mutual destruction. America and its allies, blinded by their religious nationalism, have lost sight of the fact that any anti-Islamic sentiments that nationalist Western politicians spout are gifts that IS terrorists use as propaganda and recruiting tools in their fight against the West.

Furthermore, Western civilization is made up of conflicting cultural and religious groupings that were at war in the not-too-distant past, especially when we consider the many wars between Protestant, Catholic, and Orthodox Christians, all of whom claim to be superior to the others. Based on the principle of hatred and bigotry being hierarchical, it is not beyond the imagination that renewed Christian hostilities have the potential to erupt, to the point where Christians would be tearing themselves apart.

America's promotion of the clash-of-civilizations idea is a sign of its decline. The nation is using the slogan as a last resort in the hope of arresting its decline and reviving its dying culture, which is plagued with a huge public debt, antidemocratic practices (with its elections being hijacked by money and vested interests), racism, drug use, crime and violence, inequality in health care and education, and so on. Besides its internal problems, in promoting the idea of the clash of civilizations, America is ignoring the fact that in a multicultural world, subjective identity can lead only to discrimination and conflict, neither of which is beneficial to society or the world. They become a catalyst in the fragmentation and destruction, especially in a world that is cursed with all kinds of weapons, including WMD.

In *The Clash of Civilizations and the Remaking of World Order*, Huntington wrote the following:

> In 1917, as a result of the Russian Revolution, the conflict of nation states was supplemented by the conflict of ideologies, first among fascism, communism, and liberal democracy and then between the latter two. In the Cold War these ideologies were embodied in the two superpowers, each of which defined its identity by its ideology and neither of which was a nation state in the traditional European sense. The coming of power of Marxism first in Russia and then China and Vietnam represented a transition phase from the European international system to [a] post-European multicivilizational system. Marxism was a product of

European civilization, but it neither took root nor succeeded there. Instead modernizing and revolutionary elites imported it into non-Western societies; Lenin, Mao, and Ho adapted it to their purpose and used it to challenge Western power, to mobilize their people, and to assert the national identity and autonomy of their countries against the West. The collapse of this ideology in the Soviet Union and its substantial adaptation in China and Vietnam does not, however, necessarily mean that these societies will import the other Western ideology of liberal democracy. Westerners who assume that it does are likely to be surprised by the creativity, resilience, and individuality of non-Western cultures. [119]

Western elites delude people into believing they are civilizing the world by exporting Western democracy and values to the world, even if occasionally through the barrel of a gun, as happened in Iraq, Libya, and Afghanistan. The delusion is continuing despite people becoming aware that the Western way of life and values cannot be exported, because they embody culture and religion. Although values relate to culture (including both desirable and undesirable human behavior, such as human aggression), they are generally universal, and no one civilization has a monopoly over them. The promotion of someone's values versus others' values is often associated with prejudice and in attempts to exclude and discriminate against others. Besides, the West cannot convince the people of the world of its cultural superiority when Western culture and values may also be measured by the killing, destruction, and displacing of millions of civilians throughout the world (while the West has hidden its real motives) and the notion that imperialism is the outcome of excessive greed.

In my book *Thorny Opinion* (2008), I wrote the following:

> There is no other reason, as no single group or nation has a monopoly over good or evil (or the good, the bad, and the ugly), which are the common denominators of all cultures. The only variance is the degree of emphasis on some aspects of behavior in different cultures, relevant to social conditioning, which is impacted upon by knowledge, experience, and reasoning.
>
> The majority of nations have developed identical cultures in human relations, especially in mateship, easygoing attitude, generosity, tolerance, friendliness, fairgo, and so on…Some people seem to claim their own, when in actual fact, these principles are common around the world. [120]

The hope is that, through secular education and enlightenment, ethnic and religious nationalism can be subdued as a consequence of accepting social diversity. A few signs do indicate the world is moderating, despite the fact that some countries display superiority and arrogance toward other countries. This moderation has come about because of the gradual impact of globalization and free trade on international relations, which has led to the diminishment of negative forms of nationalism. This situation occurs when genuine globalization and free-trade dynamics are driven by people, technology, and immigration, all of which lead to a lessening of politicians' influence and control over the economic management and economic sovereignty of their countries, because the economic outcome is then decided by international agreements between participating countries. Economic outcomes in turn influence social outcomes, which diminishes government manipulation and control over many aspects of the lives of a country's citizens.

Common sense dictates that the embrace and entrenchment of balanced globalization and free trade as guiding principles for international relations will have a positive outcome. Patriotism based on national identity will also be embraced, while ethnic and religious nationalism will gradually diminish. The latter will be overshadowed by common purpose and mutual benefit, especially when wise nations start to elect wise and moderate leaders who have the capacity to cooperate and compromise in order to put the world economy on a growth path rather than live in conflict and stagnation. Wise and moderate leaders understand that treating people as equals makes them fight for peace and harmony, while despising them makes them fight for survival and their dignity.

It should not escape the world's attention that the cause of most conflicts is a combination of indoctrination and conditioning by opportunistic religious and political leaders in their quest for power and glory. Misinformed and insecure people, or the groups that constitute the power bases of their leaders, are at the heart of the problem. Following dubious leaders who use religion and nationalism as motivation to designate enemies is the main ingredient for the current clash of civilizations. Throughout history, the clash of civilizations was one of the main causes behind the rise and fall of empires. Religion, nationalism, and economic expansion are behind past and current empires, and religious nationalism is a major cause for killings and destruction. To prevent a major catastrophe, all that is required for peace and harmony to prevail is the entrenchment of secularism (or at least the benign interpretation of religious texts) or, for the enlightened citizens of the world, to totally reject religious nationalism. Religious nationalism can lead only to vendettas, hatred, and warfare. Because the emergence of a universal religion is highly unlikely while the resurgence of religious fundamentalism is dominant, the other option is for the world to promote universal atheism, which can be achieved by the further separation of religion from state. With the entrenchment of science through education and scientific discoveries, the world is gradually moving away from dogmatic beliefs, which is causing a decline in religion and a rise in atheism. The statistics Huntington refers to in *The Clash of Civilizations and the Remaking of World Order* indicate that a trend is underway: the number of people classified as "nonreligious" and "atheist" rose from .02 percent in 1900 to 20.9 percent in 1980. [121] This trend was also reflected in the 2016 Australian census, released in July 2017, which indicated that the number of nonreligious people and atheists had increased to 30 percent of the Australian population. Australia may be considered typical of other Anglo-Saxon countries. [122] The shift could happen only through the spreading of modernization and urbanization; increasing levels of literacy, education, wealth, and social mobilization; and more complex and diversified occupational structures. This shift is a product of the tremendous expansion of scientific and engineering knowledge, beginning in the eighteenth century, which made it possible for humans to control and shape their environment in unprecedented ways. [123]

If we observe the period immediately following the Cold War, we will see that the world had high expectations and optimism that humanity was heading toward peace and harmony. This was soon discovered to be an illusion, however, when America's extreme capitalism and religious nationalism prepared for a major assault, with the desire to dominate the world by its hard power rather than its soft power. The triumph of Western democratic ideology over socialist dictatorship gave the illusion that Western civilization would become a universal civilization that could be imposed on the world by any possible means. In the process, America and its Western allies failed to consider that universal civilization means something to Westerners but means imperialism to others, which has led to the resistance the world is now witnessing.

The world of peace and harmony was a dream rather than a reality, a dream that was destroyed by the hawkish neoconservatives who drove America into the new cycle of hegemony.

In *The Clash of Civilizations*, Huntington also wrote the following in a section titled "Two Worlds: Us and Them":

While one-world expectations appear at the end of major conflicts, the tendency to think in terms of two worlds recurs throughout human history. People are always tempted to divide people into us and them, the in-group and the other, our civilization and those of barbarians. Scholars have analyzed the world in terms of the Orient and the Occident, North and South, center and periphery. Muslims have traditionally divided the world into *Dar al-Islam* and *Dar al-Harb*, the abode of peace and the abode of war. This distinction was reflected, and in a sense reversed, at the end of the Cold War by American scholars who divided the world into "zones of peace" and "zones of turmoil." The former included the West and Japan with about 15 percent of the world's population, the latter everyone else. [124]

I should add that people who promote the concept of an "us versus them" world and the superiority of Western civilization will turn against one another, as has happened earlier in history, especially during the European Christian and nationalistic wars for power between Protestant, Catholic, and Orthodox Christians and between European empires. This is simply because superiority is subjective and hierarchical.

With the sort of division that American hawks advocate, the world is condemned to ongoing conflict for many decades to come unless a new set of pragmatic and humanitarian leaders emerge in the West, especially in America, to guide the world into real peace and harmony. Such a leader should be psychologically strong (in order to stand up to the lobbying power of vested interests) and able to adopt a mission of changing the country, especially its economic system of extreme capitalism, into a moderate form of capitalism to subdue America's expansionist policies and its unlimited national interests. Needless to say, American-style extreme capitalism, which is driven by extreme greed, has contributed to an increase in anarchy within America and throughout the world, especially from creating poorer people within the nation and failed states across many parts of the world. The world is waiting for the emergence of such leaders who are capable of changing America from a hard power into a soft power, a country that uses military force for deterrence rather than as a force of aggression to dominate the world by bombarding, bullying, threatening, or intimidating weaker countries, including its allies. America needs to learn there is an alternative to the clash of civilizations and the subsequent threat to world peace: the peaceful exchange and tolerance of other civilizations.

If wisdom prevails, America can resume its lost leadership of the world by adopting diplomacy in its relations with other countries instead of using heavy-handedness and bullying. Hard power and tough talk can never substitute for using a rational, mutually beneficial, and balanced approach to resolving legitimate grievances by dialogue and negotiations. To achieve moral leadership of the world, America should first embrace genuine free trade and globalization to bring poorer countries into the twenty-first century; doing so will create and strengthen the middle class and convert more people into consumers instead of exploiting them to become the enemy. As another starting point, America and its European allies should lift their protectionist practices and heavy subsidies of agriculture, which prevent poorer countries from trading their most viable commodities.

To achieve economic leadership of the world, America must understand that the economic development of poorer countries is the key to the world's prosperity as a whole. Furthermore, from economic development springs intellectuals and the middle class, which then become the anchor of future democracies in developing and poor countries rather than from the imposition of corrupt regimes to serve imperialistic interests. The exploitation of poorer countries does not stack up against the principle of globalization and free trade, which is based on science, innovation, rationalization, efficiency, and universality. The principle of balanced globalization and free trade, if allowed to flourish, could have a tangible benefit to all countries as a result of the world's economic growth, which could be generated by raising the living standards of poorer countries. The other advantage would be the integration and synchronization of world economies, which could bring the world together to overcome the prevailing destructive fragmentation.

The other aspect for America to become the moral leader of the world is to abandon its obvious hypocrisy in supporting brutal regimes that contravene human rights while it claims to be the champion of democracy and human rights. We cannot be blind to this fact when we consider that America's closest allies in the Middle East are oppressive regimes and human-rights violators such as Saudi Arabia, Turkey, Egypt, Israel, and so on. It also flies in the face of America's claim to the world's moral leadership and for its promotion of Western civilization when America itself tortures prisoners and shuttles them around the world to be tortured. Its hypocrisy could not be clearer in demanding that other countries except for Israel respect nuclear nonproliferation treaties.

Finally, to achieve peace and harmony in the world, America needs to abandon the idea of building an American Christian empire through the destruction of culture and the identity of Islam, which can be seen from the many wars in recent history, most of which have been fought against Islamic countries. These wars have contributed to radical Sunni counterculture revivalism, which is being spearheaded by Islamic jihadi terrorist organizations.

Under the banner of the clash of civilizations, America is targeting many Islamic countries for the sake of its own expansion, which has created many failed states as a result of the killings and destruction. The unintended consequences of this are as follows. First, it sows the seeds for the further spread of Islamic militants' revenge as a reaction to their helplessness and misery. Second, the clash of civilizations is not helping America prosper; rather, it will cause America to decline as it gets into debt to fight unnecessary wars. In his book *Rise and Fall of the Great Powers*, British historian Paul Kennedy describes how, over the past five hundred years, nations that became great powers declined as their growth rate slowed yet their spending on defense continued to increase. The decline can be either eased or worsened by smart or stupid policy decisions. He provides convincing evidence that wars are won by economic might and because providence is on the side of the good guys. All empires are mortal and kill themselves by economic overextension. This is why American deficit spending will become a major problem in the future. [125]

Other than its confrontation with Islam, America also needs to abandon the idea of confrontation between it, as the ruling power, and the other rising world powers because the modern confrontation has the potential for the deployment of nuclear weapons that could make the planet uninhabitable to any power. The old cycle of hegemony is no longer applicable in the twenty-first century, when only the principle of coexistence should apply.

As it stands, America is in desperate need of a leader who is capable of adopting the principles of "prevention is better than the cure" and "win-win" rather than "winner takes all" in dealing with conflicts between civilizations in the hope that these principles may achieve peace and harmony in the world. This may lead to a genuine universal civilization, complete with its diversity and tolerance. America needs a leader who understands that military power can bring fear and destroy people, but fear can drive people by triggering their survival instinct to fight. And, as stated earlier, America needs a leader who understands that influence—not power—is ultimately the most valuable strategy, because influence comes through generosity of the spirit, which reaps greater gains. The use of power, on the other hand, results in resentment and counteraction, which ultimately weaken and destroy the aggressor. Such a leader will matter to the world, because individuals in history do matter.

CHAPTER 3

Summary and Possible Solutions

•••

THE ANALYSES IN THIS BOOK aim to provide space for a moderate point of view that has been narrowed by well-crafted propaganda, the prevailing mainstream-media messages, and politicians who get elected to serve vested interests. It is always my intention to highlight problems associated with terrorism, imperialism, and injustice when, as is often the case, the solutions to many problems in the world are in the hands of the powerful and the wise. As we may presently observe, however, the most internationally powerful among us do not always behave wisely and indeed appear to be infected by their corrosive and addictive power. Despite humanity's progress, the world is now governed by immoderation, which is reflected in violent actions and counteractions. The aggressive approach is currently dictated by the far-right fringe groups who are in control of the political agenda. This situation happened only because of the weakness or silence of moderating forces to achieve a desperately needed balance, both locally and internationally.

I have written this work in the belief that the political system is rigged. Corporate cash has flooded the political system, drowning out the voices of everyday people. A nexus is growing among those who are economically disadvantaged—who feel racially or religiously motivated resentment—that is overwhelming all political and international expectations. People see great wealth amassed around them in big corporations and billionaires' pockets, while they are increasingly locked out of good education, social mobility, and meaningful work. Many of them are demonized for being disadvantaged. Many families struggle with two jobs, only to fail to make ends meet. Many are angry, resentful, and ready to lash out at a political system they feel has deserted them.

Under extreme capitalism, the only voices that are heard are the powerful vested interests—the billionaires and huge corporations that are exploiting the broken political system to buy special favors and undue influence. For its expansionist nature, extreme capitalism is becoming one of the main causes of imperialism, as well as the reaction to imperialism. The only cure for extreme capitalism and corporate power is people power—that is, when the silent majority sheds its political apathy and becomes as vocal as the influential minority.

The following is a summary of some of the most critical topics that must be remedied in order to bring about peace, coexistence, moderation, and justice to secure the future of the generations who will follow.

THE US, ISRAEL, AND ISLAMIC TERRORISM

As chapters 1 and 2 of this work have shown, the United States made a mistake by expanding the war on terror—including the war in Iraq—before securing and stabilizing the Afghanistan front and completing the reconstruction of that country. It also erred by not moving toward solving the Palestinian-Israeli conflict—a situation that could have been resolved by establishing a viable Palestinian state. Both mistakes led to an increase in Islamic terrorism and became the other side of the Islamic terrorism story. The result of American and Israeli actions has been the creation of the IS and other Islamic terrorist groups who are more fanatical about Islam and more extreme than al-Qaeda and are now out of control. Terrorists employ fear as a weapon in the most potent way. They use shock and random violence to create psychological fear that exceeds the actual threat posed by their capability. One of their aims, which they are succeeding at, is to create conflict between Muslim and non-Muslim societies; this conflict is helping them in recruiting jihadists from around the world. Because of the decentralization of al-Qaeda, many of the cells of these fanatical groups are spreading throughout the Islamic and Western worlds, especially after their defeat in Iraq and Syria.

The threat they pose to the world with their barbarism has provided the justification for Western countries to kill more Muslims and to encourage Muslims to kill their fellow Muslims, which is a delusional process the West and Israel have stoked to weaken Islam in the hope that the strategy could eventually lead to Islam's self-destruction. The ambitious aim of far-right Zionists and fundamentalist Christians instead might lead to mutually assured destruction as a consequence of the never-ending cycle of violence.

The savage tactics of the Islamist terrorists must awaken America and its Western allies to the danger of provoking religious war under the banner of the clash of civilizations; such a war can never end, especially if it is aimed at 1.7 billion people. What the world is now witnessing is the consequence of the American military interventions that are embroiling the region in sectarian and tribal violence. From the time of starting the fight against terrorism, America and its allies have produced no positive results for the world except for the decentralization of terrorist groups and the spread of violent killings and destruction to many parts of the Islamic world. This destruction will not produce any positive outcome until the underlying problems are resolved, as follows:

First, in formulating its policies, America should stop listening to the far-right Zionists who control its foreign policy and its key institutions, including the financial sector and the media. It is a simple fact that the loyalty of far-right Zionists is divided between America and Israel, and the interests of America and Israel are not always in sync. This is exactly what happened in the invasion of Iraq, when America not only lost many of its soldiers but also incurred massive debt, caused turmoil in the region, and created many enemies who are now causing its decline. Satisfying the far-right Israeli government's desire to grab Palestinian land is fraught with danger, especially when Israel will stop at nothing—including apartheid, ethnic cleansing, and the killing of women and children—to achieve a Zionist project that is driven by its religious nationalism and is causing injustices and a corresponding Islamic backlash.

Second, in the new world of globalization and free trade, disturbing the balance of power in any backward or tribal country or region is an out-of-date imperialistic method that was used for the purpose of dividing and conquering. In addition, installing puppet regimes by imposing false democracy through the barrel of a gun to serve American strategic interests produces corrupt governments. This happens because of the knowledge of their temporary existence, as often happens when America replaces one puppet regime with another whenever it suits the immediacy of its strategic interests. In the process, short-term government elites gain the incentive to enrich themselves by stealing the nation's wealth as quickly as possible. This, in turn, impoverishes the country's citizens and creates resentful, impoverished people who lose hope and become desperate, with nothing left to do but fight for survival. These people usually turn against whoever is causing their plight. They often turn to religion and weapons as their only hope for their final salvation, which makes them the target of recruitment by religious fanatics; they then become martyrs on the promise of having a rewarding afterlife. History shows that fighting a nationalistic or religious war with an enemy who doesn't play by the rules of warfare is futile. Anybody who expects a victory from such a war will wait for a long time. America should use wisdom to advance its strategic interests rather than use force in its endeavors to exploit other nations; it is better to give these nations something back to satisfy their needs. Robbing the people's wealth and oppressing, dividing, and impoverishing them as part of American economic expansion and world domination cannot succeed. American leaders must examine the history of the rise and fall of empires before they repeat the mistakes of the past.

Third, America's woes are self-inflicted by its one-sided and expansionist ambitions to control the world and its resources by using all possible means, including religious war. Adding to America's woes is the decline in its future productivity as a result of its massive debt. Aggressive colonial expansion requires large amounts of financial support and manpower capacity to counter the equally large resentment and resistance it generates. The United States, in its use of power in Iraq, Pakistan, Libya, Syria, and Afghanistan, where it has heavily relied on its air force instead of its ground troops, failed to account for the extent of revolt and resistance that power would generate, especially because of the collateral damage and human casualties that occurred. The United States also failed to account for the need to protect the civilian population, which has resulted in great loss of life and has created large numbers of vengeful enemies. Its brutal approach has caused many casualties and the devastation of other nations' infrastructure and institutions. In the name of fighting terrorism—while hiding its ambition of economic expansion and the control of world resources—America has engaged in the slaughter of many innocent people.

Fourth, the American administration should stop listening to the army generals. Military culture and its history are based on attacking other nations and winning or losing wars rather than defending America. The military establishment is not a pacifist organization; it knows one thing only: war. The army, being the core of the American military complex, is designed to fight on many fronts around the world and has developed strategies for the encirclement of Russia and the containment of China, both of which are far beyond the country's military and financial capacity. America's current policies of containing China, installing a protective shield in South Korea, and arming Taiwan are the opposite of its old approach of engaging China economically and diplomatically to draw it away from Russia. On the other side of the equation, the current American policy of encircling and antagonizing Russia has become the catalyst in bringing the two giants of China and Russia together, which will be impossible for America to deal with. [1] Although the military complex, in the short term, is making money for America by militarizing and selling arms to the world, the nation's military wing is becoming a major financial imposition on the American economy and is one of the causes of America's decline. Using force to subjugate other nations—instead of employing diplomacy—to establish American hegemony is an outdated method that creates many enemies and makes America vulnerable. Its constant use of hard power instead of soft power is the main reason that so many enemies who are committed to its destruction have been created. America's military will stop at nothing to widen America's sphere of influence, and for short-term gain, they lose their moral compass and often employ their motto of "Shoot now and discuss later." Most of the time, their hasty actions are followed by unintended consequences. The American army generals are part of the nation's military complex, which has arms-manufacturing industries all over America. It has tremendous political clout, especially when congresspeople are obliged to protect these industries. This is another reason why America's own false democracy—controlled by lobby groups and money—is a curse not only for America but also for the rest of the world. It constantly leads to an arms race and an agitation for wars to facilitate its arms sales. Accordingly, we may conclude that the military is spearheading America's state terrorism and, as a reaction, it is one of the main reasons for the spread of Islamic terrorism. This fact in itself is sufficient for awakening America's allies to their blind alliance with an imperialistic country that can discard them when they reach their "use-by" date.

Fifth, as stated in chapters 1 and 2, adopting a moderate form of capitalism to curb the need for expansionist and imperialistic foreign policies and encouraging secular education and a secular system of government throughout the world are becoming key elements in avoiding the total fragmentation of the world. Without the engagement and activism of the middle class and the intelligentsia of the civilized countries to curtail the influence of ultracapitalists and fanatical religious leaders on politics, the world will be heading toward a catastrophic clash of civilizations. It is necessary for civilized countries to be a beacon for other countries by avoiding accusations of hypocrisy, especially regarding secular education.

To encourage Islamic countries to remove religious schools' influence on people—the main source of radicalization and terrorism—while Western countries do not do the same can be construed as hypocrisy. In both cases, religious dogmas are entrenched in a culture that feeds on the clash of civilizations, which is detrimental to world peace and coexistence.

Removing the direct influence of dogmatic religious leaders on conditioning children with mythology and superstition rather than reasoning and analysis, especially at an early age, is an essential step toward lessening the possibility of producing religiously fanatic generations in the world. It is inevitable that secular education, civilization, and the sophistication of people can sufficiently increase the level of political awareness to enable society to counter and prevent the political system from being exploited and influenced by these divisive religious interests.

Combating Terrorism

The world would be better off by fighting not only terrorism but also the *causes* of terrorism; the Western world thus far has glossed over its own role in provoking terrorism and in arming terrorists and potential terrorists. The clash of civilizations will continue, and the fight against terrorism will not be won, until the civilized nations of the world recognize their role in the conflict and abandon the outdated tribalistic methods of controlling the world by force and by bullying allies to join in. Doing so will be necessary as long as the world is flooded with weapons that often change hands and end up in the hands of terrorists. The modern world needs to operate on a mutually beneficial platform instead of an imperialistic model. To avoid backlashes and unintended consequences, we should always keep in mind Newton's third law of physics: "For every action, there is an equal and opposite reaction."

After the fuse was lit by encouraging religious warfare between Sunnis and Shiites, one solution could be for America and its allies to stop supplying weapons to any of the warring factions and to step back and let the fire burn itself out. In a few decades, the warring factions will be exhausted, and the region will be stable and move forward in a normal way. For the West to step back from the turmoil, it must invest in developing alternative sources of energy rather than depending on Middle Eastern and North African oil. The West must also acknowledge that Islamic terrorism is inflamed by Western military interventions and by giving Israel a free hand in its atrocities against the Palestinians. The turmoil in the Middle East and North Africa does have a few solutions. The first is for America and its allies to stop killing Muslims, destroying their institutions, destroying their countries' infrastructures, and displacing their people. The second is for America and its allies to ensure that, after the destruction is finished but before withdrawing their forces, they have a plan in place for reconstruction, especially for the restoration of the disturbed balance of power in the country. Third is for America to ensure that a two-state solution is implemented, which can happen only (1) when America realizes that Israel is not a strategic asset but a liability and (2) when the Western nations stop simply complaining about Israel's atrocities against the Palestinians and instead take urgent positive steps toward a two-state solution.

It is time to realize that the war on terror is not going to end. Instead, it is spreading by further decentralization and will get worse because of the next generations of oppressed, displaced, impoverished, uneducated, and unemployed people who will have nothing left and who will have no hope but to turn to violence, especially when driven by an ideology that will be impossible to defeat. Radicalization will continue while the focus is on only fighting terrorism instead of preventing it, especially when, as they say, prevention is always better than the cure. For terrorism to be prevented, the cause of radicalization must first be removed; second, the people must be empowered with correct knowledge to avoid the brainwashing of people with evil ideologies, especially the youth. It is essential for young people to be given the opportunity to reach their potential and to be employed and not discriminated against.

Ultimately, to defeat terrorism, the moderate countries, especially America's allies, need to understand that their first mission is to resist the threat, intimidation, and the bullying of a major imperialistic country that gives them the feeling of "If you're not with us, you're against us." America is also giving them the false feeling of being protected as a reward for belonging to its camp or being under its umbrella. The whole world should understand that the next war will be a nuclear war and that the planet will turn into radioactive ash. No country will be in a position to protect other countries, no matter how many missiles an imperialistic country can fire or how many very expensive antimissile shields it has or can sell to its gullible allies. The moderate Western countries should by now be aware that an imperialistic country is blinded by excessive greed and the desire to control the world and its resources by any possible means, which in the process will cause the leaders of such a country to lose their moral compass by engaging in killings and the destruction of those countries that own the resources. This is the main cause of the terrorism that is engulfing the world; its first and most accessible targets are the moderate Western countries, especially the Europeans, whose leaders are unwittingly aligned with imperialist America under the banner of the clash of civilizations. Under this banner, America is happily militarizing the world to protect its military complex while at the same time acting as a protection racket by seeking protection contributions from its allies.

As for the Islamic terrorists, while they're happily wearing the badge of terrorist by meeting their objective of terrorizing, they should instead be called "psychotic pigs" and be treated accordingly. They are using Islam as a tool to recruit an army of disenfranchised, alienated, and despised Muslims to commit crimes on their behalf. This is no different from the tactics of neo-Nazis, the Ku Klux Klan, or other white supremacists in mobilizing Christians against black people, Jews, and Muslims. These groups are emboldened by America's slogan of the clash of civilizations in its war against Muslims—a war that will have no winners. It should not escape the world's notice that these groups—as history shows—will eventually take aim at Jews and other minorities as further targets. This is similar to the way the Nazis categorized people hierarchically, with the Aryan race placed at the top of the pyramid.

At this stage of our analysis, it is appropriate to stimulate further discussion between readers in posing this question: if terrorists should be assigned the derogatory Islamic title of "psychotic pigs," shouldn't the tag of "terrorism" then be preserved as a badge of honor for state terrorists? Any country that engages in terrorizing other countries into submission for the purpose of domination and exploitation should be tagged accordingly and should become the subject of isolation and boycotts until it changes its behavior and denounces state terrorism. The United Nations as a whole—not just its Security Council—should have the final say in listing and eventually delisting any country that engages in state terrorism. The Security Council, with its key members having the power of veto, is undemocratic and cannot make objective decisions. Because the veto power is in the hands of past, current, and future imperialistic powers, the axis of the destructive cycle of hegemony cannot be classified as democratic. In contrast, the UN organization, with its purpose of protecting the essential sovereignty of nations, large and small, is more democratically structured; moderate and minority voices can be heard when formulating world opinion.

Accordingly, America (or any other imperialistic country) should be subjected to the scrutiny of world opinion if it uses unnecessary force that directly or indirectly causes the destruction of a defenseless nation and the killing of civilians for the purpose of subjugation or for the expansion of the sphere of influence by military means.

Finally, in discussing the subject of combating terrorism, it is necessary to refer to a March 2007 report to Congress entitled "Combating Terrorism: The Challenge of Measuring Effectiveness" by Raphael Perl, a specialist in international foreign affairs, defense, and trade. Perl points out a few critical points to consider, such as how to formulate and implement an antiterror strategy, how to prioritize and allocate resources, how to measure progress, and how to create a framework for measuring failure:

> Progress is possible using diverse strategies, under very different approaches. The goals of terrorists and those who combat them are often diametrically opposed, but may also be tangential, with both sides achieving objectives and making progress according to their different measurement systems...Policymakers may face consideration of the pros and cons of reallocating more of the nation's limited resources away from ongoing defensive projects and towards preventing the next quantum jump of terrorism, even if this means accepting losses.

Perl also points out that, as a practical matter, America cannot secure everything and everywhere because terrorist operations are relatively inexpensive to organize and carry out, especially compared with the damage they may inflict or the cost of trying to prevent them from happening. Consequently, spending more money may not necessarily increase security in a proportionate manner. The biggest damage terrorism inflicts is the erosion of civil liberties worldwide. [2]

In the same report, Perl wrote the following:

The phenomenon of terrorism can be seen as comprising human elements (supporters and hard core terrorists) and ideological elements. To the degree that terrorism is viewed as a process, the phenomenon is similar to a pipeline or factory assembly line with key stations along the way. The process includes ideological outreach, acquisition of funding and support, recruitment, organization, indoctrination, training, planning, targeting, attack, exploitation of results, financial rewards and other factors which lead to production of terrorist acts. Any such proposed anti-terrorism model would be adapted for specific terrorist groups, since such groups may operate differently.

A challenge facing those who seek to measure progress against terrorism is to identify critical, outcome-determining elements and assess how well they have been mitigated. Disrupting the process of terrorism as early as possible is vital, since it can eventually become an economic engine in its own right, with increasing numbers of individuals and businesses deriving financial benefits and developing vested interests.

As terrorism mutates, so must an effective response designed to counter it. Once terrorism has escalated to a higher level, a previous response may be less effective. Hence, terrorism requires a pro-active and quickly malleable policy of prevention and mitigation.

One concern is that the phenomenon of terror-ism, if not effectively challenged and disrupted, may at some point jump to become a regional or global pandemic of violence as an accepted modus operandi for social change. Yet another concern is that terror-ism will become the ballot box for the dispossessed, if the gap between the "haves and have nots" continues to widen.

Arguably therefore, it is important not only to measure where terrorism is, but also how close ter-rorists are to the next quantum jump. The potential quantum jump currently of greatest concern to many would be to WMD (chemical, biological or radiologi-cal/nuclear). In this view, a focal point of measurement would be how close the terrorists are to this next level, what it would take for them to achieve it, and how well the nation is preventing them from getting there. What are possible indicators that a quantum jump is imminent? [3]

Since the production of this report for Congress in 2007—es-pecially with its highlights of the negative psychological im-pact of terrorism on society, the cost of preventing terrorism, the erosion of civil liberties, and the degree to which terror-ists are able to radicalize and polarize Islam against the West and the West against Islam—America has continued with its heavy-handed approach to dealing with terrorism. Instead of combating radicalization, America has set out to further fuel Islamic radicalization by marginalizing and alienating Muslims throughout the world, which has resulted in moderate Muslims joining in the fight for dignity and survival or at least becoming the target for recruitment by terrorists. Here I should emphasize that bombarding cities; killing civilians; and creating poverty, unemployment, and a massive refugee problem are the best tools for Islamic radicalization and revenge. [4]

This is when the radicalization of Islamists culminates in the formation of vengeful terrorist cells. I should repeat that the best way to deal constructively with Islamic terrorism is by understanding the main points behind the potent mix, which are the core articles of faith in the religion: the blood feuds and revenge embedded in Islamic tradition and culture. Another key factor is the abuse behind the feuds, which may be found in the US military interventions and the Israeli atrocities against the Palestinians. [5]

AMERICA AND ISRAEL

The military interventions in the Middle East are greatly encouraged by pro-Israel lobby groups on the basis that the outcome will be mutually beneficial to both Israel and America. In the process, America has succumbed to the whims of Israeli settlers who have awesome power over Israel's policies and, indirectly, over America's Middle East foreign policy. The destructive activities of Israeli settlers are some of the main drivers of Islamic terrorism and the clash of civilizations. America is the only country in a position to stop the Israeli expansion of settlements on Palestinian lands. It can start by curtailing the power of the far-right, pro-Israel lobby groups in America, who are in control of its Middle Eastern foreign policy and of Congress. In defiance of Israel lobby groups, America can easily vote yes in the UN Security Council for the establishment of a viable Palestinian state that would go back to Israel's 1967 borders. This is the first step toward curbing Israeli aggression in the region, especially against its Arab neighbors. Failing that, American and Israeli interests around the world will be a constant target of Islamic insurgency. Rather than subject moderate Muslims to recruitment by the extremists, solving the Palestinian problem and controlling Israel's aggression would empower all moderate Muslims to turn against the extremist elements within their nations. As it stands, the terror network is evolving to become more creative, more flexible, and more agile, with a capacity to acquire WMD.

The suffering of the Jews during World War II should be a lesson that no nation should suffer the consequences of fascism. Israel's policy of segregation, ethnic cleansing, and the construction of the apartheid wall are no different from what happened in South Africa. In the process of implementing the Zionist project, Israel has tried to destroy the Palestinian nation, which has caused a tremendous Islamic backlash.

The use of Israel's armed forces has not resolved and will not resolve the deep-seated issues that divide the Israelis and the Arabs. The conflict can be resolved by the West's and America's determination to achieve a two-state solution to stop Israel from colonizing and annexing occupied Palestinian territories, to remove the apartheid wall, and to retreat to its pre-1967 borders. Because of the deep-seated element of religious nationalism involved in the conflict, medium- or even long-term direct supervision by the United Nations will be necessary. Establishing a viable Palestinian state will culminate in all Arab countries recognizing Israel and its right to exist within its own borders in total security but without the need to recognize Israel's Jewish character. Recognizing Israel's Jewish character, which is what Israel aims for, would deny Palestinian refugees the right to return to their land. Recognizing Israel as a Jewish state should not be on the agenda for settling the conflict, as its inclusion would stifle any future negotiation.

I should emphasize that Christian Zionists, Jewish far-right Zionists, Muslim fundamentalists, and all other religious fundamentalists around the world need to understand that money, nationalism, and religion are the weapons that are fragmenting the world. They should know that a fragmented world is a threat to their own survival and the survival of the human race. Despite the fact that the fragmentation of the world is a human compulsion—especially through the axis of evil of imperialism, religion, and nationalism—the human race can still avoid self-destruction by activating the instinct of the survival of the species. The need to preserve human life requires an examination of how individuals, groups, and nations contribute to the fragmentation of the world, especially in their following of sinister, extremist, and divisive political and religious leaders. To secure the future of the world, it is essential to curb extremism from all sides before it is too late. It is the duty of all moderate people around the globe to act now, as they are the best-equipped people for controlling the extremists within their own nations.

Combating Imperialism

Following the collapse of the Soviet Union in 1991, America became the main imperialist power in the world. At that time, the United States promised the world it would live without wars and with a dream for a world at peace under a single world policeman. But the single world policeman, who had the ability to command and shape the destiny of other countries, had undefined strategic and national interests. Because its undefined national interests are driven by its extreme capitalism, America has faced a headwind of resistance against its attempts to control the world and exploit the resources of other countries, especially while relying mainly on hard power. It has created enemies at a rapid rate, which has led the nation to rapid decline. The more enemies it creates, the sooner it will collapse. America's imperialistic aggression is driven by its economic capacity and its influence on the world's economic orientation, especially the nation's economic power over the G7 and the G20 countries. Although the Cold War was an economic conflict between the two opposing economic systems of capitalism and socialism, it was essentially a political war. The collapse of the Soviet Union thus has also caused the shifting of the world's earlier bipolar era of political orientation to an era of economic orientation, which has brought America's extreme capitalism to the central stage of the twenty-first century.

In a November 2010 article in the *Links International Journal of Socialist Renewal* titled "US Imperialist Aggression in the Early 21st Century," author Rasti Delizo wrote the following:

> The central aim of the imperialists was to firmly integrate the poor market economies into the neoliberal global economic regime and to widely pry their economies apart for even greater extraction of their raw materials, dumping of cheaper consumer commodities and excess financial capital, and to finally get their governments to align their states behind the imperialist camp. Inevitably, all of this was to create social-economic havoc throughout the dependent economies of the global South which sparked intermittent internal conflicts within many poor countries of the world. Understandably, this situation remains even more problematic today.
>
> Immediately after the 9/11 attacks in the US, the George W. Bush–led imperialist regime unleashed its bloody and devastating assaults across the world all in the name of Washington's so-called "global war on terror." However, I must point out here that we must accurately and correctly call this a "global war of terror" instead, and that is mainly because US imperialism

is only terrorizing the rest of the world's masses into obeying Washington's global agenda. Rather than stopping terrorism, the US is the one fomenting its own global terror in order to enforce its foreign policy agenda on the rest of the world.

The US strategic agenda is primarily economic in order to further expand access to newer regional markets across the world. These markets are needed for the export of the United States' financial capital and export commodities, and of course, to secure and ensure a near-permanent access to oil supplies, other potentially new energy sources and highly valuable raw materials. All these requirements are much needed to sustain America's economic-military-scientific-technological machine far and deep into the new century. [6]

As we discussed in chapter 1, American imperialism first occurred when the country's economic development accelerated at a high speed. This necessitated market expansion, which in turn necessitated the acceleration of military, political, and economic influence on other countries, especially through America's installation of surrogate governments and by bullying its allies. To control the world and its resources, America needed to (1) establish formidable global financial institutions to help the expansion of its rich multinational corporations grow bigger and more powerful and entrench America's extreme capitalism;

(2) expand the militarization of the country and enhance various national-security agencies, which are designed to control the world and protect the United States' puppet regimes; and (3) expand its sphere of influence through alliances, especially with the NATO countries and Israel, the latter of which is spearheading its expansion in the Middle East.

In the same article, Delizo wrote that "US imperialism urgently aims to strengthen itself as the world's undisputed hegemonic power within the next decade. It shall try to do so by having a controlling dominance over the international economy, together with its oil and other strategic resources. It will do this through American-led and influenced political alliances while maintaining its own independent stance to secure its own self-interests. Toward this end, US imperialism will never hesitate to use both its white and black (soft and hard powers) operational forces against any and all perceived global threats whenever necessary." [7]

All this is happening while America is adding more enemies (whom it lacks the capacity to counter), especially by antagonizing Russia and China through its policies of encircling Russia and containing China to restrain their legitimate right to industrial and military development. America's aggression is a major contributor to the fragmentation of the world, which is now flush with nuclear weapons and hotheaded leaders. To avert a global catastrophe, the moderate people of the world should assume their responsibility by taking politics seriously and by never leaving the destiny of the following generations in the hands of religious fanatics and extreme capitalists driven by excessive greed.

COMBATING THE CLASH OF CIVILIZATIONS

As stated in chapter 2, although millions of moderate Jews oppose far-right Zionism, millions of moderate Christians oppose Christian fundamentalism, and millions of moderate Muslims oppose Islamic extremism, extremists speak louder through their control of the religious establishments and their influence through the right-wing media. These far-right groups' hate has spread across the globe like a plague and can bring only conflict and misery to the world. The rise of the far right has coincided with the appearance on the world stage of far-right leaders who are capable of endangering world peace. Their success in getting elected is due to their ability to play on people's insecurity and by promising more than what they can deliver. Such leaders not only are unable to help the people who elect them, they also cause social and international fragmentation that will have a negative impact on society and the world. Such leaders are the main promoters of the clash of civilizations that is engulfing the world in an endless conflict; this conflict will have no winners but rather will result in mutually assured destruction. This is more so because the clash of civilizations has a religious connotation and is aimed at the world's 1.7 billion Muslims. From earlier discussions, we could conclude that the main promoters behind the slogan of the clash of civilizations are fundamentalist Christian Evangelicals, Sunni Wahhabis, and far-right Zionists. We could add that for opportunistic reasons, the Zionists have allied with the Evangelicals to ensure America's continuous and unconditional support of Israel, especially following the 1967 Arab-Israeli War, which resulted in Israel's occupation of Jerusalem and the West Bank. In turn, this emboldened various ultraorthodox interpretations of Judaic law that are founded in the Torah, the Talmud, and the Halakhah and that prohibit Jews from sharing power with non-Jews in the Land of Israel. [8]

Paul Findley wrote the following in *They Dare to Speak Out*:

In his study of Orthodox Judaism, [Vincent James] Abramo wrote: "The success of the religious parties in the 1996 and 1999 Israeli national elections vastly increased the influence of orthodox Jews in the Israeli political process. Politically influential and highly visible orthodox rabbis seek to convince Israel's religiously observant Jews that the Messiah will not arrive until Jews establish themselves as sole rulers in the biblical Land of Israel. They believe that any governmental compromise to return biblical lands to the Palestinians in exchange for a peace agreement is, in the eyes of God, a treacherous and punishable act. The orthodox are committed to derailing all Israeli government and international peace initiatives that would force them to give up any part of Jewish sovereignty, political autonomy, and administrative control over all of Israel's biblical land."

Abramo estimated that 20 percent of Israel's Jewish population is committed to these beliefs and ideology. This small percentage has proved adequate to be decisive in close elections. [9]

When we look at the power of the Zionist lobby in America, we can see the fundamentalism in Israel reflected in America's Middle East foreign policy. Couple this with what we discussed earlier about the Wahhabists' extreme interpretation of the Koran and the Evangelicals' interpretation of the Bible, and the world is ending up in conflict driven by vocal and extremely dogmatic minorities. This is especially damaging world harmony because religion is an essential part of culture and is behind the clash of civilizations. To avoid a catastrophic end of civilization as a result of dogmatic interpretations of the various religions' holy books, it is essential for the silent majorities of all cultures to shed their apathy and become more active and vocal. As a starting point, the people must elect politicians who have the courage to declare themselves to be fully secular, with a strong belief in the separation of religion from the state.

WAR VERSUS PEACE

America has a choice: continue with its costly wars and self-destruction or create a peaceful world built on win-win and coexistence principles instead of its current winner-takes-all approach. The starting point for America to become a reasonable country is by developing exit strategies to end the unnecessary wars against Islamic countries. First, it needs to remove the majority of its military bases from around the world, especially those that provoke resentment and insurgency and were set up to attack other nations rather than defend America. Second, it needs to rely mostly on diplomatic rather than military solutions to solving conflicts. To prevent mutually assured destruction, it must abandon its aggression and the desire for domination and control. The use of military power, the killings of civilians, and the destruction of homes and infrastructures all create second-class nations and sects that have no hope left but to become militant. The militancy and insurgency of the brutalized people are driven by their desire to survive rather than to consider the adoption of a moderate ideology. The brutality of America and Israel doesn't leave the brutalized a chance to think about moderation as a choice. Using the military and financial might instead of applying wisdom and diplomacy in dealing with other people and countries is a recipe for disaster for both the conquered and the conqueror. America and Israel are ignoring the simple fact that injustice creates resentment and revolt—as demonstrated in their brutal actions in Palestine, Iraq, Lebanon, Pakistan, Libya, and Afghanistan.

In denying justice and inflicting extreme pain on their enemies, or their perceived enemies, America and Israel are sowing the seeds for revenge, not only in the oppressed countries but also throughout the Islamic world. Above all, America and Israel are operating on the "rather be feared than loved" principle, without realizing that fear can either destroy people or drive them on by triggering their survival instinct to fight.

The ultimate peaceful solution can be achieved, however, when America, Britain, and their allies stop bombarding Muslim countries. Acknowledging their earlier mistakes of oppressing, killing, and displacing innocent (and not-so-innocent) people can help these nations (with Western countries' contributions) develop strategies to reestablish destroyed institutions, fight poverty, encourage secular education, solve youth unemployment, and counter the radicalization of those who are left behind and have nothing left to lose but to turn to religion and the gun. The Americans, the British, and their allies must remember that their military adventures in the Middle East have served only to fuel the terror threats to their own countries. To remedy the historical Western negligence in dealing with Islamic radicalism, they must first understand that the main source of radicalism is the Islamic religious schools; second, they must invest money and effort into encouraging and persisting with secular education in countries that have been deprived of exposure to modernity and reformation. Above all, investing in nation building is key.

In the current world of globalization and free trade, it is essential for America's prosperity, as a major exporter, to encourage economic growth throughout the world. It is necessary to maintain economic, political, and social stability to achieve world growth, especially across emerging markets where the middle class can grow and prosper. In this case, for America to be "great again," it must advance its soft power instead of its hard power. The destruction of people's livelihoods was the result of the indiscriminate bombardment of Islamic countries, which for America's undefined national interests were earmarked for regime change or for the elimination of certain religious sects. This is the main cause of world instability. This situation is coupled with (1) the current Western resentment of the millions of refugees who pour into Western countries and (2) the lack of UN funding to feed people and educate their children in refugee camps throughout the Middle East and elsewhere. I should emphasize that the outcome from millions of destitute, unemployed, hungry, ignorant, uneducated, and homeless people of the next generation will have a negative impact on the world, and the West should expect the worst rather than assume these people will have no option but to accept their destinies as second- or third-class citizens. The unintended consequences of Western countries' actions are now in full view.

THE VOICE OF MODERATION

The corruption of democracy in America is aggravated by the nation's becoming driven by money, by the sidelining of the middle-class majority from the political process, and by an all-consuming desire for power and glory. The middle-class majority, if it shed its apathy, would be in a position to challenge the disturbing trend of being sidelined and silenced by the loud voices of the extremists and the vested interests. It is the shortsighted imperialistic ambitions that are sabotaging the very notion of a true democracy by sidelining the silent majority. These ambitions allow America to use force in its endeavor to dominate the world, which is backfiring by creating a large pool of enemies of America and its Western allies. By refusing to remain apathetic, the middle class and the rest of the silent majority could bring down all the destructive elements of imperialism and terrorism. America can become a great nation again if it allowed poorer countries to prosper with stronger middle classes and more people to become consumers; this can be achieved only in a stable and peaceful world. A peaceful world cannot be achieved without curbing the excessive powers of all nations and groups whose policies are fueled by extremism.

This is a call for moderation to achieve peaceful coexistence and to heal all negative aspects of international relationships. It is a call to reject the winner-takes-all mentality and the accumulation of riches and control that are pushing the world toward a seismic shift in the balance of power. There is hope that those who are creating the imbalance of power, particularly America, can return to a humanistic approach and the use of its soft power, which would lead to a more peaceful, mutually beneficial world.

America, as a superpower, is in a position to set the security agenda for its allies and for the world. Because of America's decline, however, this task has become harder, especially while it carries such a massive debt. Securing future economic growth to pay off its debts can be achieved only by additional spending on education, health, and infrastructure and by spending less money on wars. The conflicting agendas of the Republicans and the Democrats are preventing this from happening at this stage. While most Republicans want to fight wars until the end, many Democrats want to prolong America's life by exiting these wars. The conflict between the Republicans and the Democrats has reached the stage in which the two sides loath each other and question the legitimacy of the other party. This state of affairs has contributed to America's decline, not only because of its own social-class struggle but also in the eyes of its allies. [10]

There is hope for America, especially in the awareness and the capacity of its vast army of highly educated people and intellectuals, who can arrest the demise of America both socially and internationally by curbing the power of all the religious and economic extremists who are causing the disintegration of their country. Forming a third, moderate party to counter the current partisan politics would be the first step toward solving many of America's pressing problems. In that way, America might become a country to be looked up to once again instead of being despised.

The Final Word

The purpose of this book has been to challenge students of political science and general readers to consider how manipulation by a powerful and all-consuming right-wing narrative works. This book is about identifying imperialism and terrorism as the main threats that face the world. It is meant to remind readers they are not powerless; they can defy the manipulative leaders and their destructive propaganda tools, especially their politics of fear. While engaging in fearmongering about immigration, religion, and terrorism, Western leaders are plunging the world into a period of war, famine, refugee crises, corruption, and destruction. Because of their lack of wisdom, Western leaders, especially those of the NATO countries, are guided and driven by America's aggressive foreign policy, which is leading the world into self-destructive ideologies that the elite have designed to bring the world in line with America's imperialistic ambitions.

Those Western leaders who toe the line of America's imperialistic ambition are bullied into believing that America will protect their countries from foreign aggression. Or, maybe for political reasons, they are not telling their people that America will not be in a position to protect them if a nuclear war breaks out. This is because of the following reasons. First, no country can match America's conventional military power, which leaves the only option to be a nuclear response. Second, America and Russia will be the first casualties, and the West and China will be next; everything will happen the same day or the same week. Third, no country and nobody in the world will want to survive and live after a nuclear holocaust that would turn the world into radioactive ash. Fourth, America has no permanent friends but acts only in its own self-interest ("America first"). It uses friends when it needs them and abandons them when they are useless or get in the way of its goals. A good example of this is how America used Saddam Hussein, only to destroy him later. Earlier, the Americans had used him in its relations with Saudi Arabia. To make the Saudis dependent on America and protected by it in order to remain obedient to it, Saddam was needed to be made (or appeared to be) as a major threat to

Saudi Arabia's survival. This was simply for the Saudis to continue serving America's strategic interests in the region. The Americans also used Saddam in Iraq's war against Iran to weaken Iran for being a threat to Israel. After winning the war against Iran, Saddam became the threat (or the perceived threat) to Israel and the American strategic interests in the region. Through the process of elimination, his regime was decapitated. The process of elimination is now in progress, targeting other countries. Europe, being a major competitor to America, should not assume that it is a loved partner: love is a passing phase, and a divorce can follow. As food for thought, remember how America was once a colony of Great Britain, but now their roles are reversed.

From the above analyses, we can conclude that America's military interventions in the Middle East and North Africa, and its support of corrupt Arab regimes—while it dispenses with secular regimes, fuels Islamophobia, commits human-rights abuses, and creates poverty and destruction—should be considered the main contributing factors in spreading cancerous Islamic terrorism. The cancer has spread down to single cells; it is a disease that is hard to control or cure. The problem of terrorism is aggravated by the American policy of supporting one terrorist group to defeat another terrorist group, which is not a sustainable geopolitical strategy, especially in the tribal and sectarian Middle East. To achieve the ultimate imperialistic benefit from the region, America will need a stable region rather than a region at war, as is the case with the tribal and sectarian wars that will continue for many decades to come.

The American invasion of Iraq in the spring of 2003 gave the religious Sunni fanatics the battleground they needed; the invasion helped them develop a strategy for war, not only against the "infidel" Shiites but also against Christians and Jews. Disturbing the balance of power in Iraq by disempowering the Sunnis and empowering the Shiites was sufficient for Sunni jihadists to establish the new battleground in the Middle East, especially by combining their forces with the remnants of Saddam Hussein's disbanded army, which had continually provided logistics for the armed resistance. The fact remains that the Shiites' rise to power—following the American invasion in 2003 that destroyed the secular Sunni regime of Saddam Hussein—has been responsible for turning Iraq into a broken country, a failed state, and one of the most dangerous places in the world. The consequence of empowering the Shiites in Iraq was the emboldening of the Shiite regime in Iran, which became a perceived threat to Saudi Arabia and the other Gulf states. To weaken Iran—with the help of Turkey, Jordan, and the Gulf states—America and Saudi Arabia commenced an undeclared war on the nation by mobilizing, arming, and financing jihadi Sunni terrorists from around the Muslim world to target Iran's proxy regimes of Iraq, Syria, and the Hezbollah forces of Lebanon. The undeclared war has the potential to develop into open warfare between Iran and its neighboring Sunni states—all influenced by America and Israel—and culminate in catastrophe for the region and for the world.

The conflict can be stopped when Sunnis and Shiites feel they're heading for mutually assured destruction and decide it is not in their interest to continue. This can happen when the warring factions realize the war has caused them great loss of lives and wealth and then ask themselves, "Why are we fighting, and for what?" The other option is for America and Israel to stop stoking and contributing to the conflict. It is also not in their interest to do so.

At the time of this writing, American policy in the Middle East—under the guise of fighting terrorism—is to support the Sunni autocrats by selling them weapons without asking questions about how the weapons will be used, even after people are indiscriminately killed in Yemen, Libya, Syria, Iraq, and Lebanon. This is when not Iran but Saudi Arabia is the main source of the ideology of the Sunnis' extreme interpretation of Islam, as well as arming and funding terrorists. American propaganda, in contrast, tries to convince the world that Iran is the main source of terrorism. Iran is fighting for survival to counter the threat of the Sunnis and Israel.

Ultimately, uniting the warring sects in the Middle East, instead of dividing them, is a much better proposition for a harmonious and peaceful region. Such unity could bring great benefits to America, Israel, and the rest of the world by creating economic growth and thus more consumers than enemies for the West. And, above all, an important factor in this unity is the Arabs' recognition of Israel, which could open the door for a huge market for Israel's economic expansion and a stable Middle East for America, provided that America and Israel establish a viable Palestinian state. The biggest service America and Israel can offer the world is to abandon their policy of replacing secular regimes in the region with Islamic fundamentalists who are willing to destroy not only one another but also the "infidel" Christians and Jews and their corroborators.

In the meantime, the rhetoric about defeating and destroying the Islamic State by chest-beating sounds hollow. In the short term, the Islamic State can be defeated—but it cannot be destroyed without solving the problems and grievances behind its ideology. Instead of stoking the conflict between Sunnis and Shiites with the divide-and-conquer policy, the imperialistic powers should act as conciliators to subdue the sectarian war in the region, especially knowing that sectarianism and failed states go hand in hand; from failed states is where future terrorism will expand and engulf the world, thus becoming a major element in the clash of civilizations. Above all, the imperialistic powers will sooner or later need a stable Middle East rather than a region at war. As it stands, America and its Western allies are widely considered occupying powers in the Middle East, and Muslims who are fanatical about Islam believe that the war is of Muslims against the crusaders; they are guided by their religion, which states that "God says if somebody is encroaching on you, retaliate against them." To defeat this ideology, America must simply abandon the idea of the clash of civilizations and hard-power imperialism based on the winner-takes-all approach, to be replaced with the mutually beneficial approach. If, in an extreme situation, when a military intervention is necessary as a last resort—such as in 1995, following the genocide in Bosnia—the United States must have international backing and must be accompanied with an integral plan for nation building to avoid the consequences of creating a new generation of terrorists who have nothing left to lose because they are poor, uneducated, and unemployed and have nothing to turn to but to religion and the gun.

On the ideological front—and the repeated message in this book to all extremists and fundamentalists around the world—we must avoid fragmenting the world. A fragmented world is a threat to everyone's own survival and the survival of future generations. The members of the silent majority, especially those of the middle class and the intelligentsia, have no option but to fight for their own survival and to secure a better future for the following generations. It is wise to remember that the apathy of one generation can destroy the hopes of the next.

Besides forming an independent middle-class party and adopting a moderate model of capitalism and a socioeconomic system of government that will become a beacon for Western democracies, America needs to establish itself as a trustworthy leader of the world for solving major conflicts in other countries, especially in subduing the current religious and nationalistic conflicts that are causing the fragmentation of the world. America also needs to abandon its extreme capitalism and adopt a moderate form of capitalism that embodies the fair distribution of wealth; doing so could subdue its expansionist policies and its unlimited and undefined national interests. This idea is formed on the basis that capitalism is a good thing, but when it crosses over to the dark and the extreme side, it is no longer a good thing; it becomes extremely dangerous. Extreme capitalism is driving America into aggression, especially once America became the world's only superpower after winning the Cold War.

To conclude this book, I must point out that some of the thoughts I have expressed in it were, to a certain extent, crystalized during the early presidency of Donald Trump—a bombastic and an unpolished president who is full of racism, bigotry, polarization, aggression, confusion, unpredictability, unreliability, white supremacy, extreme nationalism, psychological terrorism, unpatriotic divisiveness, global-warming denial, spontaneous gaffes, and anti-immigrant and anti-Muslim rhetoric. He is a showcase of toxic narcissism who borders on megalomania. He is the president through whom the world has become convinced that America is acting in its self-interest only and that the only allies it has are those who can be used. In the process, he is driving America away from its leading role in the world and is diminishing America in the eyes of the world. Above all, he is incapable of making "America great again." Donald Trump is the outcome of a fake democracy.

• • •

Hani Montan was born in Iraq in 1939 and has been an Australian citizen since 1973. In 1966, he earned a master of science degree in civil and industrial engineering. He has traveled extensively and has studied and worked in Iraq, Russia, Algeria, and Australia. Montan has studied a variety of subjects to keep abreast of social, managerial, and technical developments, including psychology, philosophy, project management, environmental protection, business administration, public and human relations, and political and social science.

Montan worked at Sydney Water as a project engineer and group leader for several years and has owned and managed a retail business. His early involvement in politics (starting at the age of fifteen) and his engineering instincts have contributed to his powers of observation, which have allowed him to come to logical conclusions and to offer simplified solutions to a variety of problems. The experience he has gained from working with and managing people over many years and his long-standing interest in political science have also motivated him to write about many different subjects. His other books, including *Thorny Opinion* (2008), *Dads Gags* (2009), *Israel vs. America vs. the World* (2011), *Death by Choice versus Religious Dogma* (2012), *Psyche and Personality* (2013), *Voice of Reason: In 7 Essays* (2015), and *Axis of Evil: Imperialism – Religion – Nationalism* (2016), have all been published by CreateSpace and are available from Amazon.com and other retailers in both paperback and Kindle formats. Other than his humorous book *Dads Gags*, these works are nonfiction books that discuss society, politics, religion, psychology, international relations, and other issues such as euthanasia, climate change, family relationships, and the deficiency of school education.

Montan believes in an economic system of social democracy—in which a moderate form of capitalism is pursued that includes the fair distribution of wealth—as well as a secular system of government where religion is left at the door of Parliament or Congress.

His blogs on a variety of subjects may be found on the Open Forum website (www.openforum.com.au), and his articles on the subject of dying with dignity may be found at www.dwdnsw.org.au.

NOTES

• • •

INTRODUCTION

[1] Hani Montan, *Axis of Evil: Imperialism – Religion – Nationalism* (Charleston, SC: CreateSpace, 2016), 4.

[2] Franklin D. Roosevelt, inaugural address on March 4, 1933, following the 1932 presidential election, *History Matters*: www.historymatters.gmu.edu/d/5057.

This great Nation will endure as it has endured, will revive and will prosper. So, first of all, let me assert my firm belief that the only thing we have to fear is fear itself—nameless, unreasoning, unjustified terror which paralyzes needed efforts to convert retreat into advance. In every dark hour of our national life a leadership of frankness and vigor has met with that understanding and support of the people themselves which is essential to victory. I am convinced that you will again give that support to leadership in these critical days.

CHAPTER 1: IMPERIALISM AND CONFLICTS

[1] Richard H. Immerman, *Empire for Liberty* (Princeton, NJ: Princeton University Press, 2010), 10.

[2] James Petras, "Foundation of the US Empire: Axes of Evil," July 22, 2014 in the *Information Clearing House*, 1. www.informationclearinghouse.info/article39181.htm.

[3] Ibid., 2.

[4] Montan, *Axis of Evil*, 1, 44. The second British Empire (1783–1860) refers to

the period characterized by the British Empire's change of thinking from direct military and naval control to an indirect control of its colonies. [The period featured] the expansion of dominion that was based on trade with informal control if possible and trade with rule if necessary. In Britain, early in the nineteenth century during the second empire, industrialist ideals and regulations were gradually abandoned in response to economic and political developments. Its new industrial supremacy encouraged it to give a greater force to the doctrine of free trade, which questioned the economic value of political ties between the colonies and the mother country.

[5] Oxford University, *The Oxford History of the British Empire*, vol. 5, *Historiography*, www.oxfordscholarship.com/ view/10.1093/acprof:oso/9780198205661, https://doi:10.1093/ac prof:oso/9780198205661.001.0001. This includes the following articles: P. J. Marshal, "The First British Empire," chap. 2, p.

43, https://doi:10.1093/acprof:oso/9780198205661.003.0002; C. A. Bayly, "The Second British Empire," chap. 3, p. 54, https://doi:10.1093/acprof:oso/9780198205661.003.0003. Finally, see J. W. Blake, "The First British Empire," in *History Today*, August 8, 1972, www.historytoday.com/jw-blake/first-british-empire.

[6] Hani Montan, *Thorny Opinion* (Charleston, SC: BookSurge Publishing, 2008), 115.

[7] Montan, *Axis of Evil*, 138–44.

[8] Immerman, *Empire for Liberty*, 235.

[9] Alfred McCoy, *A Question of Torture: CIA Interrogation, from the Cold War to the War on Terror*, American Empire Project (Henry Holt: New York, 2006), 1–8.

[10] Noam Chomsky, "The Torture Memos," *Info*, May 24, 2009.

[11] Mark Shields, (*NewsHour* program, a segment with Mark Shields and David Brooks on American Public Broadcasting Service, May 19, 2017).

[12] Montan, *Axis of Evil*, 32. Neocolonialism refers to

the use of economic, political, cultural, or other means such as temporary military intervention to control or influence other countries, especially by installing puppet governments. [Neocolonialism] relates to the policy of a strong country in targeting a weaker country for political and economic hegemony or for extending the sphere of influence. It involves the use of the weaker country's resources to strengthen and enrich the stronger country. It is the modern imperialistic geopolitical practice of capitalism and business globalization.

[13] Immerman, *Empire for Liberty*, 1.

[14] Robert McNamara, "The Gadsden Purchase—Strip of Land Purchased in 1853 Completed the Mainland States," on *ThoughtCo.*, updated May 31, 2017, https://www.thoughtco.com/gadsden-purchase-1773322. The Gadsden Purchase

> was a strip of territory the United States purchased from Mexico following negotiations in 1853. The land was purchased because it was considered to be a good route for a railroad across the Southwest to California. The land comprising the Gadsden Purchase is in southern Arizona and the southwestern part of New Mexico. The Gadsden Purchase represented the last parcel of land acquired by the United States to complete the 48 mainland states.

> The transaction with Mexico was controversial and it intensified the simmering conflict over slavery and helped to inflame the regional differences that eventually led to the Civil War.

[15] President Theodore Roosevelt expanded the Monroe Doctrine in his annual message to Congress in December 1904, in which he announced a corollary to that doctrine: not only were the nations of the Western Hemisphere not open to colonization by European powers, but the United States had the responsibility to preserve order and protect life and property in those countries. The Monroe Doctrine (announced in 1823) had sought to prevent European intervention in the Western Hemisphere, but now the Roosevelt corollary justified American intervention

throughout the Western Hemisphere. European intervention in Latin America resurfaced as an issue in US foreign policy when European governments began to use force to pressure several Latin American countries to repay their debts. For example, British, German, and Italian gunboats blockaded Venezuela's ports in 1902 when the Venezuelan government defaulted on its debts to foreign bondholders. Many Americans worried that European intervention in Latin America would undermine their country's traditional dominance in the region. To keep the other powers out and to ensure financial solvency, Roosevelt issued his corollary: "Chronic wrongdoing...may in America, as elsewhere, ultimately require intervention by some civilized nation...and in the Western Hemisphere the adherence of the United States to the Monroe Doctrine may force the United States, however reluctantly, in flagrant cases of such wrongdoing or impotence, to the exercise of an international police power." Roosevelt tied his policy to the Monroe Doctrine, an action that was also consistent with his "Walk softly, but carry a big stick" foreign policy. Roosevelt stated that in keeping with the Monroe Doctrine, the United States was justified in exercising international police power to put an end to chronic unrest or wrongdoing in the Western Hemisphere. In 1934, President Franklin D. Roosevelt renounced interventionism and established his "Good Neighbor Policy" within the Western Hemisphere.

[16] Noam Chomsky, *Hegemony or Survival: America's Quest for Global Dominance* (New York: Henry Holt, 2004), 17.

[17] Immerman, *Empire for Liberty*, 2.

[18] Montan, *Axis of Evil*, 31–2.

[19] Chomsky, *Hegemony or Survival*, 71.

[20] Kenneth J. Hagan and Ian J. Bickerton, *Unintended Consequences: The United States at War* (London: Reaktion Books, 2007), 7–17.

[21] Steve Coll, *Ghost Wars: The Secret History of the CIA, Afghanistan, and Bin Laden, from the Soviet Invasion to September 10* (New York: Penguin, 2004), 585–8.

[22] Hagan and Bickerton, *Unintended Consequences*, 149, 166, 188.

[23] Ewen MacAskill, "Bill Gates Warns Tens of Millions Could Be Killed By Bio-Terrorism," *Guardian*, February 19, 2017.

[24] Montan, *Axis of Evil*, 81–2.

[25] Chris Baraniuk, "Small Drone 'Shot with Patriot Missile,'" *BBC News*, March 15, 2017.

[26] "What Is 3D Printing?" 3dprinting.com/what-is-3d-printing/#whatitis.

3-D printing, or additive manufacturing, is a process of making three-dimensional solid objects from a digital file. The creation of a 3D-printed object is achieved using additive processes. In an additive process, an object is created by laying down successive layers of material until the entire object is created. Each of these layers can be seen as a thinly sliced horizontal cross-section of the eventual object...It starts with making a virtual design of the object that is to be created. This virtual design is made in a CAD (Computer Aided Design) file using a 3D-modeling program (for the creation of a totally new object) or with the use of a 3D scanner (to copy an existing object). A 3D scanner makes a 3D digital copy of an object.

[27] Hanna Rose Mendoza, "UN Secretary-General Ban Ki-Moon Lists 3D Printing among Potential Global Threats," 3Dprint.com, "editorials/opinions" section, August 25, 2016, https://3dprint.com/category/3d-printed-guns-2.

[28] Montan, *Axis of Evil*, 171–4.

[29] Ibid., 174–6.

[30] Hani Montan, *Psyche and Personality* (Charleston, SC: CreateSpace, 2013), 158–94.

[31] Montan, *Thorny Opinion*, 200.

[32] Montan, *Axis of Evil*, 181–3.

[33] Hani Montan, *Israel vs. America vs. the World* (Charleston, SC: CreateSpace, 2011), 27.

[34] Brad A. Brelinski, "US Supreme Court Issues Ground Breaking Campaign Finance Ruling." Curtis, Curtis & Brelinski (law firm), March 3, 2010, https://www.curtiscurtislaw.com/business-services/2010/03/03/u-s.

[35] Brandi Buchman, "Trump Eases Political Limits for Religious Groups," *MintPress News*, May 5, 2017, www.mintpressnews.com/tag/religious-organizations.

[36] Montan, *Axis of Evil*, 95–152.

[37] Jason Zweig, "Disturbing New Facts about American Capitalism," *Wall Street Journal*, March 4, 2017.

[38] Montan, *Axis of Evil*, 74–5.

[39] Hani Montan, *Voice of Reason: In 7 Essays* (Charleston, SC: CreateSpace, 2015), 30–2.

[40] Ibid., 32–4.

[41] Montan, *Axis of Evil*, 201. The middle class, also called the petit bourgeoisie, is

a social group between the upper class (the bourgeoisie) and the working class. It generally consists of skilled workers, subcontractors, small-business owners and some of their assistants, and the higher-educated occupational (white-collar) workers, such as professionals, administrators, and teachers. [The middle class] is the heart of the social and economic structure of a country. If it declines, the whole country declines with it proportionally. In a Western political system, because of the group's swinging nature, [the middle class] holds the balance of power between the "left" and "right." During election time, it is courted by both the left and the right wings' factional groups, often manipulated with false promises.

[42] Michael G. Roskin, "Political Science," *Encyclopedia Britannica*, https://www.britannica.com/topic/political-science.
[43] Montan, *Psyche and Personality*, 77.
[44] Montan, *Axis of Evil*, 203.
[45] Ibid., 203–5.
[46] Montan, *Voice of Reason*, 35.
[47] Das Satyajit, "America's Hard & Soft Power," *Capsule Review*, December 15, 2014, www.economonitor.com/blog/2014/12/americas-hard-soft-power.
[48] Joseph Nye Jr., "The Decline of America's Soft Power," *Capsule Review* magazine, May/June 2004, https://www.foreignaffairs.com/reviews/capsule-review/2004-05-01.
[49] Joseph Nye Jr., *Soft Power: The Means to Success in World Politics* (New York: PublicAffairs/Perseus Group, 2004), 119–20.

[50] Lawrence G. McDonald and Patrick Robinson, *A Colossal Failure of Common Sense: The Inside Story of the Collapse of Lehman Brothers* (New York: Crown Publishing Group, 2009), 3–7, 182, 241.

[51] Niall Ferguson, *The Ascent of Money: The Financial History of the World* (New York: Penguin Books, 2009), 1–14.

[52] US Senate Subcommittee on Investigations, "Wall Street and the Financial Crisis: Anatomy of a Financial Collapse," July 1, 2011.

[53] Montan, *Israel vs. America vs. the World*, 89–94.

[54] Montan, *Voice of Reason*, 24–5.

[55] Robert Weissman, "Goldman Sachs: Too Big to Rein In," interview with *Al Jazeera*, June 17, 2014.

[56] Montan, *Voice of Reason*, 31.

[57] Jeffrey D. Sachs, *The Price of Civilization: Reawakening American Virtue and Prosperity* (New York: Random House, 2012), 115.

[58] Ibid., 116–7.

[59] Ibid., 130–1.

[60] Montan, *Voice of Reason*, 39.

[61] "Cold War," *New World Encyclopedia*, www.newworldencyclopedia.org/entry/Cold_War.

[62] Montan, *Axis of Evil*, 123–4.

[63] Dana Priest and William M. Arkin, "Top Secret America" and "A Hidden World: Growing Beyond Control," *Washington Post*, July 18 and 19, 2010 (respectively). projects.washingtonpost.com/top-secret-america. projects.washingtonpost.com/top-secret-america/articles.

[64] Immerman, *Empire for Liberty*, 56.

[65] William Blum, "US Interventions—1945 to the Present," *Z Magazine*, June 1999, www.thirdworldtraveler.com/Blum/US_Interventions_WBlumZ.html.

[66] Chomsky, *Hegemony or Survival*, 42.

[67] Montan, *Israel vs. America vs. the World*, 1–17.

[68] Montan, *Axis of Evil*, 7.

[69] Chomsky, *Hegemony or Survival*, 11–2.

[70] Ibid., 15.

[71] Montan, *Voice of Reason*, 187–92.

[72] Levin Institute, "What Is Globalization?" Globalization 101. org, www.globalization101.org/what-is-globalization.

[73] Angie Mohr, "The Advantages of Free Trade in Developing Countries," *Houston Chronicle* (no date), http://smallbusiness. chron.com/benefits-trade-developing-countries-3834.html.

[74] Multiple articles on global education and global issues, www.globaleducation.edu.au/global-issues/gi-globalisation.html.

[75] Montan, *Thorny Opinion*, 110–3.

[76] M. Richard Ebeling, "Globalization and Free Trade," Quora, April 1, 2004. https://fee.org/articles/free-markets-the-rule-of-law-and.

[77] "Positive Quotes about America," Positive Quotes, www. quotes-positive.com/quotes/america.

Chapter 2: Terrorism and Conflicts

[1] Montan, *Thorny Opinion*, 113–4.

[2] Ibid., 114.

[3] Paul Findley, *They Dare to Speak Out: People and Institutions Confront Israel's Lobby*, 3rd ed. (Chicago: Lawrence Hill Books, 2003), 349.

[4] Montan, *Axis of Evil*, 100.

[5] Ibid., 101–7, 132, 145, 151.

[6] Montan, *Psyche and Personality*, 198.

[7] Samuel Huntington, *The Clash of Civilizations and the Remaking of World Order* (New York: Simon & Schuster, 1996), 130.

[8] Ibid., 130.

[9] Montan, *Axis of Evil*, 115.

[10] Montan, *Israel vs. America vs. the World*, 247.

[11] Montan, *Psyche and Personality*, 105.

[12] Emily Stephenson and Steve Holland, "Trump Vows Military Build-Up, Hammers Nationalist Themes," *Reuters*, February 24, 2017, https://www.reuters.com/article/us-usa-trump/trump-vows-military-build-up-hammers-nationalist-themes-idUSKBN-1630HH.

[13] Paul Findley, *They Dare to Speak Out*, 308.

[14] Petras, *Power of Israel*, chaps. 1 and 3.

[15] Montan, *Axis of Evil*, 86.

[16] John Mearsheimer and Stephen M. Walt, *The Israel Lobby and US Foreign Policy* (New York: Farrar, Straus and Giroux, 2008), 138.

[17] Montan, *Israel vs. America vs. the World*, 60–1, 240.

[18] Paul Findley, "The Open Secret about the Israel Lobby," Counterpunch.org, October 16, 2007, https://www.counterpunch.org/2007/10/16/the-open-secret-about-the.

[19] Ibid.

[20] Findley, *They Dare to Speak Out*, 29.

[21] Mearsheimer and Walt, *The Israel Lobby and US Foreign Policy*, 140.

[22] Ibid., 154.

[23] Findley, *They Dare to Speak Out*, 107.

[24] Ibid., 114–5.

[25] Ibid., 147–85.

[26] Ilan Pappe, *The Ethnic Cleansing of Palestine* (London: Oneworld Publications, 2007), xiii.

[27] Ibid., xiv.

[28] Montan, *Axis of Evil*, 87–8.

[29] Pappe, *Ethnic Cleansing*, 222.

[30] Ibid., 223.

[31] Ibid., 225–6.

[32] "The Apocalypse of Saint John the Apostle," These Last Days Ministries, https://www.tldm.org/bible/new testament/apoc.htm.

[33] Mearsheimer and Walt, *Israel Lobby*, 353–4.

[34] Roxane Farmanfarmaian, "Trouble for Trump: Iran, North Korea, Palestine, China." *Al Jazeera*, January 21, 2017.

[35] Jimmy Carter, *Palestine: Peace Not Apartheid* (New York: Simon & Schuster, 2007), 215.

[36] Ibid., 216.

[37] Findley, *They Dare to Speak Out*, 146.

[38] Montan, *Israel vs. America vs. the World*, 247–52.

[39] Economic and Social Commission for Western Asia (ESCWA), "Israeli Practices toward the Palestinian People and the Question of Apartheid," United Nations report, March 2017, 6–7, 21–2, www.unescwa.org:

The Apartheid Convention of 1973 classifies apartheid as a crime against humanity (in articles I and II) and provides the most detailed definition of it in international law. It also clarifies international responsibility and obligations with regard to combating the crime of apartheid. In the

1977 Protocol Additional to the Geneva Conventions of 12 August 1949, and Relating to the Protection of Victims of International Armed Conflicts (hereinafter Additional Protocol I to the 1949 Geneva Conventions), apartheid is defined as a war crime. The 1998 Rome Statute of the International Criminal Court (ICC), hereinafter the Rome Statute, lists apartheid as a crime against humanity (article 7 (1) (j)), bringing its investigation and possible prosecution under the jurisdiction of the ICC.

[40] Ibid., 62–3.

[41] Ibid., 63–6.

[42] Pappe, *Ethnic Cleansing*, 256.

[43] Norman G. Finkelstein, *The Holocaust Industry: Reflection on the Exploitation of Jewish Suffering* (London and New York: Verso Books, 2000), 149.

[44] Mearsheimer and Walt, *Israel Lobby*, 129.

[45] Ibid., 132.

[46] "Leo Strauss: American Political Philosopher," *Encyclopaedia Britannica*, May 2016, https://www.britannica.com/biography/Leo-Strauss.

[47] Francis Fukuyama, *America at the Crossroad: Democracy, Power, and the Neoconservative Legacy* (New Haven, CT: Yale University Press, 2006), 21–8.

[48] Mearsheimer and Walt, *Israel Lobby*, 126.

[49] Finkelstein, *The Holocaust Industry*, 16–21.

[50] Francis Fukuyama, *America at the Crossroad*, 40–1.

[51] Montan, *Israel vs. America vs. the World*, 138–40.

[52] Andrew Erdmann and Suzanne Nossel, "Are We All Nation Builders Now?" Stanley Foundation, June 2007, www.stanley-foundation.org/publications/other/Erd.

[53] Derek Chollet, Tod Lindberg, and David Shorr, *Bridging the Foreign Policy Divide* (New York: Routledge, 2008), 124.

[54] Stephen E. Ambrose and Douglas G. Brinkley, *Rise to Globalism: American Foreign Policy Since 1938*, 8th ed. (London: Penguin Books, 1997), 316–51.

[55] Montan, *Axis of Evil*, 35.

[56] Ibid., 35–6.

[57] Mearsheimer and Walt, *Israel Lobby*, 292–93.

[58] Ibid., 293.

[59] John Mearsheimer, "The Iraq War: Realism versus Neo-Conservatism,"

Open Democracy, April 4, 2005, mearsheimer.uchicago.edu/pdfs/A0037.pdf.

[60] Huntington, *Clash of Civilizations*, 125–54.

[61] William Kristol and Robert Kagan, *Present Dangers: Crisis and Opportunity in American Foreign and Defense Policy* (San Francisco: Encounter, 2000), 20.

[62] Montan, *Israel vs. America vs. the World*, 55–6.

[63] Immerman, *Empire for Liberty*, 209–10, 225.

[64] Montan, *Axis of Evil*, vii–viii.

[65] Mearsheimer and Walt, *Israel Lobby*, 49.

[66] Ibid., 50.

[67] Ibid., 77.

[68] National Security Archive, "The Iraq Project," www.nsarchive.org/project/iraq-project; Unredacted: The National Security

archive blog, "Colbert Uses Declassified Doc to Grill Rumsfeld: 'It Is Big,'" https://nsarchive.wordpress.com/2016/02/03/colbert-uses.

[69] Mearsheimer and Walt, *Israel Lobby*, 251.

[70] Montan, *Israel vs. America vs. the World*, 181–2.

[71] Ricks E. Thomas, *The Gamble: General Petraeus and the American Military Adventure in Iraq* (New York: Penguin, 2010), 295–8.

[72] Montan, *Axis of Evil*, 50.

[73] Montan, *Voice of Reason*, 207.

[74] Ibid., 46–7.

[75] Chomsky, *Hegemony or Survival*, 124–5.

[76] Mearsheimer and Walt, *Israel Lobby*, 36.

[77] Peter Beaumont and Joanna Walters, interview with Alan Greenspan following the publication of Greenspan's book *The Age of Turbulence: Adventures in a New World, Guardian*, September 16, 2007, www.theguardian.com › World › Iraq. https://www.commondreams.org/news/2007/09/16/greenspan-admits-iraq.

[78] Montan, *Israel vs. America vs. the World*, 249.

[79] The Iraq Inquiry, "The Chilcot inquiry," vol. 4, section 4.1; vol. 6, section 6.2; published July 6, 2016, www.iraqinquiry.org.uk/the-report.

[80] James Bamford, *A Pretext for War: 9/11, Iraq, and the Abuse of America's Intelligence Agencies* (New York: Anchor Books, 2005), 258–82.

[81] Fukuyama, *America at the Crossroad*, 181–95.

[82] Ibid., 35–6.

[83] Montan, *Israel vs. America vs. the World*, 165.

[84] Montan, *Axis of Evil*, 138–9.

[85]Huntington, *Clash of Civilizations*, 247.

[86]Montan, *Axis of Evil*, 19.

[87]Ibid., 149–51.

[88] Ibid., 159.

[89]Montan, *Israel vs. America vs. the World*, 10.

[90]Montan, *Axis of Evil*, 19–20.

[91]Ibid., 147.

[92]Ibid., 85.

[93]Chomsky, *Hegemony or Survival*, 122–3.

[94] Pew Research Center, "Mapping the Global Muslim Population," October 8, 2009, www.pewforum.org/2009/10/07/mapping-the-global-muslim-population.

[95]"Wahhabism," *New World Encyclopedia*, web.newworldencyclopedia.org/entry/Wahhabism.

[96]"Wahhabism to ISIS: How Saudi Arabia Exported the Main Source of Global Terrorism," *New Statesman*, November 27, 2014, https://www.newstatesman.com/world-affairs/2014/11/wahhabism-isis.

[97]"What Is the Muslim Brotherhood?" Egypt *Al Jazeera*, June 19, 2017. www.aljazeera.com/indepth/features/2017/06/muslim-brotherhood, "The Muslim Brotherhood and Trump's Terror list." *Aljazeera* February 2, 1917, "Tilleson: Black listing Muslim Brotherhood problematic." *Aljazeera* June 15, 2017, www.aljazeera.com/indepth/features/2017/02/muslim-brotherhood.

And Montan, *Axis of Evil*, 135–6. Also, refer back to subsection "Saudi Arabia's Role in Terrorism" in chapter 2 of this book.

The summary of the above is as follows:

The Muslim Brotherhood (MB) is the oldest political Islamist group in the Arab world and…is banned to operate as a political party in many…Arab countries. It was founded in Egypt in 1928 by…Islamic scholar Hassan al-Banna. He had a vision of a universal Islamic system of rule that could be attained by promoting Islamic laws and morals and by engaging society through offering social services. [The Muslim Brotherhood's] ideology is mainly focused on adherence to the ideal of society governed by Islamic laws and morals and to the reform of existing political systems in the Arab world. It embraces the idea of political activism and social responsibility, organizing charitable works and social support programs as part of its outreach to its core support base of lower-income populations. In its early days in Egypt, the MB was involved in the active struggle against British occupation, and also cooperated with the Free Officers movement to liberate Egypt from the monarchy.

[The Muslim Brotherhood] suffered a major set-back in the Arab world following their attempt in 1966 to assassinate the popular and secular leader…Gamal Abdel Nasser, which led to [the jailing and execution] of its leader, Sayyid Qutb. In 1970, however, the Muslim Brotherhood officially renounced violence during the rule of Egyptian President Anwar el-Sadat. They formally adopted a mandate of democracy in 1995 and their influence became apparent in professional work syndicates and social welfare work circles. In 2012, [the MB] ran a candidate in the post-"Arab

Spring" presidential elections in Egypt. Mohamed Morsi won the election and was Egypt's first democratically elected leader until a coup by the Egyptian armed forces in 2013 overthrew and jailed him along with many individuals in the MB leadership. Its supreme leader in Egypt is Mohamed Badie, who is currently in prison, having been sentenced to a number of life in prison and death sentences for a variety of charges. Because [the MB] offered a different model of Salafi Islamist politics to that of the Saudi State, the Saudis decided to support the military coup in Egypt and the subsequent brutal crackdown on Muslim Brotherhood supporters. Opponents of [the] Muslim Brotherhood, such as Saudi Arabia, Egypt, and the UAE consider it…a terrorist organization only because it is an existential threat to their rule. In March 2014, the Saudis designated the group as terrorists. However, according to US Secretary of State Rex Tillerson in his testimony before the House Committee on Foreign Relations on June 14, 2017, "Classification of the Muslim Brotherhood in its entirety as a 'terror' group complicates the security and politics of the Middle East." He added, "It was problematic to place the entire organization—whose members amount to more than five million, some of whom occupy positions in governments across the region—on a 'terror list.'" He pointed out…the fact that the Muslim Brotherhood have become parts of governments and parliaments in countries such as Bahrain and Turkey. Therefore, the Saudis' designation of the Muslim Brotherhood as a terrorist organization can have unpleasant consequences in making over five million followers fighting for their life and becoming real terrorists. Finally, it is worth noting that the Saudis were supportive of the MB, until it decided to welcome the Iranian revolution in 1979, which got worse following its condemnation of Saudi Arabia's invitation of American troops during the first Gulf War against Iraq in 1991.

[98] Montan, *Voice of Reason*, 212–13. Salafi jihadists are

an Islamic group who believe that violence and terrorism are justified to realize political objectives. Violent jihad is part of the rejection of any non-Islamic teachings and the adherence to a strict interpretation of the sacred text of the Koran in its most literal form, which advocates the absolute commitment to jihad. The Salafi jihadists consider the Muslim Brotherhood an excessively moderate organization. Currently, America and its puppet regimes are perceived as the greatest enemy of Islam. The power of [the Salafi jihadists] will intensify, especially in Egypt following the military coup. [The coup] will open another front for the West and Israel to fight. [The Salafi jihadists'] ideology is equal to that of the Islamic State in Syria and Iraq. [Their] loyalty and violence are shifting toward the Islamic State as a result of the destruction of the middle class, high unemployment, and extreme poverty, which coup leaders won't be able to solve. Egypt will become a failed state, joining many other countries in Africa and the Middle East, especially since the world is in recession and no multinational company will have the desire to invest in countries that are very risky. The removal of mainstream

Islamic movements like the Muslim Brotherhood, which was trying to work within the democratic process, is convincing the radical Muslims to use brutal force to achieve better results rather than wait for the kindness of their enemies, the Christian fundamentalists and the extreme Zionists.

[99] Comments from Bob Corker (current US senator and former US ambassador to Israel) on July 12, 2017, while addressing a legislative committee hearing.

[100] Interview on *BBC Arabic* on May 5, 2009, with Sheikh Adel al-Kalbani, imam of al-Haram Mosque in Mecca, and earlier with *al-Arabia (ABBC) TV* on February 27, 2009, sheikyermami.com/2009/05/saudi-imam-drive-the-jews-and the-christians-out-of-the-arabian-peninsula.

[101] James Petras, "Foundation of the US Empire: Axes of Evil," *World News Daily*, July 22, 2014, 4–6, www.petras.lahaine.org/?p=1995 and www.informationclearinghouse.info/article39181.htm.

[102] "London Attack: Corbyn Criticises Tories in Terror Speech," *BBC*, June 4, 2017.

[103] "London Bridge Attack," *ABC News*, June 5, 2017.

[104] Montan, *Axis of Evil*, 158.

[105] Ibid., 59–60.

[106] Chomsky, *Hegemony or Survival*, 210.

[107] Guy Taylor, *Washington Times*, February 9, 2016, on James Clapper's statement to the Senate Armed Services Committee on North Korea, www.washingtontimes.com/news/2016/feb/9/james-clapper-intel-chief.

[108] "Barack Obama at Nuclear Summit: 'Madmen' Threaten Global Security," *Guardian*, April 2, 2016.

[109] Montan, *Axis of Evil*, 89.

[110] Huntington, *Clash of Civilizations*, 20.

[111] Zbigniew Brzezinski, foreword to Huntington, *Clash of Civilizations* (2011), 6.

[112] Hani Montan, *Death by Choice versus Religious Dogma* (Charleston, SC: CreateSpace, 2012), 46.

[113] Sharon White, "Universal Civilization," Articles Factory, January 27, 2007, www.articlesfactory.com/articles/travel/universal-civilization.html.

[114] Rohitarora, "Modernization vs. Westernization: Universal Civilization?"
World Geo-Politics, posted June 12, 2009, adopted from Huntington, *Clash of Civilizations*, worldgeopoliticsblog.blogspot.com/2009/06/modernization-vs.

[115] Montan, *Psyche and Personality*, 32.

[116] Ibid., 72–4.

[117] Montan, *Thorny Opinion*, 149–50.

[118] Ibid., 179.

[119] Huntington, *Clash of Civilizations*, 52–3.

[120] Montan, *Thorny Opinion*, 199.

[121] Huntington, *Clash of Civilizations*, 64–5.

[122] Australian census of 2016, released July 11, 2017,
www.abs.gov.au/ausstats/abs@.nsf/mediareleasesbyCatalogue.

[123] Huntington, *Clash of Civilizations*, 68.

[124] Ibid., 32.

[125] Montan, *Israel vs. America vs. the World*, 19–20.

Chapter 3: Summary and Possible Solutions

[1] Montan, *Voice of Reason*, 205–7.

[2] Raphael Perl, "Combating Terrorism: The Challenge of Measuring Effectiveness," special report to Congress, updated March 12, 2007, 2–4, https://fas.org/sgp/crs/terror/RL33160.pdf.

[3] Ibid., 5–6.

[4] Montan, *Axis of Evil*, 38.

[5] Ibid., 126.

[6] Rasti Delizo, "US Imperialist Aggression in the Early 21st Century,"
Links International Journal of Socialist Renewal, November 27, 2010, links.org.au/node/2088.

[7] Ibid.

[8] Findley, *They Dare to Speak Out*, 282.

[9] Ibid., 281–2.

[10] Montan, *Axis of Evil*, 215.

BIBLIOGRAPHY

• • •

ABC News. "London Bridge Attack," June 5, 2017.

Al Jazeera. "What Is the Muslim Brotherhood?" June 9, 2017.

Al Jazeera. "Tillerson: Blacklisting Muslim Brotherhood Problematic," June 15, 2017.

Ambrose, Stephen E., and Douglas G. Brinkley. *Rise to Globalism: American Foreign Policy Since 1938.* 8th ed. London: Penguin Books, 1997.

Australian census of 2016. Released July 11, 2017, www.abs.gov.au/ ausstats/abs@.nsf/mediareleasesbyCatalogue.

Bamford, James. *A Pretext for War: 9/11, Iraq, and the Abuse of America's Intelligence Agencies.* New York: Anchor Books, 2005.

Baraniuk, Chris. "Small Drone Shot with Patriot Missile." *BBC News,* March 15, 2017.

BBC News. "London Attack: Corbyn Criticises Tories in Terror Speech," June 4, 2017.

Blum, William. "US Interventions—1945 to the Present." *Z Magazine*, June 1999.

Brelinski, A. Brad. "US Supreme Court Issues Ground Breaking Campaign Finance Ruling." Curtis, Curtis & Brelinski, March 3, 2010.

Brzezinski, Zbigniew. Foreword to Samuel P. Huntington, *The Clash of Civilizations and the Remaking of World Order.* New York: Simon & Schuster, 2011.

Buchman, Brandi. "Trump Eases Political Limits for Religious Groups." *MintPress News*, May 5, 2017.

Carter, Jimmy. *Palestine: Peace Not Apartheid.* New York: Simon & Schuster, 2007.

Chollet, Derek, Tod Lindberg, and David Shorr. *Bridging the Foreign Policy Divide.* New York: Routledge, 2008.

Chomsky, Noam. *Hegemony or Survival: America's Quest for Global Dominance.* American Empire Project. Reprint, New York: Holt Paperback, 2004.

———. "Exterminate All the Brutes: Gaza 2009." *Info.* January 19, 2009 (Revised June 6, 2009).

———. "Guillotining Gaza." *Peace and Justice Post*, July 30, 2007.

———. "The Torture Memos." *Info* (testimony in the Senate Armed Services Committee report). May 21, 2009 (Revised May 24, 2009).

Clarke, Richard A. *Against All Enemies: Inside America's War on Terror*. New York: Free Press, 2004.

Coll, Steve. *Ghost Wars: The Secret History of the CIA, Afghanistan, and Bin Laden, from the Soviet Invasion to September 10, 2001*. New York: Penguin, 2004.

Corker, Bob. Address at the Senate Legislative Committee hearing, July 12, 2017.

Das, Satyajit. "America's Hard & Soft Power." *Capsule Review*, December 15, 2014.

Ebeling, Richard. "Globalization and Free Trade." Quora.com, April 1, 2004.

Economic and Social Commission for Western Asia (ESCWA) of the United Nations. "Israeli Practices toward the Palestinian People and the Question of Apartheid," March 2017.

Encyclopaedia Britannica. "Leo Strauss: American Political Philosopher," May 2016.

Erdmann, Andrew, and Suzanne Nossel. "Are We All Nation Builders Now?" Stanley Foundation, June 2007.

Farmanfarmaian, Roxane. "Trouble for Trump: Iran, North Korea, Palestine, China," *Al Jazeera*, January 21, 2017.

Ferguson, Niall. *The Ascent of Money: The Financial History of the World*. New York: Penguin Books, 2009.

———. *Colossus: The Price of America's Empire*. New York: Penguin, 2004.

Findley, Paul. *They Dare to Speak Out: People and Institutions Confront Israel's Lobby*. 3rd ed. Chicago: Lawrence Hill Books, 2003.

———. "The Open Secret about the Israel Lobby." Counterpunch. org, October 16, 2007.

Finkelstein, Norman G. *The Holocaust Industry: Reflection on the Exploitation of Jewish Suffering*. New York: Verso Books, 2000.

———. *Beyond the Chutzpah: On the Misuse of Anti-Semitism and the Abuse of History*. Berkeley: University of California Press, 2008.

Fukuyama, Francis. *America at the Crossroad: Democracy, Power, and the Neoconservative Legacy.* New Haven, CT: Yale University Press, 2006.

Gardner, Howard. *Intelligence Reframed: Multiple Intelligences for the 21st Century.* New York: Basic Books, 2000.

———. *Multiple Intelligence: New Horizons in Theory and Practice.* Reprint, New York: Basic Books, 2006.

Gates, Bill. Speech on the threat of bioterrorism. Munich Security Conference, February 19, 2017.

Goleman, Daniel. *Emotional Intelligence.* 10th anniversary ed. New York: Bantam Books, 2006.

———. *Social Intelligence: The New Science of Human Relationships.* Reprint, New York: Bantam Books, 2007.

Greenspan, Alan. *The Age of Turbulence: Adventures in a New World.* Reprint, New York: Penguin Books, 2007.

Guardian. "Barack Obama at Nuclear Summit: 'Madmen' Threaten Global Security," April 2, 2016.

Hagan, Kenneth J., and Ian J. Bickerton. *Unintended Consequences: The United States at War.* London: Reaktion Books, 2007.

Hart, Alan. *Zionism Is the Real Enemy of the Jews*. Atlanta: Clarity Press, 2009.

Herman, Edward S., and Noam Chomsky. *Manufacturing Consent: The Political Economy of the Mass Media*. New York: Pantheon Books, 2002.

Huntington, Samuel P. *The Clash of Civilizations and the Remaking of World Order*. New York: Simon & Schuster, 1996; reprinted in 2011, with a new foreword by Zbigniew Brzezinski.

Imam Sheikh Adel al-Kalbani. Interview with *BBC Arabic*, May 5, 2009.

Immerman, Richard H. *Empire for Liberty: A History of American Imperialism from Benjamin Franklin to Paul Wolfowitz*. Princeton, NJ: Princeton University Press, 2012.

The Iraq Inquiry. "The Chilcot Inquiry," July 6, 2016.

Kennedy, Paul. *Rise and Fall of the Great Powers*. New York: Random House, 1987.

Kristol, William, and Robert Kagan. *Present Dangers: Crisis and Opportunity in American Foreign and Defense Policy*. San Francisco: Encounter, 2000.

Levin Institute. "What Is Globalization?" Globalization 101.org, 2015.

McCoy, Alfred. *A Question of Torture: CIA Interrogation, from the Cold War to the War on Terror.* American Empire Project. New York: Holt, 2006.

McDonald, Lawrence G., and Patrick Robinson. *A Colossal Failure of Common Sense: The Inside Story of the Collapse of Lehman Brothers.* New York: Crown Publishing Group, 2009.

Mearsheimer, John. "Hans Morgenthau and the Iraq War: Realism versus Neo-Conservatism." *Open Democracy*, May 19, 2005.

Mearsheimer, John, and Stephen M. Walt. *The Israel Lobby and US Foreign Policy.* New York: Farrar, Straus and Giroux, 2008.

Mendoza, Hanna Rose. "UN Secretary-General Ban Ki-Moon Lists 3D Printing among Potential Global Threats." 3Dprint. com, August 25, 2016.

Mohr, Angie. "The Advantages of Free Trade in Developing Countries." *Houston Chronicle*, no date.

Montan, Hani. *Axis of Evil: Imperialism – Religion – Nationalism.* Charleston, SC: CreateSpace, 2016.

———. *Death by Choice versus Religious Dogma.* Charleston, SC: CreateSpace, 2012.

———. *Israel vs. America vs. the World*. Charleston, SC: CreateSpace, 2011.

———. *Psyche and Personality*. Charleston, SC: CreateSpace, 2013.

———. *Thorny Opinion*. Charleston, SC: BookSurge, 2008.

———. *Voice of Reason: In 7 Essays*. Charleston, SC: CreateSpace, 2015.

National Security Archive, Washington, DC. "Colbert Uses Declassified Doc to Grill Rumsfeld: 'It Is Big,'" February 3, 2016.

New Statesman. "Wahhabism to ISIS: How Saudi Arabia Exported the Main Source of Global Terrorism," November 27, 2014.

New World Encyclopedia. "Wahhabism."

Nye, Joseph Jr. *Soft Power: The Means to Success in World Politics*. New York: PublicAffairs/Perseus Group, 2004.

———. "Soft Power: The Means to Success in World Politics." *Capsule Review*, May/June 2004 issue.

Pappe, Ilan. *The Ethnic Cleansing of Palestine*. London: Oneworld Publications, 2007.

———. *A History of Modern Palestine: One Land, Two People.* Cambridge, UK: Cambridge University Press, 2006.

Perl, Raphael. "Combating Terrorism: The Challenge of Measuring Effectiveness." Special report to Congress, updated March 12, 2007.

Petras, James. "Foundation of the US Empire: Axes of Evil." *World News Daily*, July 22, 2014.

———. "Foundation of the US Empire: Axes of Evil." Petras's personal website, July 19, 2014.

———. *The Power of Israel in the United States.* Atlanta: Clarity Press, 2006.

Pew Research Center. "Mapping the Global Muslim Population," October 8, 2009.

Priest, Dana, and William Arkin. "Top Secret America." *Washington Post*, July 19, 2010.

Rasti, Delizo. "US Imperialist Aggression in the Early 21st Century." *Links International Journal of Socialist Renewal*, November 27, 2010.

Ricks, Thomas. *The Gamble: General Petraeus and the American Military Adventure in Iraq.* New York: Penguin Books, 2010.

Roskin, Michael G. "Political Science." *Encyclopaedia Britannica*.

Sachs, Jeffrey. *The Price of Civilization: Reawakening American Virtue and Prosperity*. New York: Random House, 2012.

Scheuer, Michael. *Imperial Hubris: Why the West Is Losing the War on Terror*. Dulles, VA: Potomac Books, 2007.

Smith, Anthony D. *Nationalism: Theory, Ideology, History*. 2nd ed. Cambridge, UK: Polity, 2010.

Smith, Grant F., and Michael Scheuer. *Spy Trade: How Israel's Lobby Undermines America's Economy*. Washington, DC: Institute for Research of Middle Eastern Policy, 2009.

Taylor, Guy. "Intel Chief Warns of Widening Array of Terror Dangers." *Washington Times*, February 9, 2016.

United States Senate Subcommittee on Investigations. "Wall Street and the Financial Crisis: Anatomy of a Financial Collapse," July 1, 2011.

Weissman, Robert. "Goldman Sachs: Too Big to Rein In." Interview with *Al Jazeera*, June 17, 2014.

White, Sharon. "Universal Civilization." *Articles Factory*, January 27, 2007.

World Geo-Politics. "Modernization vs. Westernization: Universal Civilization?" Adopted from Huntington, *Clash of Civilizations*, June 12, 2009.

Zweig, Jason. "Disturbing New Facts about American Capitalism." *Wall Street Journal*, March 4, 2017.

I N D E X

• • •

Note: Arabic names beginning with "al" or "el" are listed by the name following the article (e.g., Ayman al-Zawahiri is listed under "Zawahiri, Ayman al"). The names "Ibn" and "Abu" are similar to "Mc" or "Mac" in being part of the name; such names are listed as, for example, "Ibn Abdel Wahhab, Muhammad." Group names such as "Jaish al-Mohammad" are listed in the usual alphabetical order (under *J* in this case).

3-D printing 24, 288

9/11 attacks 143, 205, 210, 263

Abdullah (king of Saudi Arabia) 164

Abramo, Vincent James 267-8

Abu Bakr al-Baghdadi 187

Abu Ghraib prison 7, 8, 144

Acton, Lord *viii*

Afghanistan 11, 16, 17, 18, 23, 50, 53, 68, 78, 93, 100, 148, 149, 152, 159, 160, 168, 169, 177, 185, 190, 201, 202, 211, 233, 245, 248, 269, 288, 307

Ahrar al-Sham 93

AIPAC 104-105, 108, 112-14, 140

Al Jazeera 60, 291, 294, 298, 305, 308, 314

Algeria 92, 175, 176, 281

al-Nusra Front 22, 93, 187, 205

Amazon.com 23, 282

America. *See also* United States xi, xvi, 3, 6-29, 31-8, 41-5, 47-59, 62-90, 92-5, 98, 100, 102, 104-10, 112-15, 117, 119-22, 124, 126-133,

www.ingramcontent.com/pod-product-compliance
Lightning Source LLC
Chambersburg PA
CBHW051037250726
48656CB00001B/18